GrassRoutes

Northern California Wine Country

 **GrassRoutes**

Northern California Wine Country

Green Road Trips

Serena Bartlett

with Julia Dodge, Daniel Ling,
and Ilsa Bartlett

SASQUATCH BOOKS
SEATTLE

*To small-scale farmers and their families, for considering humane
treatment of animals, soil health, and organic and biodynamic practices
that prolong our planet.*

*Certainly, travel is more than the seeing of sights; it is a change
that goes on, deep and permanent, in the ideas of living.*

—*Miriam Beard*

Printed in the United States of America
Published by Sasquatch Books
Distributed by PGW/Perseus
15 14 13 12 11 10 09   9 8 7 6 5 4 3 2 1

Cover design: Rosebud Eustace
Cover and interior illustrations: Daniel Ling
Interior design and composition: Rosebud Eustace
Interior maps: Map Resources / Emily Ford

Library of Congress Cataloging-in-Publication Data
Bartlett, Serena.
  Grassroutes Northern California wine country : green road trips / Serena Bartlett.
    p. cm.
  Includes index.
  ISBN-13: 978-1-57061-607-5
  ISBN-10: 1-57061-607-8
  1. California, Northern--Guidebooks. 2. Ecotourism--California, Northern. I. Title. II.
Title: Northern California wine country.
  F867.5.B37 2009
  979.4'10454--dc22
                              2009018159

Sasquatch Books
119 South Main Street, Suite 400
Seattle, WA 98104
(206) 467-4300
www.sasquatchbooks.com
custserv@sasquatchbooks.com

SUSTAINABLE FORESTRY INITIATIVE

Certified Fiber Sourcing

www.sfiprogram.org

CONTENTS

The Quiet Coast

Acknowledgments

I am unendingly grateful to all the people who have helped me with this book, and to the beautiful Northern California wine country for inspiring me. I'd especially like to thank Daniel Ling for his love and support throughout this process; Julia and Ilsa for their contributions; and the small-business owners who have dedicated themselves to making positive impacts on their community.

The GrassRoutes Story

Like cracking open a dusty geode, travel has revealed to me the many facets of the world, allowing me to compare my known surroundings with the previously unexplored. No other activity has had quite the same impact, offering a unique experience of both commonalities and differences in the quilt of humanity.

After each journey my reality was challenged with new ways of thinking and acting, and I found I had new interests and an altogether different perspective. The most important souvenir I brought home wasn't tangible—it was a more open mind.

I became a detective of sorts, unearthing cultures and becoming familiar with local customs by seeking out nontraditional attractions and cities off the beaten path. Wherever I was, the locals gave me the chance to have unique experiences rather than manufactured ones. When I returned home I kept up the habit, discovering a wealth of intrigue in my own country. Whether trekking across another continent or walking a few blocks to a nearby neighborhood, no matter what my pocketbook dictated, I always managed to find new cultural gems.

GrassRoutes was born out of my growing collection of ideas and inspirations drawn from my journeys. I made up my mind to promote world citizenship, but search as I might, I found no vehicle that expressed my ideas about travel, so I decided to create one.

The concept evolved from a bundle of notes collected on the road. Since I have always viewed cities as whole entities, I didn't want my guides to be divided into chapters covering specific neighborhoods. Also, chowing down on some messy barbecue doesn't equate with dining on braised rabbit, so I chose not to organize the guides simply by activity. GrassRoutes guides had to be designed around the mood of the traveler and the timing.

But organization wasn't the only thing I wanted to do differently. GrassRoutes, true to its name, champions local businesses and their corresponding contributions to the greater good of the community. Restaurants that serve sustainably grown produce share these pages with shops that showcase works by local artists. Wildlife preserves are in the mix with amusements that use energy-saving techniques. Volunteer listings give visitors the opportunity to interact with residents while giving back. Being conscientious about society and environment is a recipe for peace: this is one message I hope to convey.

Another is that travel can fit a limited budget. GrassRoutes is more than a guide to a city's attractions—it is a reaffirmation that authentic cultural experiences are not out of reach for anyone.

As you enjoy your travels, you can be satisfied knowing that you are a conscientious consumer. With such a bounty of local businesses dedicated to the spirit of positive change, it is becoming easier to support such a philosophy. Each listing in every GrassRoutes guide meets this standard in one aspect or another. So while you are venturing out into the world and meeting real people in new places, your dollars are staying in the community.

In this spirit, I bring you GrassRoutes guides, created to benefit readers and communities. I hope you will try something new, even if you thought it was not possible. All you need to have a genuine cultural escapade is an inquiring mind, a detective's spirit, and the desire to get acquainted with the world around you.

Read more about the GrassRoutes philosophy: *www.grassroutestravel.com/story*.

Urban Eco-Travel Tips

To help you prepare for your adventure, here are some tips that I have compiled over my years of world travel.

Trip Planning

Don't overplan. Pick dates that make sense, and make the fewest reservations you can get away with to take into consideration factors of time, exhaustion, and exploration.

Before embarking on a trip, tell as many people as will listen where you are going, and get their feedback and tips. Have the same talkative approach when you get to your destination so you can meet locals and learn their favorite spots.

Look at books and magazines featuring the culture and history of the area before embarking on your trip, and keep a well-organized travel guide and a clear map with you while you are exploring.

Time Allotment

When picking dates, consider what kind of trip you want to have. One game plan is to spread out your time between different sights as a good introduction to an area. Another is spending prolonged time in one or two cities to truly get to know them. Either way, in my experience it is good to slow down the tempo of travel enough to smell the proverbial roses.

Reservations

Be sure to reserve a hotel for at least the first night so you have somewhere to go when you get off the plane. Even if you prefer to travel on a whim, I recommend starting on day two—after you get your bearings.

Before you book a room, try to get an idea of your destination first, so you can place yourself in the area that most interests you. If your entire vacation will be spent in the same area, I suggest staying in the same centrally located hotel the whole time so you avoid having to carry your stuff around. After all, you probably didn't travel to see different hotels, but to see the city itself!

Whenever you do book a hotel, make sure you know its cancellation policy.

In general, don't reserve many transit engagements. That way, if you want to extend your stay in a given spot, you can do that without too many trials and tribulations. Local transit arrangements are usually easy to book without much advance notice.

Restaurants tend to have widely varying policies on reservations, so check ahead to see whether your dream meal requires one. Or forgo the reservations: when you get to your destination, look around and act on a whim, or best of all, get the locals' advice. It is hard to get a good sense of a restaurant from its web site.

Be sure to reserve tickets for any special events you'd like to attend.

Packing

Pack light, but anticipate a variety of activities. I like to have a good pair of pants that can match with different shirts. I also bring one dressier outfit and a bathing suit.

Bring more than enough underwear, but wear clothing that can keep its shape for two or three days of use, especially pants or skirts. You'll be meeting and interacting with new people every day, so no one will know you wore the same outfit two days in a row.

Buy sundry items like sunscreen after you arrive. Remember, you will have to carry what you bring, so don't weigh yourself down.

Check the climate and current weather conditions of your planned locations and pack accordingly.

Try taking your luggage for a stroll in your own neighborhood before hitting the road. Then you'll know right away if you've overpacked, with enough time to do something about it.

Read GrassRoutes' latest packing tips and gadgets: *www.grassroutestravel. com/packing_tips.*

Safety

All major cities around the world have some amount of crime. Please use your wits and stay safe. Try to avoid traveling alone to new places at night.

En Route

Travel with equipment that helps make the journey to your destination peaceful. When I travel, I bring earplugs, headphones, and a sleep mask so my voyage will be blissfully quiet. I find this is easier than asking others to tone it down.

Get enough sleep before you fly. I recommend drinking lots of water the day before traveling and the day of—more if you tend to get dehydrated easily or are prone to headaches from dry plane air. Boosting your dose of vitamin C won't hurt either. To prevent your ears from popping on takeoff and landing, purchase a natural gum, like rain forest–friendly, chicle-based chewing gum.

When You Get There

Don't plan two activity-heavy days back to back. In general, it is good to have a combination of restful, educational, and physical experiences. Balance your time rather than trying to jam in too much activity. Ask yourself what you really want to see, and cut out the rest. Keep in mind that you can always come back, and be realistic about what you and your friends and family have the energy for.

Consider breaking into smaller groups when people in your party have different ideas of what they want to see and do.

Carbon Offsets

Despite the debate about the effectiveness of carbon offsets, they represent an important stop-gap measure that can really do a lot of good. Carbon offset providers use a calculator programmed to estimate what a given trip will rack up in carbon dioxide emission. This mechanism considers factors like trip distance and the number of passengers on the vehicle so you'll only be responsible for your share. To offset the estimated carbon dioxide emission, you then pay one of these providers to plant trees or otherwise reduce carbon elsewhere.

You aren't throwing your money away if you know where to get certified offsets. For instance, some of the best carbon offset products are certified by Green-e, a consumer protection program run by Center for Resource Solutions. Other carbon offset providers doing a stellar job, and thus endorsed by Environmental Defense Fund (*www.fightglobalwarming.com*), are Carbon fund.org and AtmosClear (*www.atmosclear.org*).

Major travel web sites are helping out by making carbon offsetting a click option when you purchase your ticket.

Green Travel

Air travel is not great in terms of being carbon neutral, but many airlines are starting to spend money investing in energy efficiency to make up for their jet fuel emissions. When you book, pressure them to do so, or buy your own credits when you fly from one of the certified carbon offset providers. Travel often necessitates flying, so when you can, try to use airlines that are more conscientious, and you are sure to make a more positive contribution to the greater good. Weigh your options and do the best you can.

Public transit and biking are the greenest solutions around, but other great ways exist to get around, like using vehicles that run on compressed natural gas, electricity, fuel cells, or biofuels. In these pages, I point you to the latest and greatest green transit solutions in the area you'll be visiting.

Read more about green travel: *www.grassroutestravel.com/green_travel*.

Eating

These days eating green is a tricky undertaking. Here are some tips to stay conscientious and also get your grub on whether you're away or at home.

- Lots of smaller farms operate organically but just don't have the bucks to maintain an organic certification stamp. Search these out on your next farmers market excursion.

- Organic produce that's out of season, shipped from far away, can be more taxing on the environment than buying conventional, local produce in season.

- Biodynamic farming is a wonderful philosophy of growing that takes into consideration many factors beneficial to the earth. It isn't always easy finding biodynamic produce; try farmers markets or search online for a biodynamic farm. Some are a part of CSA (community-supported agriculture) programs. Otherwise, buy local, in season, and organic.

- For more affordable and accessible organics, buy from a local farm, join a CSA, or subscribe to an organic food box service.

- Find out which conventional produce you should avoid because it's grown unsustainably, or requires soil sterility and high levels of chemicals that stay on board when you take a bite. Stone fruit and leafy veggies are two examples of things to buy organic, always.

- Conventional produce that doesn't require a large amount of pesticides or to which pesticides aren't as apt to stick, such as fruits and vegetables with thick peels, are safe to eat.

- When you are ordering at one of the restaurants in this book, you may find some ingredients that aren't sustainable on the menu. Just go for the dishes that you know have ingredients that can be sustained.

- Kosher, halal, and organic, hormone-free meats are always better choices in terms of taste, quality, humaneness, and sustainability.

- Be especially careful when it comes to seafood. Shrimp, tuna, big-fin fish—all no-nos. Squid, catfish, tilapia, anchovies, and mackerel, on the other hand, are all totally tasty and easy to sustain. The Monterey Bay Aquarium has an up-to-date explanation of the best seafood choices: *www.montereybayaquarium.org/cr/seafoodwatch.aspx.*

Read more about eco-friendly dining: *www.grassroutestravel.com/eating.*

Banking

Did you know that the most important factor in true sustainability is economic? Think local jobs, banks that give loans to new small businesses, and more. Business owners who live where they work care more about the longevity of their community and local environment, and when you spend your money at locally owned businesses, you support that sincere effort.

Most of the businesses in these pages have direct links to the local economy, injecting most of their revenue right back into the community. Don't consider the sustainability movement without looking into the economics of it—indeed the solution to many challenges in society today lies in the communion between green industry and economics. For more info, check out Van Jones's Green For All (*www.greenforall.org*) or Business Alliance for Local Living Economies (*www.livingeconomies.org*).

For specific establishments and more about keeping money circulating locally, see Local Banking on page 71, and refer to *www.grassroutestravel.com/buy_local.*

Using GrassRoutes Guides

Organization by type of venue runs the risk of muddling, say, an upscale restaurant with a drive-thru, just because both are technically restaurants. Instead, shouldn't guides be organized by what kind of experience you are looking for?

GrassRoutes guides employ a new system of organization that makes searching for activities, restaurants, and venues easy. This guide is organized by situation, with chapters such as "Up Early," "Do Lunch," and "Hang Out" that pay attention to your state of being.

All phone numbers are in the 707 area code unless otherwise stated.

There is a price range key and also a "who to go with" key to highlight great spots to go with friends, family, solo, or for romance.

As authors, we want to tell our experiences from our own perspectives. The initials after each review denote the author:

SB: Serena Bartlett   DL: Daniel Ling
JD: Julia Dodge   IB: Ilsa Bartlett

Our Criteria

Urban eco-travel is defined by businesses and activities that give back to their local communities through environmental, social, or economic means. To appear in a GrassRoutes guide, a business or activity *must* have a local presence or be locally owned. In addition, if we can answer yes to at least one of the following questions, the destination passes our test:

- Does it bank locally?
- Does it hire locals?
- Does it use energy-efficient appliances?
- Does it sell fair trade merchandise?
- Does it have a positive community benefit (for example, bringing people together or providing community outreach)?
- Does it use fair trade, organic, or locally grown products?
- Is its location environmentally sound (for example, the building is not on a landfill, or the building is made with green materials)?
- Does it participate in reuse/garbage reduction?
- Does it care about the environment, community, and economy around it?
- And last, but certainly not least, do we love the place? Does something make it special? Does it blow our minds?

With these considerations in mind, we've created a series of icons to accompany our reviews. These icons (see key on opposite page) indicate which of the criteria above are particularly noteworthy at a particular business or organization.

🖌	art/cultural/historic preservation	Ⓢ	free
🏦	banks locally	🧴	green cleaning
🚲	bikeable	💡	green energy use
CO	cash only	🏠	hires locals
🗑	community pillar	💡	inspirational
🍌	composts	🍅	local organic produce/ ingredients
$	cost: cheap	🏪	locally owned
$$	cost: moderate	🚌	on public transit route
$$$	cost: pricey	📓	recycled material use
🐕	dog friendly	♻	recycles
📖	educational	R	reservations recommended
🚗	electric vehicle use	💘	romantic
✚	employee health care	V	vegetarian
🤝	employees reentering workforce	((ọ))	Wi-Fi available
🞕	fair trade		

The GrassRoutes Team

Serena Bartlett

A natural born contrarian, Serena has lived and traveled in more than 25 countries. She is an award-winning author and an active spokesperson for inspiring ways to tread more lightly on the planet. With degrees from Friends World College (now Global College) and Long Island University, she had the world as her classroom. Serena is a regular contributor to a number of national and Bay Area publications, having written stories on everything from shampoo-making with garden ingredients to green business tips to an interview with one of her role models, Riane Eisler. She has appeared on KRON4's *Bay Area Backroads* as a green travel expert as well as on other programs, and has been a featured guest on KPFA and KGO radio. Serena revels in creative solutions for becoming more self-reliant, like sewing her own sheets and quilts, designing jewelry, making wild forays in the kitchen, and growing her own edible garden. She is a ski bum at heart and a swimming junkie, equally comfortable on a pack trip with her poodle or as a city slicker. Discover more about Serena at *www.serenabartlett.com* and at *www.grassroutestravel.com*.

Daniel Ling

Born and raised in Oakland, Daniel's style of freehand line drawing continues to evolve with each new GrassRoutes guide. His art has been shown at several galleries, design studios, and cafes. Daniel studied anthropology at UC Berkeley, where he learned to see beyond the superficial by putting aside preconceived notions. He can be found zipping around the streets of Oakland and San Francisco on his speedy bike, scaling the bouldering walls at the local climbing gym, in the front row of a Sonic Youth concert, or buried in a book. See more of Daniel's designs and artwork at *www.grassroutestravel.com/illustrations*.

Julia Dodge

Julia Dodge has been a connoisseur of Bay Area culture since her tenure at San Francisco State University's journalism program. Fascinated with the diversity and uniqueness of her lifelong home, as well as with the quirks of American society, Julia enjoys exploring new places in her own backyard. She has written lifestyle and travel pieces for *San Francisco Magazine* and *Valley Lifestyles* magazine, and has been the managing editor of *Bay Area Business Woman* since 2006.

Ilsa Bartlett

Ilsa has been dreaming of California since a young age, making the state her home in 1999. She has previously written on food science and spirituality, and she worked as a journalist on the East Coast. Her blog, Institute for Rewiring the System (*www.hotlux.com/angel.htm*), focuses on basic breathing meditation.

Dutsi Bap

Our cheerleader, research assistant, and referee, Dutsi boosts morale and provides support crucial to the GrassRoutes team. When he's not on the road testing out new locations, he visits local nursing homes to spread joy and fluffiness. He completed therapy dog certification and believes that the meaning of life is to eat roast chicken, run in the park, and take long naps at the feet of our writers. Dutsi also loves our freecycled leather couch!

Northern California Wine Country Overview

Northern California Wine Country Regions

Napa and Suisun Valleys

Livermore Valley and Beyond

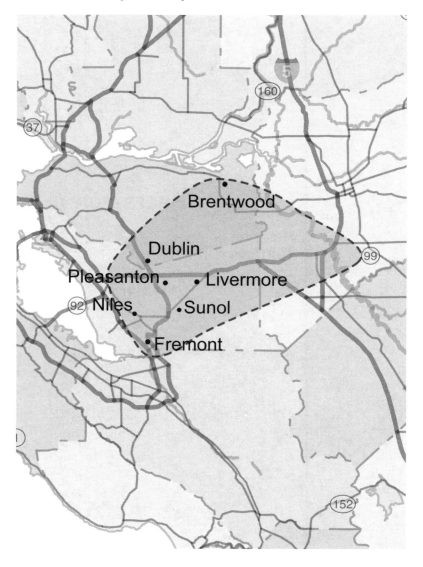

Inland Sonoma County

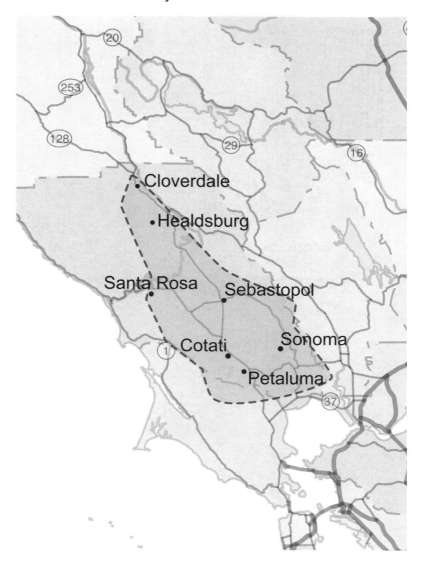

Northern West Coast from Point Reyes to Westport, and Mendocino County

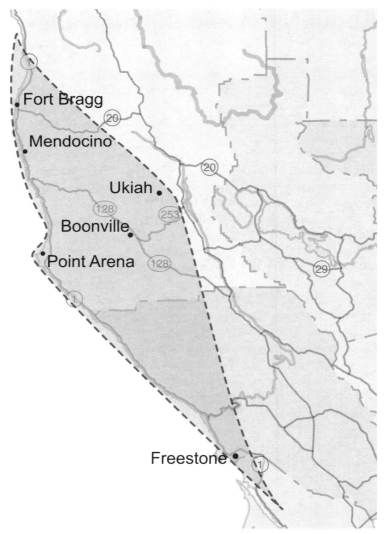

NOUVEAU HIGHLANDS

About Napa and Suisun Valleys

Napa is old in many ways. Old in the sense that the region was as popular for the same chardonnays and cabernets in the late 1800s as it is today; old like the 50-, 60-, and 70-year-old zinfandel vines that seem to writhe with time; but also old as in tired, because the same image-conscious set of mostly white, mostly prosperous wine drinkers has been coming here now for generations, and Napa bends over backward to uphold its image as a picture-perfect paradise for them. Few questions seem to be asked about what constitutes enjoyment in this mecca of indulgence. It seems to me there is an implication of visitors having something to gain here that they are missing, something more akin to status than to renewed self-awareness, which is my usual motivation to travel.

But this means that the environment challenges me. I am acutely aware of the lack of diversity, the assumption that paradise can be bought, the lavishness enjoyed on the backs of unnamed others. I wriggle and struggle to find something real in this land of façades. In the end, Napa offers me all I could ask for in a journey: the chance to look at something that makes me uncomfortable and find value in it. And I believe I have found a new Napa, one where biodynamic agriculture is honored, workers are paid a living wage, and interaction between various people is promoted. Of course there is room for elegance, celebration, and the odd duck breast in a cherry-balsamic reduction, but there are also plenty of questions to be asked, plenty of things to be learned, and plenty of new inspirations, even in what I previously thought of as a homogenous greenbelt of garish pleasures. Next door to Napa is the underappreciated Suisun (pronounced "sue-soon") Valley. The best farm trails are here, and lush fruits and vegetables tangle the rolling hills. Try the olive oils, black-eyed peas, and summer corn at roadside stands and u-picks, or delve into homemade jams and local honey from the plentiful hives that prove the agricultural health of this place. The wines from this region are lovely, and the relaxed vibe is a happy contrast to the packed popularity of Napa. I like going to both Napa and Suisun valleys in one day. It is a reasonable bike ride between the two valleys, and the differences are complementary when experienced back to back.

Getting Around
Helpful tips to get from point A to point B

Solano Napa Commuter Information
800.535.6883
www.solanolinks.com/commuterinfo
Find a carpool, a vanpool, or another super-savvy method of smaller-scale mass transit with the resources here. The site includes a bike links map and offers a convenient Matchlist service that will hook you up with a ride—it is not just for locals, so get with it and go carpool style!

Vallejo Baylink Ferry
877.643.3779
www.baylinkferry.com
$6.50–$13.00 one way
The City of Vallejo and San Francisco's Blue & Gold Fleet make possible one of the most breathtaking and practical trips in the Bay Area. Travel from San Francisco across the bay, sideswiping the Carquinez Bridge and winding around Mare Island to the Vallejo landing, where you can bike the paved paths or pick up a Napa VINE or Solano Express bus. When you leave your car in San Francisco and get to Wine Country via mass transit, you take in more views, meet more people, and take care of the planet.

If you are vacationing in San Francisco, Oakland, and Wine Country, I recommend taking BART from either the San Francisco or Oakland airport, staying in a central location (taking a Zipcar if you need it for a day), riding the ferry over to Vallejo, and then traveling by bus around Wine Country, sans rental car.

Solano Express
424.6075, www.sta.dst.ca.us
800.535.6883, www.solanoexpress.com
$1.50–$4.50, monthly unlimited pass $50
This network of buses, including Vacaville City Coach, Fairfield/Suisun Transit, Vallejo Transit, and Solano Express, just got a boost that put some 25 new vehicles on the road. With the goal of promoting public transit, the Solano Transportation Authority provides one of the best ways to get around just

east of the bay. Download a free map from the STA's useful web site and get updates on new routes and services.

When I am in San Francisco I take the Vallejo-bound ferry to Solano Express, which drops me off at a Suisun Valley connection and leads on to the Suisun Harvest Trail (see page 16). On the Solano Express web site you can request a "duo pass" voucher for the Baylink ferry-to-bus option.

Napa VINE

800.696.6443
www.nctpa.net/vine.cfm
Free–$4.50 for entire loop (Vallejo-Calistoga); punch passes are $20 (15 percent off regular fares) and have no expiration date, so if you are planning a future trip, these are a great bargain

This fixed route takes you from Vallejo all the way to Calistoga and beyond to Santa Rosa. VINE Route 10 is the main bus, but each stop has a transfer point to a local VINE or Calistoga HandyVan shuttle. At the base of the Veterans Home of California-Yountville you can take the Yountville Shuttle for just $1 door to door; it's free for stops on the fixed route. In St. Helena a VINE shuttle loops around the main shopping route, while the American Canyon Transit shuttle follows a zigzag route that covers points east and west. Calistoga HandyVan is the best public transit in that rural region, and Vallejo and Suisun Valley are serviced by the most advanced system in the nouveau highlands region, the Solano Transportation Authority. I've found bus drivers in this part of the Bay Area to be helpful—just ask and they'll guide you. Free VINE maps are available at all the local visitors bureaus and chambers of commerce, and at many hotels. Paratransit service is also available in Napa County; for more information call 252.2600.

This bus system is the only reliable public transit in Northern California Wine Country, and I wish there were more of it. It is a great chance to take in the views rather than having to keep your eyes on the road.

Up Early

Early-bird specials and morning treats

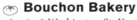 Bouchon Bakery

6528 Washington St, Yountville

944.2253

www.bouchonbakery.com

$$

Daily 7a–7p

On an early-morning walk, I'm lured to Bouchon by the bakers pulling out trays of treats. A French couple enters with me, and we chat about their travels. They tell me Bouchon is just like the bakeries at home, except that the pain aux raisin aren't in an *S* shape back in Paris, and the croissants aren't cut open to insert the framboise preserves. I'll forgive these differences, because after one bite I'm completely won over. Try a cinnamon bun if you're interested in one of the bakery's American offerings, or go traditional with a macaroon or the signature chocolate *bouchon*, a tiny dark chocolate bit of bliss. I pack up a loaf of whole wheat "country" bread and a slice of rich quiche for later. Dutsi turned up his nose at the doggie biscuit I got for him here, but then again, he is a British poodle, so I wouldn't expect him to go gaga for French food. *SB*

Balloons Above the Valley

 603 California Blvd, Napa
 253.2222
www.balloonrides.com

Yes, $200 is a lot to drop on a morning excursion, but early risers will be entertained until the early afternoon with an incredible, high-flying view of the corduroy vineyards. Get your toes wet with dew while you watch your transporter inflate. Then launch into the sunrise in a woven basket with some knowledgeable guides, who will not only ensure your safety up in the clouds, but also point out landmarks from above, possibly the best vantage point from which to see the valley. Save your pennies for this excursion by picnicking instead of eating out for a few days prior, and wake up with the sun for a unique journey in the Napa skies. *SB*

Golden Bagel Café

 3240 Jefferson St, Napa
258.1413

There's no substitute for a New York bagel, but a bagel from the Golden Bagel Café in downtown Napa comes pretty darn close. Egg bagels, glazed with whole yolks for a glowing sheen, go perfectly with the smoked salmon schmear made in the cafe from wild sockeye flown in from Alaska. I always go for a caraway pumpernickel bagel (which is supposed to be deep brown, but I'll accept the lighter version here) with a pile of cheesy eggs squished inside and topped with slices of red onions and tomatoes. This is a good spot to grab a quick breakfast before a day of valley explorations. *SB*

Morning Garden Walk in Yountville

Get up before the rest and go on a solo stroll around the quiet town of Yountville. Start on the main drag, in front of V Marketplace. This walk provides a great opportunity to meet the skillful gardeners who keep the town so prim and pruned. I try to practice Spanish with a busy rose pruner by asking for his eatery tips and complimenting his handiwork. The Vandeleur Park garden is a rose-covered triangle, complete with fountains, sculptures, and an old oak tree. After winding along the narrow path, head north to the French Laundry (see page 49), where the kitchen garden for Thomas Keller's three Yountville restaurants will fill your nostrils with sweet, dewy smells. After peering into the restaurant's quiet courtyard garden, head east a few blocks on Creek Street, and you'll see the children's garden in front of the Yountville Community Hall. As the town wakes up, any walk through Yountville will yield peeks at line cooks and bakers prepping for the day of cooking ahead amid the flowering lanes of a pristine vacationers' village. *SB*

The Tillerman Tea Company

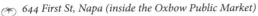

644 First St, Napa (inside the Oxbow Public Market)
265.0200
www.tillermantea.com
Mon–Sat 9a–7p, Sun 10a–5p

This pretty tea shop reminds me of exploring Fortnum & Mason when I lived in London. The teas are fresh off the boat from China and Taiwan, and each purchase comes with a detailed description of how to brew the specific blend. The same passion that Napa fosters for refined palates in wine drinking can be carried over to tea drinking, and at the Tillerman Tea Company it is. Whether you need a morning jolt or you're sneaking out to bring back treats for your fellow travelers, afternoon tea is best got in the morning when "the Davids" (owners David Campbell and David Wong) can give you the time and attention to teach you the right method for a proper cup. Come back later for a Chinese tea ceremony class or a seasonal tea tasting that includes loads of take-homes. *SB*

Gillwoods Cafe

1320 Napa Town Center, Napa (second smaller location in St. Helena)
253.0409
www.gillwoodscafe.com
Daily 7:30a–2:30p

A classic breakfast is not beyond this posh county. Join locals at Gillwoods Cafe for a veritable feast of American classics: cheesy omelets, high-stacked pancakes, and bottomless coffee. This is also one of the most patient eateries

around, with a truly relaxed vibe and no pushy waitstaff bugging you to put down the novel you've got your nose in and finish up. *SB*

Ritual Roasters

610 First St, Napa (inside the Oxbow Public Market)
253.1190
Mon–Sat 8a–7p (Tues 8a–8p), Sun 9a–5p

One of my favorite coffee shops is has migrated up the bay from San Francisco and in high demand among Napa foodies. Grab a cup of the special blend or a bag of freshly roasted beans to gift a lucky houseguest. Ritual Roasters brews each cup to order and never serves beans that have been out of the roaster for more than a day. *SB*

Vallejo Farmers' Market

Georgia and Marin sts, Vallejo
Year-round, Sat; July–Aug, Wed
www.pcfma.com

Each week another fruit or vegetable is bursting with ripeness at this farm-to-table market. In the early morning on a September Saturday, I catch the aroma of fragrant pears, their juicy scent wafting along the bay breeze. Bosc, Bartlett, and Comice varieties are perfectly ripe today, but no matter what the season, you'll find something farm fresh at this market due to the amazing growing climate of the region. Eat up! *SB*

Get Inspired

Museums, tours, and awe-inspiring exhibits—anything that aims to enthuse

 Great Olive Tours
 Various locations
 968.9978
www.greatolivetours.com
Cost: $75, including samples, take-home treats, meals, and luxe transportation

When it comes to certain things, like skiing and vegetables, I can get pretty nerdy and gear-headed. That's just how Great Olive Tours guide Carol gets about olives. She knows the ins and outs of the olive cycle and is ready to share her contagious excitement with you. Arriving in with a clean palate (no coffee on the morning of the tour!) helps get your taste buds extra sensitive and ready to distinguish the subtleties of each unique olive and its oil. Follow the Wine Country olive trail, which is the new big thing for winemakers and chefs alike, and then end with a demo in Carol's kitchen. Don't scrape the bottom of the barrel with other clueless olive oil buyers—most of the "dipping oils" that have been infused with basil or lemon are the lesser-quality stuff with flavors to cover up blunders. Here you'll learn how to avoid the big no-nos and where to buy the best oils in California. You'll want to get creative in your own kitchen after tasting this kind of inspiration. *SB*

 Elmshaven House
 125 Glass Mountain Ln, St. Helena
963.9039
www.elmshaven.org
Sun–Thurs 10a–5p, Fri 10a–1p, Sat 2–6p

I come with light-hearted cynicism to Ellen Gould White, who was a prolific writer and proponent of a strange and quite emboldened breed of religiousness as a Sabbatarian Adventist. That said, her house is really gorgeous, and it is fully restored to its original 1900s grandeur, giving visitors a window into St. Helena's past. I like old furniture, and especially old kitchens, so the tour is a treat for my imagination and a definite walk down history lane. *SB*

The Hess Collection

4411 Redwood Rd, Napa
255.1144
www.hesscollection.com
Daily 10a–5:30p

Donald, the founder of Hess Collection Winery, has a penchant for buying beautiful things. He's assembled an art collection from Europe, Asia, Africa, and the Americas, including paintings and sculptures that somehow make the wine taste better. This collection has a magic effect on me—it transports me to a New York gallery, wine glass still in hand. Linear works by Frank Stella are my favorite, and pieces by naturific Andy Goldsworthy and famous Francis Bacon are also here. Step outside into the picnic area with an expansive view of the vineyard valley below. *SB*

Baksheesh Fair Trade

1327 Main St, St. Helena (two other locations in Sonoma and Healdsburg)
968.9182
www.vom.com/baksheesh
Mon–Sat 10a–6p, Sun 11a–5p

When I get the urge to tiptoe around in a beautiful store, I go to Baksheesh. The artifacts, all made by traditional craftspeople paid over and above a living wage for their handiwork (and certified by Fair Trade USA), are simply beautiful. Let me also give fair warning: it is near impossible to leave without buying something. I have a treasured blue walrus finger puppet my mom bought me here that goes with me everywhere in my luggage, and my wooden bowls for garden salads were also found on this store's shelves. This is one of the few places where you will be inspired and able to afford to bring home a new find even if you are on a tight budget. The colorful shelves have something for everyone, and I mean *everyone*. I was originally told about this place by the son of a grape picker, who is as manly as manly can be. If he shops here—and shopping isn't his main fascination—then I can safely say it is one St. Helena place that brings together all the kinds of people who live and travel here. *SB*

Di Rosa Preserve

5200 Sonoma Hwy, Napa
226.5991
www.dirosapreserve.org
Wed–Fri 9:30a–3p, tour times vary
Admission: Gatehouse Gallery is free, $10–15 for tours

Yeah! Finally a place in Wine Country that honors, let alone mentions, the artistic might of its southern neighbor: Oakland. On a recent trip to this premier Napa art space, I witnessed a show made up completely of the vast talents in Oakland, both past and present. But Oaktown isn't the only city where the di Rosa spotlight is shed. The entirety of Northern California is given a stage at this gallery-cum-museum surrounded by a Seagram-owned winery property. The stone building that makes up the Gatehouse Galley has an interesting past, first as a winery, then as a moonshine distillery, then as a mushroom shed, then a winery again, and now a gallery of the best art around. I highly recommend putting down a few extra bucks for a complete tour of the permanent collection, grounds, and behind-the-scenes views. Here is one inspiration in Napa that doesn't involve wine, just beautiful views and an amazing art collection. *SB*

Napa Firefighters Museum

1201 Main St, Napa
259.0609
www.napafirefightersmuseum.org
Wed–Sat 11a–4p

I didn't know that my adventures around Napa Valley would bring me to an old firehouse full of restored historic engines, but then again, isn't the unexpected what adventure is all about? This fun hideaway, a unique space on Main Street, which is otherwise strictly eateries, drinkeries, and boutique eyeglass shops, brings me back to my childhood. I used to follow family friends to the country to experience old-school Americana on the Fourth of July, and getting a chance to ride one of those bright-red engines was the clear highlight—well, other than the caramel apples and fireworks. The exhibit here features firefighting gear from as early as 1859, like the Jeffers Hand Pumper that rode on a horse-drawn firefighting cart. I like the photographs of the Napa days of old and the revolving exhibits put on by local historians and groups like 4H. Go back in time and bring out your inner child in the same visit. *SB*

Lincoln Theater

100 California Dr, Yountville
944.1300
www.lincolntheater.com
Mon–Fri 10a–4p, Sat 10a–2p

Old on the outside and brand-spankin'-new on the inside, the Lincoln Theater is where Bill Cosby comes when he's in town and where the best singers, from flamenco to Motown to opera, take the stage. This is a great place for a date in Napa, with fine eateries nearby at which to get a meal before or after the show. The world-class shows with a small-town feel are the ultimate way to make a night of it. *SB*

Blue Heron Gallery

6525 Washington St, Yountville
944.2044
www.blueheronofnapa.com

Images of grapes, vineyards, cellars, bottles of wine—you guessed it, it's Napa Valley–inspired art. But the beauty of Blue Heron, as you saunter past gold-framed paintings and large-scale photographs, is that this upscale art gallery is completely local. Co-owner Betty Jo March, who is responsible for most of the watercolors on display, is very happy to talk about the world-class artists, many of whom live only minutes away. And if you're like me and traditional art (or wine) isn't your forte, you must check out Phil Glasshoff's scrap-metal army. OK, they're not assembled for battle, but these robotlike creatures made of old garage parts look like the Tin Man's kin. *JD*

 Napa Valley Open Studios

Last two weekends in September
www.nvopenstudios.com

Delis, wineries, inns, and galleries are all venues at this free, self-guided tour around Napa's art scene. Trek to the Oxbow Public Market, then to the Schaer Gallery, and then to the Randolf Inn for a mini-tour in close proximity to the river, all within an easy bike ride of Napa's main hub. Circling around the shows closest to the river is a special treat; I like to make believe it is filled with passenger steamboats as it once was, taking revelers and grape growers to and from their country-city destinations. These imaginings make the art seem more vivid to me. *SB*

Get Active

Hikes, bikes, runs, and rapids—anything and everything to keep you moving

Backroads Bike Tours

Various locations
800.462.2848
www.backroads.com/biking-trips (search on "California")

If you aren't up for your own self-planned bike trek around the valleys of vino, catching up with a Backroads tour of Napa (and Sonoma) is a surefire way to see the highlights without having to design your own itinerary. Four- or five-night excursions feature some of my favorite wineries, and you can choose your group size and the type of hotels you stay in, either high end or casually comfortable. The Napa-Sonoma route winds through five different appellations, the countryside, and redwood forests, and is punctuated by wine tastings and picnics. Each ride ends at a cozy nook, where you'll rest up before another day of exploration. *SB*

Mare Island Shoreline Trail

www.mareisland.org

Mare Island is in line to be the next big Bay Area destination—its wide, winding bike trails, ideal location, and historical context make it an amazing trip for people young and old. Best of all, it hasn't yet been "discovered," so the crowds making their way through San Francisco's Fisherman's Wharf and Embarcadero area haven't migrated to this interesting island. I love the old buildings, some of them with chipping paint, others well maintained to tell Mare Island's history as a port checkpoint and military base. (In fact, it was the very first Naval base established on the entire Pacific Coast in the 1850s.) Eucalyptus trees scent the air, and most of the flat, bikeable sidewalks are in view of the water. Take the path parallel to Highway 37 over the Mare Island Bridge, and then explore the various structures of the island. Whether you walk, run, bike, or blade, you'll be peacefully traveling around the Bay Area's secret island. *SB*

⑤ Napa River Ecological Preserve Walk

Yountville Cross Road at Silverado Trail

In the middle of wine-chic Napa Valley is a glimpse of the area's natural past—still home to some 150 species of birds. Thanks to many wineries that have signed on to help maintain their facilities in a way that protects the watershed and minimizes or entirely does away with pesticides and chemicals, the area will still be home to beautiful flora and fauna into the future. Turn off Silverado Trail or, if you are in Yountville, head north to Yountville Cross Road, and about 2 miles from Silverado Trail you'll find the staging point at the base of the riverside trail. You can park cars and bikes in the dusty lot and then head along the winding trail, past oaky shrubs and weeping willows ripe for bird-watching. The park is almost 80 acres, largely concentrated along the river watershed, so head back in the same direction you came from rather than searching aimlessly for a loop. This walk is one of the best ways to see the real Napa, the Napa of old that hasn't been touched by the big bucks or the grapevines. It is a crucial part of the ecosystem, and the river park is a testament to Napa locals' dedication toward preserving it. *SB*

Solano Avenue and Silverado Trail Biking

My two favorite bike rides in Napa are complementary: one is shorter and has fewer cars, and the other is a bit more strenuous and has the best wineries in the area.

Solano Avenue is a relatively flat and nearly car-free parallel to the more trafficked Highway 29. It is known as Frontage Road to many, but its actual name is Solano Avenue, and it runs from Napa to Yountville, passing by rows of vines, sunflower-lined driveways, and fun tasting rooms like Silenus Vintners (see page 27). If I am staying in one of the nearby towns, it is my preferred way to traverse back and forth, to grab lunch at the Oxbow Public Market from a bed-and-breakfast in Napa, or to dine at Ad Hoc while staying in Yountville.

Silverado Trail is much more of an excursion. Take a long afternoon or an entire day to wind around the curves and bends of this popular bike route. Just be sure, as always, to wear a helmet and go dorky with reflective gear and bright-colored clothing so you can easily be seen. If you are staying in Napa, turn off Soscol Road onto Trancas Road, which is on the right if you are heading north. Wide bike lanes run for most of the 30-mile route from Napa to Calistoga, and you'll find lots of wineries, some big and corporate like Andretti and Duckhorn, and some smaller and organic like Sinsky, ZD, and Dutch Henry. Take your pick, but make sure not to miss some of the places in Napa that aren't just doing grape monocropping, like Long Meadow Ranch (see page 16) and Omi Farm (4185 Silverado Trail, Napa; 800.532.0500). I'm no pro biker, and if I get a gaggle of friends together I am comfortable on this trail, as long as I wear my disgusting neon-green vest, a modified piece from my old ski racing uniform. Then no one messes with me, and I am free to explore the open road, vines and all. *SB*

$ **Bocce Ball at Crane Park**

S Crane Ave, St. Helena; 963.5706
St. Helena Bocce Club; 963.1663; http://sthelenabocceball.com

What's the national sport of Napa? Bocce, of course—the sport that goes best with wine or pinot grape juice. Sunday through Friday nights at Crane Park the St. Helena Bocce Club is in full swing, taking up most of the bocce courts to score their way to the bocce championships. Get an earful from the locals on the rules and culture of this imported pastime. You can have your own chance to play by calling ahead and asking about the availability of the courts. All the equipment are available for your use. *SB*

And if you can't cram in at Crane, the local's choice for a bocce court, you can look for bocce at one of the other 30 or so courts around Napa. Other courts I recommend are as follows:

The Carneros Inn
4048 Sonoma Hwy, Napa

Dutch Henry Winery
4300 Silverado Tr, Calistoga

Fuller Park
Jefferson and Oak sts, Napa

Robert Sinsky Vineyards
2950 Sage Canyon Rd, St. Helena

Summers Winery
1171 Tubbs Ln, Calistoga

Turnbull Wine Cellars
8210 St. Helena Hwy, Oakville

Yountville Veterans Park
Washington and California sts, Yountville

Volleyball in Veteran's Park
Washington and California sts, Yountville

Something free in Yountville? Yes, it is true, you can strike up an impromptu game of v-ball with your travelin' crew just about any time at this towny park. It comes complete with free use of a well-strung net and old-oak shade. There's also a quarter-mile lemniscate track running around the sandy court, so you can make the losing team run laps. Let's play! *SB*

Napa Valley Bike Tours
6795 Washington St, Bldg B, Yountville
944.2953
www.napavalleybiketours.com

For the employees of Napa Valley Bike Tours, bicycling is not just a job, it's a lifestyle. Owner Abraham bikes 40–60 miles per day, and the staff, who he regards as a big family, won the 2008 Bike to Work Challenge. Ordinarily I would be intimidated by such cycling professionals, especially since my ass hasn't seen a bicycle seat since high school, but instead I felt at ease, thinking that perhaps even I could hop on for a ride again (the staff has taught beginners on the driveway the morning of their first ride ever!). And what better way to reintroduce myself to cycling than by cruising through sunny, rolling vineyards among the birds and bees, truly experiencing the sights and sounds? The terrain is not only harmonious and classically Californian, but also relatively flat for those who want to save energy to sip vino in traditional Napa Valley style. *JD*

Gardens
Blossoming bounties and picnic places

Ⓢ Suisun Harvest Trail
www.suisunvalley.com/map.asp

With clearly marked numbers and easy-to-follow maps online and at most of the highlighted locations, this harvest trail has a little of everything. U-pick farms where you can gather berries and black-eyed peas, wineries, and lunch spots that feature local veggies are all on the trail. Hit one or two spots or go for a farmstead marathon in this hidden gem of a valley. *SB*

Rubicon Estate Gardens
1991 St. Helena Hwy, Rutherford
968.1100
www.rubiconestate.com
Daily 10a–5p

Rubicon is owned by the Coppola family, and they've gotten smart. The entire estate vineyard is certified organic, and its lush gardens serve as home to butterflies and bees, which keep the ecosystem healthy. If you are nixing a long list of winery visits and just want to focus on one, $25 will get you valet-parked and into these gardens, complete with a wine tasting and historic tour. Wandering around the estate is a lovely way to while away the hours in opulence. *SB*

Long Meadow Ranch
1796 S St. Helena Hwy, Rutherford
963.4555
www.longmeadowranch.com
Wed–Fri 1–6p, Sat 9a–5p

Don't get me wrong, I'm gaga for a good California wine or a zesty olive oil, but these are both in high supply all over these valleys, and the monocropping can get a bit tired after days of swilling cabernet sauvignon and slurping evoo. Biodiversity is king at Long Meadow Ranch, where you can purchase grass-fed beef, fresh chicken eggs, and fruits and veggies from the garden. Keeping the soil healthy and the community happy is of primary importance to Long Meadow, and sustainable, organic practices are maintained to hold up these lofty ideals. When you think about it, everything in the universe is somehow interconnected, and this mentality is an obvious component at Long Meadows. Some of Napa's finest restaurants grab their grub here, but you can also taste the goods direct from the source at the tiny restaurant, complete with epic views. *SB*

Frog's Leap Winery

8815 Conn Creek Rd, Rutherford
963.4704
www.frogsleap.com
Mon–Sat 10a–4p

I wish I were Peter Rabbit, so I could hide in Frog's Leap's toolshed and live in the amazing organic garden forever and ever. Time, attention, and love have been sown into the soil—I don't know how else to explain the utter bounty of these always-blooming patches. My favorite time to visit is autumn, when winemakers are walking the vineyard, trying to decide when to harvest the grapes, and the garden is full of my favorites: kohlrabi, bright-red nantes carrots, white full-moon pumpkins, Fuyu persimmons and rosy pomegranates, leeks, celery, and radishes, as well as bok choy and celeriac, one of the best soup additions on the planet. Degge, the head gardener, is in tune with the seasons, using a mix of highly trained intellect and instinctual know-how to fertilize with compost, sow seeds, and turn the beds. Traipse around the grounds, watch the nitrogen-rich purple vetch flowers smile in the sun, and then go home and start building your own edible garden. The winery received a Gold LEED certification, so practicing responsible land stewardship isn't just talk at Frog's Leap. *SB*

Nickel & Nickel Gardens

8164 St. Helena Hwy, Oakville
967.9600
www.nickelandnickel.com

This 42-acre winery was originally settled as a farmstead in the 1880s. Eating a picnic lunch in the shadow of one of the historic barns on the farmstead, among irises and sweet-smelling alyssum, is the highlight of a visit to these rolling hills. Walk the grounds aimlessly afterward, peek into the fermentation barn, or take photos of the rustic red siding on the Gleason barn. *SB*

Barney's Backyard

1492 Library Ln, St. Helena (behind the St. Helena Public Library)
www.shpl.org/barneysbackyard.htm

The St. Helena Wine Library Association has a little vineyard of its own for people like me, who like to taste the grapes before they get "winified." Named for beloved member Bernard Rhodes, these vines are right behind the public library, with views of Robert Louis Stevenson's cabin in the distance and "mixed blacks," made up of St. George stock petit syrah, zinfandel, and Carignane grapes, in the foreground. Here you can explore a nonwinery vineyard set up to preserve these great grapes and inspire the library and its future members. *SB*

Do Lunch

Outstanding midday eating of every sort

 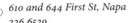

Oxbow Public Market

610 and 644 First St, Napa
226.6529
www.oxbowpublicmarket.com
Mon–Sat 10a–6p, Sun 10a–5p (individual merchant hours vary)

Elsewhere on these pages I've written about Oxbow Public Market merchants, but this new market has even more to offer. Taylor's Automatic Refresher's hamburgers (see page 22) are on the grill next to the market, and around the corner from this 1950s-style burger stand and next to the Model Bakery (see page 24) is the Fatted Calf (644 C First Street; 256.3684), one of the best places to spend your bones getting into meat. The authentic rillets made of duck or pork are spread on bread from the bakery next door. Or go for the reasonably priced mortadella (my favorite) laced with pistachios. All the meats are organic and hormone free, most come from farms within walking distance, and the curing room is right behind the meat counter. Pica Pica is located inside the main hall of the market and specializes in Venezuelan *pupusas*, or corn pockets, stuffed with flavorful local ingredients. Hog Island Oyster Company is another highlight—everything sold here has passed strict sustainability and taste criteria. You can get an amazing-tasting roasted chicken from Rotisario and with a side dish spend less than $15. Olive oil and cheese can be found when snooping around the main hall, and for dessert, nothing is better than a cupcake from Kara, another San Francisco transplant. *SB*

 Oakville Grocery

78566 St. Helena Hwy, Oakville
944.8802
www.oakvillegrocery.com
Daily 8a–6p (general store), 7a–6p (espresso bar)

I don't know about you, but a big, fancy picnic shared with my honey and some friends is my favorite way to spend a lazy afternoon. Oakville Grocery caters to my most luxuriant picnic plans, with oodles of high-end cheeses, fresh salads and breads, and, of course, vino. Sesame chicken skewers together with a handful of local olives and a few slices of summer melon and I am good to go. I bring my oversized wicker basket purchased from the excellent Vallejo SPCA Thrift Store (1121 Sonoma Blvd; 925.685.0908), and by the time I'm out it is brimming with choice comestibles. *Choice*, I tell you. And if we are all too famished to find a spot at one of the winery picnic grounds or off the trails of a nearby park, there is a roadside garden planted with fragrant roses right outside the market, ideal for immediate munching. *SB*

Napa General Store

540 Main St, Napa
259.0762
www.napageneralstore.com
Daily 8a–4:30p

The quickest lunch solution for gourmands on the run is a boxed option made with only the finest local ingredients from the Napa General Store. Mediterranean-style marinated chicken sandwiches with fresh basil pesto, two side salads, and dessert make a complete and easily portable meal, but the fresh Vietnamese spring rolls are my standby. You can even have these boxes delivered to your home or hotel for a few extra bucks. The Napa General Store also offers wine, olive oil, and Wine Country–inspired gifts and decor, but being one who avoids most gift-y stores, I stick with the yummy nosh and catering from the fab, homegrown kitchen. *SB*

Valley Cafe

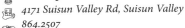

4171 Suisun Valley Rd, Suisun Valley

864.2507

Mon–Thurs 6a–2p, Fri–Sun 6a–3p

$

The bell jingles as I enter, and steam from the fresh-baked bread pudding wafts over the register as I place my order. Thirty-year veterans of this cute corner cafe have their names emblazoned on mugs hanging about the bubbling soup pot. A Veggie Bennie comes with homemade biscuits and hollandaise, and a smattering of whatever vegetables the cooks can find at nearby farm stands. Today it was large beefsteak tomatoes, torpedo onions, and spinach from Larry's down the road. With everything on the menu under $10, it is hard to believe the creamy, béschamelly clam chowder is really made here, in this cozy dinerlike setting. But it is true; this cafe cooks up fine lunches from local bounty every day of the week, and if you don't believe me, ask Skip, Dino, Steve, or Barbara—they've been taking lunch breaks here since the 1970s. *SB*

Boon Fly Café

4048 Sonoma Hwy, Napa

299.4870

www.thecarnerosinn.com/thecarnerosinn/restaurant_boonfly.aspx

$$

Daily 7a–9p

When you're biking toward the Napa-Sonoma County line, over the uppermost rivulets of the bay waters, and past the grape-crusher statue, hunger and thirst set in. Boon Fly Café, which is part of the Carneros Inn, is ideally located right off the road, so I take a break from the bike lane and head inside the welcoming red, barnlike building for a delicious lunch. The daily flatbread special is always enticing—one day it might be local Point Reyes blue cheese and caramelized onions, and the next, smoked river salmon right from the nearby coast dabbed with lemon crème fraîche. Ingredients come from the most reliable sources, and sausages are made right in the kitchen. You won't be turned away if you're on a budget—a hearty Reuben sandwich, baby-greens salad from the Carneros Inn garden, and house-made potato chips all together runs under $20. No better bike break, I say, and if I'm feeling too sore to go on for the day, I'll stay the night or opt for a massage at the inn's full-service spa. *SB*

Genova Delicatessen

1550 Trancas St, Napa

253.8686

Mon–Thurs 8a–7p, Fri–Sat 8a–8p, Sun 9a–5p

Genova Delicatessen creates personalized sandwiches from an array of snazzy ingredients. Slop a pile of New York–style coleslaw on your roast beef, or try one of the varieties of domestic or imported prosciutto. Pick your bread—the ciabatta is my favorite—and your own heap of fillings. Authentic Italian pasta and white beans are also available in the grocery section. This store is the Little Italy of Napa. *SB*

Pacific Blues Cafe

6525 Washington St, Yountville

944.4455

www.pacificbluescafe.com

Daily 8a–10p

The main drag of Yountville can be a real drag when you just want simple, inexpensive eats. In fact, I discovered that you're plain out of luck if you're looking for a quick bite as you pass by numerous bistros that will put a dent in your wallet (well, at least my wallet). So here appears the Pacific Blues Cafe, with sandwiches, salads, and a delicious Blues Burger with jalapeño jelly and fries. Even with a beer you are still looking at no more than $20 per person. Flying solo on a particularly scorching-hot day, I chose to pass on the bustling main patio area and sit at the more secluded four-table front patio to enjoy a cooling cross-breeze, as recommended by the hostess. It enhances the dining experience when it feels like you got the VIP table. *JD*

Mustards Grill

7399 St. Helena Hwy, Oakville

944.2424

www.mustardsgrill.com

Mon–Thurs 11a–9p, Sat 11a–10p, Sun 10a–9p

I recently heard that eating mustard, curry, and turmeric on a regular basis improves brain function and plasticity, so even more reason to stop by this Napa Valley tradition for a done-up lunch. A midday trip to Mustards Grill allows for the same quality food experience as an evening visit, but on a smaller budget and without the wait list. Check out the namesake ingredient growing wild along the roadside, which is also reflected in rich dressings and meat rubs. Rabbit, pork, beef, and various fowl found on this menu are almost exclusively sourced from Wine Country ranches. Try as I might, I can't be swayed from ordering the lemon-lime meringue the restaurant is famous for, even after a hearty feast. *SB*

Taylor's Automatic Refresher

933 Main St, St. Helena
963.3486
www.taylorsrefresher.com
Daily 10:30a–9p

In my estimation, Taylor's Automatic Refresher is responsible for two important things: inventing the San Francisco–style garlic fry now replicated all over the Bay Area and being the only really laid-back eatery in Napa County. Sure, it is a famous stop off St. Helena Highway, but after picking grapes, turning soil, or selling the Napa image to tourists, the locals gather here for no fewer than eight variations on the hamburger. A burger, fries, and a milkshake never had a better view, especially when blueberries are in season and they're stuffed in the blender with milk and ice cream. *SB*

Red Rock Cafe

1010 Lincoln Ave, Napa
252.9250
www.backdoorbbq.com/cafe.html
Daily 11a–9p

In between walking the bridges of Napa proper, I find a meaty lunch gets me ready for an evening of wine sipping and slurping. Chuckburgers made with hormone-free meat from a local ranch are served with Red Rock Cafe's famous sticky-sweet barbecue sauce and a side of crispy, house-made coleslaw. This is a refreshingly hokey spot that represents the charm of Napa, not the typical image of the region as welcoming wine drinkers only. Checkered tablecloths and window seats that look out on one of Napa's central streets provide a view of the real town to go along with the taste of slow-cooked perfection. *SB*

Sweet Tooth

A convergence of sweet things—the best places to discover your soft spot for sugary treats

 Alexis Baking Company

 1517 Third St, Napa
258.1827
www.alexisbakingcompany.com
Mon–Fri 6:30a–4p, Sat 7:30a–3p, Sun 8a–2p

Doesn't an Iced Lemon Dream sound fantastic? Well, I can tell you, it doesn't just *sound* fantastic, and the other sweets and breads at Alexis Baking Company, elevated by a menu of comfort-food classics for breakfast and lunch, are delish, too. I opt to carry out a couple of German chocolate cupcakes and a rosemary or walnut wheat loaf of bread as the backbone of a great picnic. Find your own sweet answers here. *sb*

 Cups & Cones

 6525 Washington St, Yountville
944.2113
www.vmarketplace.com
Daily 10a–5:30p

Downtown Yountville's V Marketplace, although designed as a rustic barn, is a high-end shopping mall of fashion and wine, so wandering into Cups & Cones is a refreshing reminder that you haven't died and gone to yuppie hell. It's easy to appreciate this quirky ice cream and candy shop, not only for its sweets, which are, of course, always a delight, but for its art deco wall murals of sultry figures and shelves of kooky merchandise. While the Exotic Blast smoothie is fruity and the coffee's organic, I recommend visiting for the dashboard hula girls, bacon bandages, birdbaths, and life-size cardboard cut-out of Beyoncé. Your friends will thank you for not returning with the typical wine-themed souvenir. *jd*

Three Twins Ice Cream Absurdities

610 First St, Napa (second location in San Rafael)

257.8946
www.threetwinsicecream.com
$ *Mon, Wed, Thurs 11a–7p, Tues, Fri 11a–8p, Sat 10a–8p, Sun 10a–6p*

Why choose between Mexican chocolate or bittersweet chocolate ice cream when you could have both? In fact, while you are at it, why not go completely bonkers and order the Ultimate Sundae, where Three Twins will fly you to the Himalayas and serve you and your rich friends a 100-scoop sundae on the spot? I'm not sure if Three Twins has actually been taken up on it, but their Strawberry, Mint Confetti, and Mocha Difference are pretty stellar. You'll find Neal's special recipes at farmers markets, a few restaurants, and in the freezer section of a number of local grocers, the company's dedication to organic ingredients remains. If you want to dream big, really big, you can call Neal and order up a trip across the world to celebrate this icy cream. *SB*

Model Bakery

1357 Main St, St. Helena; 963.8192
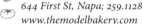
644 First St, Napa; 259.1128
www.themodelbakery.com
$ *Daily, hours vary by location*

Wine Country's original bread is still baked in the oven built by Italians in the 1920s, but I come here for the sweet stuff. If you are hungry or have a hole to fill in your picnic basket, you are covered, but please, oh please, don't leave without at least one almond macaroon or lemon bar. *Tres leches* and old-fashioned carrot cakes vie for my attention, but there are also seasonal cakes featuring local fruits throughout the year. Do me a favor and grab me a slice while you're at it. *SB*

Vines

Don't listen to anything but your own taste buds to discern your likes and dislikes when it comes to Wine Country's namesake

Ledgewood Creek Winery

4589 Abernathy Rd, Suisun Valley
426.4424
www.ledgewoodcreek.com
Daily 10a–5p

Drive along Abernathy Road, through the rolling terrain of Suisun Valley, and rows of vines bookended by red roses will catch your eye. I followed the flowers up Ledgewood Creek's dusty driveway to the tasting room, where pours of all their estate-grown wines are offered seven days a week. Beginning with a comparison of 2005 and 2006 vintages, I found that sauvignon blanc, viognier, and chardonnay were all vastly different between years. The 2005 I found more sophisticated in the case of the sauvignon blanc, but 2006 (and likely years to come) has benefited from more time under the watchful eye of UC Davis–trained viticulturist Larry Langbehn. Never was the pizza-and-wine combo more respected than with Ledgewood's GSM (grenache, syrah, mourvèdre), a blend of juicy reds that varies from year to year, running the gamut from quiet (with mostly mourvèdre) to loud (when syrah is the primary grape). Norm, the guy working the tasting room, poured my mother and me a special taste of 2007's "baby sauvignon blanc," which will undergo further aging before being bottle-ready. It was a refreshing treat; the cloudy stuff had a lively taste, like a snapshot of the fermentation process. I left with a bottle of 2005 GSM for my next pizza party and a chewy merlot, stereotype-defying in its almost smoky complexity. Next time I'll bring a picnic, as there are several umbrella-covered tables enclosed within an insectary garden of lavender, wild sage, and roses, which attract bugs that protect the grapes. This open and friendly tasting room is slow-paced and attentive to your every whim as a weekend taster—a far cry from the hullabaloo at most Napa wineries. *SB*

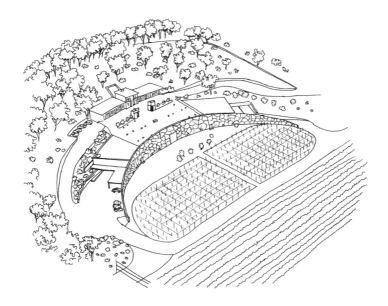

 ### Napa VinJus

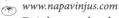 *www.napavinjus.com*

Drink your chardonnay in a nonalcoholic way with virgin wine, that is, Napa VinJus, made of mostly white wine varietals and served at a bunch of yummy places, like Fatted Calf (644 C First Street; 256.3684) and Bounty Hunter (see page 40). You don't have to "drink" to drink this. *SB*

 ### ZD Wines

 8383 Silverado Tr, Napa

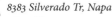 *963.5188*

 www.zdwines.com

 Daily 10a–4:30p

This family vineyard has been growing organic grapes almost since it opened, and the lofty tasting room is a great place to enjoy the fruity splendor of a classic Napa cabernet or a unique chardonnay. Not all the wines are organic, but just ask the knowledgeable pour staff and they'll direct you to the ones that are. *SB*

Quintessa

1601 Silverado Tr, Rutherford

967.1601

www.quintessa.com

Traditions fuse at top-notch winery Quintessa, where biodynamics, fine design, and local chefs converge to celebrate one of Napa's best vintages. The insectary is home to friendly bugs that help keep vines safe and happy, and no other winery I've found does as extensive a barrel tasting when blending its wine (there is a single blend each year). Make a reservation and you'll be spoiled with a tour of one of the most beautiful vineyards in the valley, two glasses of Quintessa wine (from different years), and a food pairing from a chef whose name you'll remember after one bite. *SB*

Frog's Leap Winery

8815 Conn Creek Rd, Rutherford

963.4704

www.frogsleap.com

Mon–Sat 10a–4p

These vines are some of the happiest in the valley. They are interspersed with gardens and orchards, and all are organic and punctuated by nitrogen-rich cover crops to keep the soil blissful. The wines, both red and white, reflect the earth-friendly joy, but a trip here will inspire much more than the wine drinker in you—that's a guarantee. Read more about their gardens (see page 17). *SB*

Silenus Vintners

5225 Solano Ave, Napa

299.3930

www.silenusvintners.com

Daily 10a–4p

Families wanting to get their hands purple have bonded together to form Silenus, a group tasting room where mostly hobbyist winemakers and boutique vintners strut their stuff. Try the cabernet franc from Gridley and you'll realize these guys mean business. *SB*

Dutch Henry Winery

4310 Silverado Tr, Calistoga
942.5771
www.dutchhenry.com
By appointment only

One of Silverado Trail's organic boutique wineries is also one of the most beautiful to visit. The fun, hip ambiance seems to make the wines taste better, too. The cabernet, which the region itself is known for, is beyond great in my humble opinion, but come taste it and decide for yourself. *SB*

Grgich Hills Estate

1829 St. Helena Hwy, Rutherford
963.2784
www.grgich.com
Daily 9:30a–4:30p

The oversized barn of a tasting room is covered with passionflowers and English ivy, a symbol of how Grgich Hills Estate puts the nature around the winery first. This family-run vineyard is one of the largest on Highway 12 to have gone organic and biodynamic, using algae "soups" to protect vines from sunburn and unwanted visitors, and using sheep to transform healthy cover crops into fertilizer. Plus Grgich has gone solar, and the wines aren't too shabby either. The zinfandel is a shining star here; with just the right balance of zest and perfume, this complex wine tells a story in your mouth. *SB*

Robert Sinskey Vineyards

6320 Silverado Tr, Napa
944.9090
www.robertsinskey.com

The smaller size and attention to detail of this premier winery makes it the most recommended by chefs and sommeliers I've talked to all over the Bay Area. Everything is done with pleasure in mind: the soil is pleased to have royal treatment and organic-farming practices, the herbs and veggies explode during each harvest season, and the wines go well with everything. Take the time to visit this place if you go anywhere on Silverado Trail. *SB*

Charbay Winery and Distillery

4001 Spring Mountain Rd, St. Helena
963.9327
www.charbay.com

This is the best place to taste brandy in the valley. Charbay Winery and Distillery makes its version from gorgeous pinot grapes (grown in cooler climates), distilling them so that your ice cream never has to be lonely again. As someone who isn't usually moved by strong spirits, I found this brandy surprisingly tasty, with the flavors layered in an accessible way rather than a knockout concoction. Try the olive oil, too—it is beautiful! *SB*

Vezér Family Vineyard

2522 Mankas Corner Rd, Suisun Valley
888.823.8463, 429.3935 (cafe)
www.vezerfamilyvineyard.com

For being located in an often-overlooked pocket of winemaking geography, Vezér Family Vineyard sure sets itself apart. Its La Salette has won the attention of the know-it-all wine columnists at the *San Francisco Chronicle* multiple times, and its cabernet sauvignon is a beautiful embodiment of berry and smoky cedar, like the definition of the grape. A visit to the winery gives you tasting access to all of its success stories, plus there's a cute cafe where you can lunch and chat about your top picks. *SB*

Hagafen Cellars

4160 Silverado Tr, Napa
888.424.2336
www.hagafen.com

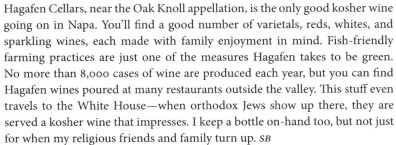

Hagafen Cellars, near the Oak Knoll appellation, is the only good kosher wine going on in Napa. You'll find a good number of varietals, reds, whites, and sparkling wines, each made with family enjoyment in mind. Fish-friendly farming practices are just one of the measures Hagafen takes to be green. No more than 8,000 cases of wine are produced each year, but you can find Hagafen wines poured at many restaurants outside the valley. This stuff even travels to the White House—when orthodox Jews show up there, they are served a kosher wine that impresses. I keep a bottle on-hand too, but not just for when my religious friends and family turn up. *SB*

Wooden Valley Winery & Vineyards

4756 Suisun Valley Rd, Suisun Valley
864.0730
www.woodenvalley.com

I go back in time when I drink these old-world wines. Primitivo, the great-grandfather of every American zinfandel, is Wooden Valley's punchy big red. The winery also has some über-sweet wines for you sugar cravers—one is made from white gamay and has a refreshing honey-citrus flavor. The family who owns and runs the vineyard is as sweet as their dessert wine, and a trip here is nothing like visiting the crowded, pompous rooms of many of the wineries in the neighboring valley. *SB*

Staglin Family Vineyard

1570 Bella Oakland Ln, Rutherford
944.0477
www.staglinfamily.com

Chardonnay is a hard sell for me, but at Staglin Family Vineyard it is the first thing I ask for in the beautiful tasting room. Nonmalolactic fermentation and a mix of oak resting barrels make it rise above the rest. That's not to say Staglin doesn't have a classic incarnation of the area's famed cabernet sauvignon—its juicy but balanced flavors make me giddy with joy! All the grapes are organically farmed, and this family-owned winery puts on a huge music festival each year and donates all the proceeds to various mental-health clinics. You'll be blown away, I tell you. *SB*

Pamper

Shelters from the hustle and bustle, simple enjoyments, and all things feel-good

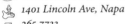
Relaxation Company Day Spa

1401 Lincoln Ave, Napa
265.7733
www.relaxationco.net

With walls covered with curtains and calming paint colors, there is nothing sharp about this soft place. It is just a nice spa—a nice, cute spa—where massages and relaxing baths are waiting for you. Choose a treatment, either solo or duo, and get ready to let go. *SB*

Health Spa Napa Valley

1030 Main St, St. Helena
967.8801
www.napavalleyspa.com

Although this spa offers some treatments I wouldn't go near, there are some I seriously covet. The Outrageous Indulgence package is just that—four hours of freedom from worries, complete with hot stone massage, facial, and sugar scrub, with a poolside lunch, for under $500. The facilities are gorgeous—near hotels and restaurants—and steps away from St. Helena's Chamber of Commerce. *SB*

Mud Baths in Calistoga

A trip to Calistoga is practically equivalent to taking a dip in some mineral-y mud. Here are a number of ways to get muddy yourself, whether you are staying for a week or just driving through:

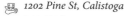 Euro Spa & Inn

1202 Pine St, Calistoga
$$$ *942.4056*
www.eurospa.com

Euro Spa & Inn has one of the tidiest ways of experiencing this area's naturally occurring mud. The spa staff brushes it on and pairs it with an excellent massage for a discount. *SB*

$ Dr. Wilkinson's Hot Springs Resort

1507 Lincoln Ave, Calistoga
942.4102
www.drwilkinson.com

Dr. Wilkinson's is the longest-running mud and mineral bath spa, with mineral pools and whirlpools to go with a full-coverage mud soak session. Even with all the bells and dingles, you can't spend more than $129, and if you are so relaxed you can't drive away, it is equally reasonable and comfortable to stay the night at the resort. *SB*

Golden Haven

1713 Lake St, Calistoga

942.8000

www.goldenhaven.com

\$\$

Golden Haven is set up with several identical rooms, each with side-by-side mud baths and chlorine-free hot tubs and showers, complete with luxurious bath products. You can sit and chat with a friend from the vantage point of a vat of weightless mud or make it romantic with a partner—either way, it is your room and you'll feel at home. *SB*

 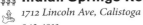

\$\$\$ ## Indian Springs Resort and Spa

1712 Lincoln Ave, Calistoga

942.4913

www.indianspringscalistoga.com

The fanciest mud baths are here at the side of the geyser-fed mineral pool. No matter what treatment you schedule, you can use the healing mineral pool surrounded by gorgeous terraces and poolside lounges, and also take a dip in "the waters," a rock pool shrouded by fountains and full of Indian Springs geyser water with natural salts. The volcanic mud here is a much darker shade than what you'll find elsewhere, and the treatments are more like excursions through various pools, baths, soaks, and scrubs. Select from the spa menu and then sit and contemplate your good fortune at the foot of a gleaming white Buddha sculpture by a koi pond. *SB*

Solage Spa

755 Silverado Tr, Calistoga

866.942.7442

www.solagecalistoga.com/solage

\$\$\$

Rather than having you dip into a tub full of maroon mud, this spa paints the stuff all over you, with each batch specially formulated for your skin type. The rooms are beautiful, and various amenities aid your complete relaxation, inside and out. Wash off the mud in geothermal waters, and then take time to sit in a "sound chair," the closest thing to zero gravity outside of NASA Ames Research Center. Facials and massages, solo or for couples, round out the spa menu, and all the products and procedures are done with your well-being, and that of the earth, in mind. *SB*

Acorn Thrift Store

657 Main St, St. Helena

963.7489

Mon–Sat 10a–4p, Sun 9a–12p

Pamper yourself with some feel-good retail therapy—all for a good cause, of course. This little shop is full of knickknacks from Napa locals' homes and contains interesting wineglasses, baskets of various sizes, and vintage T-shirts, all prettily set around the shop for you to gaze at. I took home a little wineglass with a wobbly green stem etched with grape leaves. Find your own unexpected treasures for cheap compared to this usually pricey valley. *SB*

Face It Beauty and Bath Spa

503 Georgia St, Vallejo

552.4021

Every facial mask, bath oil, and massage oil is mixed for you, right at the time of your scheduled service, from organic herbs, pure essential oils, and fresh fruits and vegetables. The idea here is to incorporate your whole self in the process of getting a beauty treatment. Pair a signature rose petal facial, which includes a heavenly spearmint scalp massage, with a *bain du lait*, made up of organic milk, honey, and chamomile essential oil. Deep tissue and prenatal massage are both offered, as well as the spectrum of massage pressure in between. Owner and operator Sharon Rose has a kind touch, and at a fraction of the cost of most Napa spas, her unique baths and facials are hard to top. *SB*

Bookish
Reading retreats in every flavor

Napa City-County Library

580 Coombs St, Napa (other branches in American Canyon, Calistoga, and Yountville)

253.4241

www.co.napa.ca.us/library

Mon–Thurs 10a–9p, Fri 10a–5:30p, Sat 10a–5p, Sun 2–9p

Quiet is key at this library filled with reading nooks. Each subject area is housed in its own cubbylike section, with a low reading table in the center. Pore over travel guides and cookbooks like me, look into learning Spanish, or research vino. The librarians are helpful in an old-school kind of way, catering to silence and the organization that makes the collections here perennially available for Napa residents and visitors from all walks of life. *SB*

Copperfield's Books

1330 Lincoln Ave, Calistoga (other locations in Healdsburg, Napa, Petaluma, Santa Rosa, and Sebastopol)
942.1616
www.copperfields.net
Mon–Thurs 10a–8p, Fri–Sat 10a–9p, Sun 10a–6p

Wine Country's local bookstore chain brings the pages to life with near-daily readings from both local newbie authors and big-time, nationally known writers. My favorite events are the "word temple" poetry nights, when a slew of complementary poets share their concentrated words in a passionate flurry of dramatic sequence. Find an awesome array of magazines and all the newest sustainability volumes here. *SB*

Vineyards in the Watershed

www.nswg.org/book2002.htm
To order, e-mail nswg@naparcd.org or call 252.4188

Published by the Napa Sustainable Winegrowing Group, this volume details the experiences and best practices of several Napa Valley farmers growing wine sustainably within a watershed. The book covers not only the importance and possibility of protecting wildlife and water quality, but also how to steward the land for the long term, be a fair employer, and go organic. Although it does get pretty technical, this is a comprehensive and serious book about real-world successes undoing some of the damage the rampant expansion of the wine industry has done to Napa's environment. It was written so we can continue enjoying this terroir long into the future, and it's an interesting read, even if you aren't a big wine drinker. *SB*

Learn

Courses, classes, and places to take on new challenges

Suscol House Intertribal Grounds

Chiles–Pope Valley Rd, Napa

256.3561

http://suscol.nativeweb.org/suscolHouse.php

Through generous donations and community support, this parcel of land has been secured for a traditional arbor, in the style of the Towa and Choctaw Indians. It is an outdoor arena shaded with willow branches, perfect for powwows and ceremonies. The arbor, off Chiles–Pope Valley Road, is part of a native Californian cultural preservation complex, including an outdoor kitchen, sweat lodge, barn, and Suscol House, the main education center. The complex hosts regular events, each unique and special, and if you are interested in joining in a powwow and there isn't one scheduled here, you can give the Suscol Council a buzz and they'll direct you to one going on elsewhere in the state. *SB*

Robert Louis Stevenson Silverado Museum

1490 Library Ln, St. Helena

963.3757

www.silveradomuseum.org

Wed–Sun 12–4p

The impoverished genius with health issues found respite with his beloved Fanny in the dry Calistoga climate. It was near the very spot of this educational museum that the author of *Treasure Island* spent his honeymoon and in the process developed some of the rich details used in his most famous tale. The wild nature that abounded in his time (the 1860s) was a total contrast to his native Scotland and added inspiration to his works. You can inspire your own discoveries when the history of the area comes to life for you at this well-organized museum. I must say, I find it funny to call the artifacts here "Stevensoniana" as classified in the exhibits, but it is a huge collection of original books and writings from the great man. It is one of the coolest free things to do around Napa Valley, especially for a bookish chick like me. *SB*

Napa Valley Museum
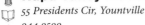

55 Presidents Cir, Yountville

944.0500

www.napavalleymuseum.org

Wed–Mon 10a–5p

Admission: $2.50–$4.50, free for children under 7

Right in the shadow of the Veterans Home of California–Yountville (see page 39) is a funny-looking modern construction housing the keys to Napa's future and its past. Even though the region has been greatly manicured by family vineyards and wine-loving businessmen, this museum is a testament to those who are interested in preserving the land and the cultural heritage of this world-famous area. Quite a few talented artists live nearby, and the museum often has shows incorporating their beautiful works. A recent exhibit I saw featured paintings and sculptures by Nancy Willis, Eleanor Coppola, Jill Strohm, and Deanna Forbes, all artists whose work has been inspired by Napa's special natural environment. With an aim to preserve, the Napa Valley Museum has classes and events dedicated to specific ways of meeting that goal—basket-weaving classes and dance parties with local mariachi music are just two examples. The permanent interactive exhibit on California wine is a great primer for understanding the terms used at the wineries and the process by which the luscious fruit of these vineyards is bottled and enjoyed together with local cuisine. *SB*

Napa Valley College

2277 Napa-Vallejo Hwy, Napa

253.3000

www.napavalley.edu

At the heart of Napa for many locals is this bustling community college, which supports continuing education and events related to the themes in Napa Valley. Learn English or brush up on Spanish, take a quarterly class in viticulture, or attend a free poetry reading. If you're staying for a month, why not take a class here to keep your brain active? It will at least give you an excuse to have an extra taste or two at a new winery. What other school do you know of where you can get credit (if needed) for olive-tasting and soil-management classes? Financial aid is available, and many of the classes are offered online, so you can actually study in Napa Valley, something I previously considered an oxymoron. *SB*

Vallejo Naval and Historical Museum

734 Marin St, Vallejo
643.0077
www.vallejomuseum.org
Tues–Sat 10a–4:30p
Admission: $1–2

Mare Island's historical significance and edgy rawness make it a unique discovery no matter how many times you think you've got its number. This heady museum is the only place to clearly glean facts about the area's colorful past and put into perspective the huge changes and wide range of historical periods the Bay Area has been through. It was the first place to be deemed a Naval base on the entire West Coast, and learning about this port makes it impossible to underestimate the importance of Vallejo and Mare Island ever again. *SB*

Cooking Classes

Yes, food is big here. But if you aren't already a talented chef, ready with food-and-wine-pairing ideas, don't sweat—part of your vacation can be becoming one. Here are my picks for cooking classes in Napa:

Gourmet Retreats at Casa Lana

1316 S Oak St, Calistoga
942.0615
www.gourmetretreats.com

Casa Lana's Gourmet Retreats are my top pick if you're really ready for some culinary education. You can opt to spend five days at a swank retreat, cooking on the professional steel equipment and making plans for epic meals once you get back home. All the recipes you study are bound up for you to take back to your own kitchen, and learning quick and impressive knife skills over the period of a few days will make them stick. *SB*

Culinary Institute of America

2555 Main St, St. Helena
967.1010
www.ciachef.edu/California

Perhaps the most famous place to learn a cooking skill or two is St. Helena's outpost of the CIA, and no, I don't mean the undercover agency. At the Culinary Institute of America, the only undercover work you'll do in your new starched white chef outfit is deseeding a hot pepper or discovering the true meaning of seared meats. At the DeBaun Theater you can watch demonstrations by many local favorite chefs. Sometimes they'll even let you in on their restaurant recipe secrets, and you always get to taste what they create. *SB*

Cooking with Julie

Various locations
227.5036
www.cookingwithjulie.com
Cooking with Julie isn't the same as cooking with Julia (Child, that is, for those of you who haven't read her *Mastering* books or watched her long-running show), but it is a run through Napa's seasonal cuisine. Start by following this bubbly chef through the farmers market, picking out ingredients that will go into your new recipe learnings. Simple, beautiful fare is as important as technique, and finding the best artisan products will make your end result all the more delicious. *SB*

Volunteer
Fun, quick, and easy ways to give back to the community

The California Maritime Academy
200 Maritime Academy Dr, Vallejo
654.1139
www.csum.edu
This rolling-admission school has a progressive education department for new immigrants and English-language learners. Come volunteer to teach a class! The diversity in the community is responsible for the local economy working well and all the food and wine production. There are many ways you can take part—even if you don't already communicate in multiple tongues. *SB*

Migrant Workers' Resource
2425 Jefferson St, Napa
253.3537
Spend a few hours of your time aiding migrant workers' well-being and education either at this location or at the resource center inside Napa Valley College. Call ahead to see how you can be of help to the entire Napa community. *SB*

Church Women United Clothing Center

2473 Second St, Napa

224.1341

When you aren't flipping through the racks to find something for yourself at this community-run thrift shop, you can get behind the counter and volunteer your time to pick up donations and organize the inventory of the only spot in Napa that gives clothes away. Men, women, and families in need can come and get new duds with help from the tidy church ladies. *SB*

Sunrise Horse Rescue

1098 Lodi Ln, St. Helena

963.7783

Few volunteering opportunities are this glamorous—well, except for the barnyard cleanup time! Play with these majestic horses and help out a stable that aims to provide happy lives to previously mistreated horses, many of which were expelled from a laborious racing career. *SB*

St. Helena Family Center

1440 Spring St, St. Helena

963.1919

Given that every hour another 300 or so Americans lose their access to health care, it's no wonder there is a need for free health services like those offered at this community resource. Lend a hand toward supporting local families here—you can take part in a variety of ways. *SB*

Veterans Home of California–Yountville

100 California Dr, Yountville

944.4600

There are many ways to volunteer time at this huge veterans' complex; you can read aloud, garden, and even help keep the pool facility up and running. Spend time with these wise folks who have participated in keeping America safe. They have really lived, and their stories alone make a trip here worthwhile. *SB*

Napa Emergency Women's Services

1141 Pear Tree Ln, Napa
255.6397

Help fundraise and plan fundraising events for this organization that aims to provide crucial services to local women at all stages of life. *SB*

Imbibe
Where to sip and swill with a local feel

Rockville Inn

4163 Suisun Valley Rd, Fairfield
864.4325
Daily 11a–10p

Grape growers and winemakers alike come here for casually romantic dates, to sip and swill the valley's best vintages and some inexpensive pints. In the dining room, roses grace each table and kindhearted waitstaff serve the same extensive drink menu as the bar next door, where all the locals hover after a long day's work in the hot sun. Come find some pleasant nosh and a drink to toast with your newfound friends. *SB*

Bounty Hunter

975 First St, Napa
226.3976
www.bountyhunterwine.com
Sun–Thurs 11a–10p, Fri–Sat 11a–1a

"Where do I go to find the good stuff?" This is a question I often ask myself on my wine-tasting travels, especially when there are huge estate wineries lining the streets and rural routes like those in Napa and Suisun valleys. But the good stuff is easily found at Bounty Hunter, where rare and uncommon vintages can be tasted or purchased for later imbibing. This week the seasonal special was an intoxicating 2005 Gaja Barbaresco—just my style and hard to contend with. Hourglass and newish Justice cabernet sauvignons vie for my attention. "Wine Scout" Jeff makes wine fun to drink and easy to understand, and inspires confidence in your own wine tastes rather than imposing the "should-like" tone of voice. His muttonchop sideburns crinkle up when he laughs at himself, as he harvests a bottle from the wall wine library like it's a delicate bunch of grapes. Come chat, giggle, and learn about your own taste buds, and when you get hungry, partake in the mean barbecue served at the stylish mahogany bar. The folks here somehow stay sober even though they taste some 5,000 wines a year, rejecting more than 90 percent of them to include only the best for sale in their coveted catalog. *sb*

Napa Smith Brewery

1 Executive Way, Napa
255.2912
www.napasmithbrewery.com
Mon–Fri 8a–5p

Enter Napa through its back door, Highway 12, and after a mile or so of grapevines you'll be stuck at a light next to some very large beige structures with noticeably castlelike wooden doors.

As I pulled up, I beheld Steve, the new president of Napa Smith Brewery, with rolled-up sleeves, watching the cellar master tip a forklift load of raisined zinfandel grapes into the crusher. Three or four men were overseeing every detail, checking off boxes on clipboards and stealing a grape or two to pop in their mouths. They gladly demonstrated their process of making a 2008 zinfandel—a new venture—that will be ready to drink in 2010.

Just next door is where hops from California and about 10 different countries are made into Napa Smith beers, which are found at more taps in the valley than any other brew, and for good reason. The pale ale is brighter than most, crisp and great with cheesy food like the flatbreads at Ubuntu (see page 54). Napa Smith's pilsner is clean, and I enjoyed mine with a light lunch of chicken salad with nasturtium flowers from the GrassRoutes garden (yes, you can find Napa Smith by the six-pack and even in 22-ounce bottles at markets around town). Brewmaster Don Barkley of Red Tail Ale fame is "let loose," according to Steve, to make the best beers, following the whim of his genius.

Sneak up on the Smith family like I did and you'll glimpse their family operation, set apart by fine brews and, recently, fine wines to match. *sb*

Cole's Chop House

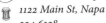

1122 Main St, Napa
224.6328
www.coleschophouse.com
Sun–Thurs 5–9p, Fri–Sat 5–10p

The bar at Cole's Chop House is one of my favorites in all of Napa. Although this place is all about perfectly dry-aged steak, a 24-ounce porterhouse steak shipped from Chicago isn't exactly the picture of sustainability. I head to the bar instead for an amazing list of cocktails made from the freshest ingredients (with names inspired by literature) and Napa wines from the most prestigious vines. Seasonal menu additions, many sourced from local farms, pair with my raspberry gimlet and my beau's Hemingway daiquiri with white rum and fresh-squeezed grapefruit juice. Pork loin from a nearby ranch, seared with apples and bacon and apple cider from Philo, is a great dish to split when it's available. Get into the masculine dark-wood atmosphere and taste a piece of true Americana the Napa way. *SB*

Oxbow Wine Merchant and Wine Bar

610 First St, Napa
257.5200
www.fpwm.com
Sun–Wed 9a–9p, Thurs–Sat 9a–10p

There's always a flutter of commotion around the Wine Merchant at Napa's Oxbow Public Market. That's because the central snack bar is the apple of everyone's eye, serving crisp picholine olives, fine-shaved cheeses, and colorful pasta salads for easily diverted shoppers. Take home the ingredients of any of the dishes you taste, but better yet, talk to the pourers and they'll match up your bite to a wine you've never heard of—even me, a wine writer. On a recent trip into the internationally stocked cellar, I came upon two rare Barolos, made in the old-country, Slovenian way with a rustic punch and some "floaties," as I like to call them. I went home with some forceful aged goat cheese and a big chewy red, a match made in heaven. In Oxbow Market this store is the first to open and the last to close, so even more reason to play matchmaker with your taste buds. *SB*

Pancha's of Yountville

6764 Washington St, Yountville
944.2125
Hours vary

This spot stands out mostly because of its sheer shock value. Amid the chichi diners of Yountville's single-pointed main street sits Pancha's, a dyed-in-the-wool dive bar. Cheap draft beers, shots of hard liquor, and beatable video games are here, with the crowd to match. I am so glad this place exists, and I'm not even a huge fan of dive bars, but it makes me more relaxed and easier with Yountville itself, a place trying so hard to project a specific image that I often don't feel like it is real. Take a breather from the pomp and circumstance at this locally owned Yountville staple. *SB*

Downtown Joe's American Grill and Brewhouse

902 Main St, Napa
258.2337
www.downtownjoes.com
Mon–Fri 8:30a–12a, Sat–Sun 8a–12a

Downtown Joe's is the first place on the Napa circuit for a beer. It stands out, literally, because it reaches over the bubbling Napa River with a gracious porch lit up even in the early afternoon, twinkling lights, and a buzz of locals and tourists clinking pint glasses. During the summer months the nights are always busy here, so it is near impossible not to meet your neighbor or a stranger-turned-friend. Often on Thursday and Friday nights live bands play at the riverside amphitheater below, and unless they sound like the garage band I heard on my last trip, the music should be a pleasant partner for unbeatable fries and a couple of pints of what's on special. *SB*

Stay In

The best take-out and take-home activities in town

La Luna

1153 Rutherford Rd, Rutherford
963.3211
Sun 8a–6p, Mon–Thurs 8a–7p

Burritos are an important part of life, wouldn't you agree? So I skip the fancy Ameri-Mexican joints on the main drag for La Luna, where you can buy an

entire extra bottle of salsa verde if you want your burrito "wet." Gather up snacks and ingredients while you wait your turn behind the winegrowers and their friends and family—carnitas burritos are the usual order. Fresh juices and cinnamon-y horchata are a grand relief for summertime thirst under the hot Napa sun. It's funny, even hoity-toity food writers and chefs (including Thomas Keller himself) tout their love for this spot, so I'm guessing they want to either eat "real food" just as much as any of us or investigate how to bring authentic, mouthwatering flavor combinations to their own cooking and are inspired by the wafting smells at this little gem. *SB*

Peters Video

1200 Main St, St. Helena (second location in Calistoga)
963.2739
Sun–Thurs 10a–9p, Fri–Sat 10a–10p

Peters Video is one of the few, if not the only, locally owned video stores in rural Napa, and the film buffs behind the counter (when local teenagers aren't manning the place) help me find the right movie for my mood. Most bed-and-breakfasts in the area offer pricey pay-per-view of horrid recent releases or have a gratis VHS sampling in their living room including the usual muck: *Jurassic Park, Honey, I Shrunk the Kids,* and something with Denzel Washington. Peters Video offers hard-to-find foreign gems that are ideal for those nights you want to explore the silver screen from inside your room. *SB*

 Lawler's Liquors

2232 Jefferson St, Napa

226.9311

$

Abraham, the man behind the counter, didn't know how Grandma Lawler got into the *malfatti* tradition, but he does know how to keep it alive, and the flavor and value make this my favorite Napa spot to find what the Italians call "badly made" and I call heaven in a blanket. *Malfatti* are spinach or chard dumplings, and the freshly cooked versions at Lawler's are only a few bucks a dozen. I get mine with a cup of house-made minestrone to go and add a six-pack for a sudsy variation on Napa's favorite drink—you'll find some interesting brews here. Pictures of Jesus, the family's kids and grandkids, and a few lucky horseshoes make up Lawler's backdrop to this authentic, low-maintenance food tradition. *SB*

Back Door Barbecue

1010 Lincoln Ave, Napa

252.9250

www.backdoorbbq.com

$

Daily 4:30–9p for takeout

Enter Red Rock Cafe from the back door and your to-go order of barbecue and fixins will be ready shortly. I like staying in and playing board games at least one night of my vacation, and nothing goes better with that than hot links and tri-tip doused in molasses-rich barbecue sauce. Keep your vacation going even when you are on the down-low with a carry-out meal from this back door. *SB*

Napa Taco Trucks

Various locations on Soscol Rd, Napa

$

I promise, this will be the only time I ever direct you to find and move toward a Wal-Mart. But the portion of Soscol Road opposite Napa's big-box store is home to several taco trucks of varying names and people. Come on a hot summer night, and the makeshift outdoor restaurants are exploding with happy taco-munchers. During the winter months there may be only one truck, but that's all it takes. To-go orders often come with a foil-wrapped goodie bag of pickled carrots, cauliflower, and jalapeños. The *lengua* (beef tongue) and carnitas (fried pork) are my top two picks, but no matter what you order you'll enjoy this fragrant, festive feast. Enjoy your meal roadside or get out of the glare of Wal-Mart and head back to your den to tempt your traveling companions with a taco. *SB*

Casual Night Out
Dining and delighting in a relaxed atmosphere

Villa Corona Cocina Mexicana

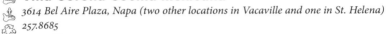
3614 Bel Aire Plaza, Napa (two other locations in Vacaville and one in St. Helena)
257.8685
www.villacoronamex.com
Mon–Fri 9a–9p, Sat 8a–9p, Sun 8a–8p

Smoky ranchero sauce, red rice, and smooth pinto beans are elements of the home-style Mexican cuisine at Villa Corona. Some specialties are the sopitos, fat corn patties piled with crunchy cabbage, shredded roast chicken, and cheese, and the tortugas, crispy flour tortilla triangles stuffed with grilled vegetables and Monterey Jack cheese and then drizzled with chili-infused sour cream over a salad. I get hungry just walking into this place—even though it looks like nothing special, with the exception of finger puppets strung from the ceiling, it smells like something very special. Finally, a relaxed place in Napa with amazing food and zero attitude. The Villasenors, second-generation Napans, run the business as a family, and you can feel the personal touch. *SB*

Bleaux Magnolia

1408 Clay St, Napa
252.2230

http://bleauxmagnolia.com
Mon–Sat 11:30a–2:30p, 5–9p; Sun 11a–2:30p, 5–8p

Creole makes an entrance to quiet little Napa here, and the effect is rather fabulous. Take classic French cooking techniques, layer on some Acadian adaptations and a smattering of Louisiana regional ingredients, and boom—Bleaux Magnolia. Gumbo, duck breast jambalaya, and cornbread catfish are impossible to decide among, but I start with fried green tomatoes so I have a bit more time to decide. All ingredients are carefully chosen by chef Matt Mermod, and many of them come from less than 100 miles away. The restaurant has no corkage fee for those who prefer to bring their own wine, and the cheese plate is glorious, crested with local triple-cream brie, dotted with fiery nuts, and slathered with honey. Considering the measures Bleaux Magnolia takes to impress with its lavish desserts, including bananas Foster and homemade root beer floats, you might not have room to fit in the cheese course. Come on Sunday when there is a brunch featuring classic beignets and jambalaya breakfast burritos. SB

El Tapatio Cafe

2982 Rockville Rd, Fairfield
434.8464
Daily 11a–9p
$

Smothered and spicy wet burritos, crispy taquitos, and mushy tamales are house favorites at this excellent, low-key family joint. The whole family can eat for around $20, which is unheard of anywhere else in the region, so eat up, get your hot-pepper fix, and recover from all your wine tasting with some home-style Mexican grub à la El Tapatio Cafe. SB

Ad Hoc

6476 Washington St, Yountville
944.2487
www.adhocrestaurant.com
$$$
Daily 5–9p, Sun 10:30a–2p for brunch

In my work, a great enjoyment is being able to make choices rather quickly, to ensure I get the behind-the-scenes look when a reservation becomes available or to discover a new region that had been overlooked. I often benefit from acting in the moment, and I wonder at a restaurant's ability to be in the moment, too, when planning menus. Thomas Keller's adored protégé, Dave Cruz, whom my waitress referred to as a "cuddly guy," determines each evening's four-course meal at Ad Hoc, where the menu can be made in freestyle fashion. He'll look over the local butchers' offerings, take a stroll through the French Laundry garden, sniff the air, and put the season together with his own daily inspiration, rolling out a $48 prix fixe menu each night.

Carpaccio, salads, and chilled soups are the usual beginnings of this rather huge dining experience (even a single order of the family-style menu guarantees leftovers). Meat, fish, or pasta is the main affair; tender veal scaloppine with buttery noodles and haricots verts decorated my most recent plate. Next up is the cheese course, in which braised endive or local wildflower honey might make an appearance. The meal finishes with classic American desserts that send patriotic shivers up my spine, especially when irresistible strawberry shortcake or peach cobbler made from Brentwood organic fruit is on the menu.

I recommend an early meal to ensure a bench seat facing the front of the restaurant. The dappled sunlight mingling with the veils of grape leaves and oak-covered hills is perfection with a bite of the local bounty and a taste of the terroir. *SB*

Dress Up

Don your shiny shoes and head out to one of these fancy places

French Laundry

6640 Washington St, Yountville
944.2380
www.frenchlaundry.com
$$$ *Daily 5:30–9p, Fri–Sun 11a–1p*

When a chef gets three Michelin stars for not one but two restaurants, it is hard to eat his food without the highest of expectations. But that is no problem for chef Thomas Keller. He likes the expectation game—in fact, I think he fans its flame.

On the French Laundry's menu (your only choice here is whether to opt for the vegetable menu or the everything menu) are small servings of flavor combinations. You are left wanting more, and then the next course comes and you repeat the feeling of desire. No ingredient shows up twice, and the flavor rainbow, together with the soft and velvety space and quiet din, make this a most sensual dining experience.

Though reinvented by this passionate cook, the French Laundry has been interesting since its beginnings, when the Schmitt family, now apple farmers, owned the stone-walled space. Make a reservation no less than two months in advance, and come early to watch the sun set over the restaurant garden across the street or sit by the flowering hedge in the courtyard. Pick out a special outfit, but stay comfortable—the last thing you'll be thinking about is how you look when you are biting into aiguillette of Liberty Farms Peking duck with Swiss chard, chanterelle mushrooms, Tokyo turnips, and sauce Colbert; or butternut squash tortellini with pomegranate kernels, butternut squash confit, and brown butter emulsion; or honeycomb sabayon glacé with spiced tuile, tupelo honey ice cream, and Santa Rosa plum confiture. *SB*

Étoile Restaurant

1 California Dr, Yountville
204.7529
www.domainechandon.com
$$$ *Thurs–Mon 11:30a–2:30p, 6–9:30p*

Part of Domaine Chandon, the large sparkling-wine producer, Étoile is an elegant yet comfortable place to celebrate life with someone special over bubbles and beautiful plates. Not all of the entrées pass the sustainability test, but they include plenty of local ingredients elevated with the fanfare of a gorgeous space and no shortage of wine pairings. Oyster tastings, featuring local shellfish, are served raw, fried tempura style, and poached, and in the entrée category, seared duck breast with white peaches and baklava pâte is the shiniest star on the menu. *SB*

Redd

$$$ 6480 Washington St, Yountville
944.2222
www.reddnapavalley.com
Daily 11:30a–2:30p, 5:30–10p; bar menu available 2:30p–12a

Following the trail of chef Richard Reddington of Redd shines the light on what sets his contemporary California cuisine apart: he's been the menu maker at Masa's, Jardinière, and Napa's own Auberge du Soleil restaurant. Each ingredient is given serious consideration, but humor enters with his brilliant pairings of chorizo, sausage, and saffron, or burdock and soy caramel with glazed pork belly. Most of his ingredients are from producers near the restaurant. Napa is known for beautiful and artful food, and Redd is one more reason why. *SB*

Martini House

1245 Spring St, St. Helena
963.2233
www.martinihouse.com
$$$ Daily, hours vary

I drove up St. Helena's main drag hungry, watching posh people slip into the rows of Main Street eateries. I turned the bend, hoping to find something different, something set apart, literally and figuratively. And what did I discover but Martini House—designed by the man behind the restaurants Boulevard and Jardinière (both in San Francisco)—which welcomed me with its candle-covered backyard dining room and manly, regal interior. The menu lived up to the ambiance—I had three different amuse-bouche before I had even made a decision to order the duck breast, rare, with two preparations of figs: fresh puréed and macerated Missions. Nothing is more beautiful than gracious, authentic service, and that is another standout at Martini House, where I was more respectfully taken care of than at any other restaurant in

town. Don't miss the prehistoric walrus head set atop the shimmering bar (the owners found it on a trip to Alaska) or the fun frog prince paintings in the loo. Every detail is fun and enjoyable, including the luscious food. *SB*

Auberge du Soleil

180 Rutherford Hill Rd, Rutherford
800.348.5406
www.aubergedusoleil.com
$$$ *Daily 7–11a, 11:30a–2:30p, 5:30–9:30p*

As if slowly sinking into wriggling oak branches and stripes of vines, you can have this complete escape for a short evening if you can't stay for a few days in total retreat. I choose the vegetarian tasting menu every time—it is simply the most amazing assemblage of herbivore delights, like roasted cherries with pistachio sable, and potato gnocchi with black summer truffles, pea shoots, and foraged mushrooms. There is no better way to become a whisper in your own reality, by focusing on textured flavors while in view of only the dry veils of wrapping hills and the luxurious abode around you. The memory of a meal here stays with you, so that you can be there once more in your daydreams without a flinch. The hotel and spa are wonderful and tempting, but this restaurant is not one to miss. After all, what other hotel do you know of that was started by a chef as a restaurant and branched out to hospitality from a food perspective? *SB*

ZuZu

829 Main St, Napa
224.8555
www.zuzunapa.com
Mon–Thurs 11:30a–10p, Fri 11:30a–11p, Sat 4–11p, Sun 4–10p

Few Napa eateries offer the same level of refined indulgence at this price point. Feast on a table full of small plates with friends and family, who follow you because they've learned to trust your tastes. My favorites are *boquerones*, a mix of fresh anchovies with hard-boiled eggs and a flavorful rémoulade, and the quinoa salad with shredded duck breast. Moroccan rack of lamb and never-chewy Monterey squid are two bigger dishes I can't avoid ordering, the steam still rising from the fresh-cut meat as it arrives at my crowded table. Chef Angela Tamura is choosy about where her ingredients come from, and I am happy to say she rarely puts seafood on her tantalizing menu that doesn't pass my sustainability test. Spicy red wines are a good choice for this authentic cuisine, which is influenced by the world and created with California love. *SB*

FARM

4048 Sonoma Hwy, Napa
299.4880
www.thecarnerosinn.com
Mon–Sat 11:30a–2:30p, 5:30–10p, Sun 10:30a–2p

The Carneros Inn complex is home to some of Napa's most indulgent and simultaneously sustainable luxuries, and FARM has a lot to do with that. FARM is the drop-dead delicious fine-dining room (Boon Fly Café, see page 20, has great casual fare and lunch), where romancers staying at the inn go to toast their special occasion. Chef Jeff Jake treats his guests like Italian royalty; the restaurant wraps around a courtyard and bocce court, the sport of Napa. And although the menu has echoes of far-off lands, it sings the praises of its own terroir and incorporates only organic or sustainably farmed ingredients. As long as you avoid the tuna and halibut dishes (both types of fish are nearly impossible to eat sustainably, as their habitat has been halved in the last decade), you can rest assured that the meal's subtle elegance will be perpetuated for future generations. The late-night menu is a grand way to stay up into the wee hours, gaze at the sparkling stars, and throw around a bocce ball or two before you turn in. *SB*

Angèle

 *540 Main St, Napa*

 252.8115

 www.angelerestaurant.com

$$

Mackerel and spiced chickpeas, frisée salad with poached eggs and de Puy lentils, lamb sausage with duck confit—just reading Angèle's menu makes my mouth water. I get gussied up in a pretty dress so I look good for the food, which is plated so artfully it inspires me to go the extra mile myself. Make a reservation ahead of time and be sure to also read the menu online in advance, otherwise it may be nearly impossible to narrow down the possibilities on the spot. *SB*

25°Brix Restaurant and Gardens

7377 St. Helena Hwy, Napa

944.2749

www.25degreesbrix.com

$$$

Mon–Thurs 11:30a–9p, Fri 11:30a–9p, Sat 11:30a–9p, Sun 10a–9p

The menu at Brix, named for the sugar-to-water ratio of dissolved solids in grapes, comes from 14 raised garden beds surrounding the restaurant. Luxurious incarnations of these vegetables find themselves on your white-clothed table, together with organic meats and sustainable seafood. Order Brix wine and you'll taste the grapes planted on the very hills the window-side tables face. Meyer lemons, ripe figs, and many berries add to the particularly outstanding desserts, one of the highlights of a meal here. I order the lemon-blueberry parfait or the strawberry and peach pot de crème after my Monterey calamari or white corn risotto with beans from the garden. *SB*

Ubuntu

1140 Main St, Napa
251.5656
www.ubuntunapa.com
$$$ *Mon–Thurs 5:30–9p, Fri–Sun 11:30a–2:30p, 5:30–10p*

From the outside, all I could see were strawlike curtains shrouding in mystery this restaurant, a place many claim to be the world's most inventive vegetarian dinner spot. Throughout my Wine Country travels, whether in Sonoma, Mendocino, Suisun Valley, or even the tiny northern towns of Napa, I'd heard that Jeremy Fox and his wife Deanie were doing something truly unique and amazing in their restaurant-slash-yoga-studio in the city of Napa. "Don't leave without trying the cauliflower pot," recommended the brewmaster at Napa Smith. "You're going to fall head over heels for the *carta da musica*— nothing that crispy ever tasted so good," said the concierge at Auberge du Soleil. From my own experience eating at top restaurants, from Seattle's Canlis to Yountville's French Laundry, I wanted to see a chef work wonders with vegetables, without the "crutch" of meat to add texture and flavor.

I was taken under Jeremy's wing on a culinary adventure through his inspirations and his garden, this week bursting with tomatoes. The first course, the aforementioned *carta da musica*, was indeed a delicate, crispy wafer covered in wild baby greens and shaved truffle pecorino with trumpet mushroom chips, each ingredient added to create a symphony of flavor. Chef Jeremy showcased his limitless innovation in the tomato tasting menu, pairing slow-roasted tomatoes with creamy zucchini hummus, a dab of reduced olive caramel, and neat spoonfuls of eggplant caponata, which must also have received the same, slow-cooked treatment. Tomato consommé was next, enlivened with garlic confit, okra from biodynamic winemaker Benziger's garden, and shell beans. The effect reminded me of Vietnamese dessert soups, where mung beans and tapioca balls float in sweetened coconut broth. Paired with a breathtaking rosé, the potato salad and cauliflower in a cast-iron pot were brought to life. The potatoes, boiled and fried, were huddled together with tarragon and caper cream, and decorated with *ficoïde glaciale*, a palate-stretching ice plant with a citrus aftertaste and crispy texture. The nuance of creamed cauliflower, scented with *vadouvan* (a French variety of curry) and layered with roasted florets and raw "couscous," also made from cauliflower, was perhaps the most unique use of that vegetable I have sampled to date.

Other highlights of the six-course feast were salty chickpea fries, cubed and scattered as crouton alternatives in my salad, Deanie's brioche with butter and roasted cipollini onion and three-day tomato sofrito, local polenta with smoked corn and the same sofrito, and shiso dumplings, made with my favorite Japanese herb and toasted bread to resemble something like upscale matzo balls swimming in tomato broth.

Needless to say, I didn't miss the meat, and Jeremy's menu was uninhibited to the point of an exhaustive vegetarian adventure, where all the norms are challenged, all the taste buds are engaged, and complementary textures are in full force. Even if you can't get into the artistic means with which food is expressed here, you can at least say that the restaurant is evolving cuisine, one menu at a time. I'll be back for another food voyage with Ubuntu and perhaps a pre-meal yoga class in the glass-enclosed studio upstairs. *SB*

Listen

Any auditory experience you can imagine

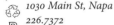

Napa Valley Opera House

1030 Main St, Napa
226.7372
www.nvoh.org

Don't let the name miff you—I've seen Ahmad Jamal, one of my favorite jazz pianists, at this so-called opera house. But that's not to say there isn't opera here. The historic building housing this modern, fully equipped stage plays host to string quartets, real jazz (none of that canned "easy listening" stuff), and yes, opera. Musicians wanting a respite from city performances happily accept invitations to perform in this magnificent space in the hospitable Napa Valley, and I am just as happy to play audience for the occasion. *SB*

Sunday Jazz at Sardine Can

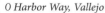

0 Harbor Way, Vallejo
553.9492
www.sardinecan.net
Sun–Thurs 8a–9p, Fri–Sat 8a–10p

At Harbor Way right by the Mare Island Causeway is the good old Sardine Can, a local hangout for 20 years, where crab sandwiches and clam chowder come with live music nearly every night. Owner Nanette cooks up classic American-style seafood treats to the sounds of local musicians. My favorite time to go is on a lazy Sunday, when a long bike ride is too ambitious and a Bloody Mary with celery and jazz is the perfect seaside spectacle, without the boisterous buzz of Napa Valley on a weekend. *SB*

Vallejo Music Theatre

Fetterly Playhouse for the Arts, 3467 Sonoma Blvd, Vallejo
552.2789
www.vallejomusictheatre.org

Home to Vallejo's vivid performing-arts scene, including the Vallejo Symphony and the Vallejo Choral Society, this stage sees all the Broadway hits to boot, directed and performed by local talents. Founded in 1967, this theater brings people from all over the Bay Area to indulge their fetish for classic musicals at affordable prices. Come early and join neighbors for supper at the theater's Supper Club, and get yourself and your family away from the TV screen for a night of true entertainment in rich American fashion. *SB*

Napa Valley Symphony

Lincoln Theater, 299 California Dr, Yountville
226.6872
www.napavalleysymphony.org

Classical music is sexy again, when great concerts are marketed by theme à la Napa Symphony. Find Handel, Saint-Saëns, Ravel, and de Falla on a bill called "Fireworks," or Vivaldi, Borodin, Mahler, and Tchaikovsky selections at a "Heart Strings" concert with strings only. The tone and pitch of the concerts are surprisingly good; however, there are some concerts where only one movement of each piece is played, and I've never been into the whole classical mix-tape thing. Pops concerts lull those who don't want to go to a real classical concert, but I think once they see this symphony playing behind a popular sax player or singer, they'll want to come back and hear some of the heavyweights. You know I'll be there—if I have a choice of concert it's the symphony first, but hey, that's me. *SB*

Napa Valley Youth Symphony

Various locations
916.600.4228
www.nvyso.org

Adults aren't the only ones who play instruments in Napa. This youth orchestra, started in 2002, has been recognized as one of the best in the state. Hear them all together at the Lincoln Theater (see page 11) or in sinfonia (with the youngest musicians) or quartet ensembles at other locations around the valley. Since the musicians practice all year long at least once a week together, they mean business when they sit down to perform. SB

The White Barn

2727 Sulphur Springs Ave, St. Helena
251.8715
www.thewhitebarn.org

Once upon a time this big barn housed carriages traversing the Sierras on those tricky western migrations. Now there is no sign of the Civil War general who built the place back in the 1870s, just lively shows that benefit local charities. This is one of the coolest places to see a concert. The barn is no longer full of hay; rather, it contains comfy seats for bardic Irish music, jazz choir, and blues shows. Each and every paid ticket contributes to the well-being of the community—when you purchase your ticket, the staff will tell you which fund your money is supporting. SB

Jarvis Conservatory

1711 Main St, Napa
255.5445
www.jarvisconservatory.com

The Jarvis Conservatory is my favorite place to go at night in Napa (OK, aside from one of the schmancy eateries). Where else can you see a Louis Bourgeois film? Where else can you find a puppet festival? Where do the best ensembles come to play, sing, and act? Jarvis. The conservatory hosts a slew of local performances, including high school plays, but I go for the choral concerts (sometimes groups come up from San Francisco) and the art films, which show at least once a week. I am an art-house cinema junkie, so the prospect of seeing *Trouble the Water* or *Man on Wire* is an easy sell. *Othello*, *The Barber of Seville*, and *Don Giovanni* are just a few of the popular operas performed on this stage. Performers are trained at the conservatory, and this place makes a determined effort to shed light on the rich Hispanic culture that lives here, too. Don't say you can't get real culture in Wine Country—it just ain't true! *SB*

Brannan's Grill

1374 Lincoln Ave, Calistoga
942.2233
www.brannansgrill.com
Mon–Sat 11:30a–close, Sun 11a–close

Each and every weekend of the year, Brannan's Grill brings live musicians to its small stage, hosting mostly jazz performers who lull you to eat with their smooth vibes or lively saxes. I always take a seat at the carved wooden bar, where locals and tourists alike enjoy $5 pints and peppered conversation when the music is in full swing. On a recent visit the trio was so inspiring that I found myself turning in small, romantic circles in the arms of my beau along the row of linen-swathed tables. One of my favorite Brannan's combinations is free-range roast chicken or local oysters with a Sprecher cream soda, which tastes extra delish when the jazz is in full swing. *SB*

Lodge
Great places to rest your noggin

El Bonita Motel

195 Main St, St. Helena
963.3216
www.elbonita.com

As much as I love luxury, it is sometimes hard to actually get ZZZs when everything is über-chic and royaltylike. I get the best rest at El Bonita, where there are beautiful pools and amenities, but a more relaxed atmosphere and no major 'tude. The vintage sign makes this place stand out when whizzing by on Highway 12 on a weekday. *SB*

Auberge du Soleil

180 Rutherford Hill Rd, Rutherford
963.1211
www.aubergedusoleil.com
$$$

No other Napa Valley hotel creates the kind of complete retreat fostered at Auberge du Soleil. In fact, if you opt to make a reservation here you'll likely stay on the property your whole visit and have the best of the valley come to you. Exquisite rooms are a portal to another reality, where no worries can exist, and between the spa, the restaurant, and the amenities, you won't be wanting for more. The hotel has huge, private maisons and smaller, cozier rooms with a view, but there is no wrong room to book at this lush oasis. You will feel pampered just setting foot here. *SB*

Poetry Inn

6380 Silverado Tr, Napa
944.0646
www.poetryinn.com
$$$

The luxurious outpost of Cliff Lede Vineyards, Poetry Inn is a lofty set of huge rooms overlooking the Stags Leap appellation. No part of your stay here shies away from royal treatment, and while I adore the attention to detail, I sometimes wonder why an escape like this is seen as the be-all end-all of vacations. For a couple of days of ultimate tranquility with a high price tag, Poetry Inn can't be beat—just expect to have a removed experience. *SB*

Oleander House

7433 St. Helena Hwy, Yountville
944.8315
www.oleander.com
$$

A homey—and yes, a tad hokey—bed-and-breakfast that typifies the soft side of this lush valley, the Oleander House is a comfortable place and not in an artificial sense. You get to meet everyone who's staying, chat over a home-cooked breakfast, cuddle and sleep in, or use the place as a home away from home to explore the surrounding regions. This is an inn the whole family will be happy residing at, and after a day or two it'll feel like you live there. *SB*

The Cottages of Napa Valley

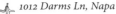 *1012 Darms Ln, Napa*

252.7810

www.napacottages.com

$$$

Little rows of colorful cottages decked out on the inside with freestanding tubs, classy country decor, and fireplaces offer more than meets the eye for the lucky folks who find their way here. Though you'll pay a pretty penny for a night basking in laid-back luxury, it is well worth it for a special occasion when all your focus is on your loved one, and the only interruption you want is to find breakfast waiting at your doorstep at an appointed time. *SB*

 Solage

 755 Silverado Tr, Calistoga

942.7442

 www.solagecalistoga.com

$$$

Although many Napa-bound tourists are of either the lover or star-crossed type, the whole family can experience laid-back luxury at Solage, where the 89 studios are so well contained that the lovers can be left well alone and the families can adore their playful children without too much commingling. Your hard-won pennies go toward a complete sensory overload, where details have been given more consideration than you ever thought possible or necessary. But they also go toward something more important, something often passed over in the name of luxury: a sustainable future. Hemp curtains, paraben-free sunscreen samples (did you know that when using most sunscreens you were putting carcinogens on your skin?), nontoxic laminates and paints, air-flow architecture, solar panels, wool upholstery, and reclaimed cedar exteriors are just a smattering of the people- and environment-friendly choices Solage has made. You won't find a plethora of plastic water bottles at your bedside here—just cotton sheets so soft you'd think they were silk, smooth pebble showers, and an excuse to stay in your room all day, whether you're a kid or just one at heart. *SB*

Rose Garden Inn

1277 St. Helena Hwy, St. Helena

963.4417

www.rosegardeninn.net

Lodging in luxury is possible for under $200 even in Napa—you just have to know where to go. Finding the Rose Garden Inn, located just off the St. Helena Highway, was such a discovery. Stay in the reasonably priced Rose Room or the fancier Tulip Room and you'll have the same comfortable treatment, including a better-than-average breakfast. Wi-Fi, flowering gardens, and big tubs complete the amenities. *SB*

Gaia Napa Valley Hotel and Spa

3600 Broadway St, American Canyon

674.2100

www.gaianapavalleyhotel.com

While on a mission to Wine Country, there's a stop at "the gateway to Napa Valley" that no earth-conscious traveler should miss: the greenest hotel in the nation. Yes, we in Northern California are that blessed—the Gaia Napa Valley Hotel and Spa takes the green concept and hits the ground running, bringing the beauty and bounty of the outdoors right into the comfort of a luxury hotel.

Architecturally, Gaia, which is Greek for "Mother Earth," is a strange creature: it appears that you're walking into Venus's shell. Decorated in earth tones, the 131-room hotel is composed of Forest Stewardship Council lumber, carpet containing recycled content, recycled tiles and granite, and low VOC (volatile organic compound) sealants, adhesives, and paints. Upon entrance, guests can view the lobby's real-time display of how much water and electricity the hotel is (or isn't) using.

The rooms, which sport names like Grasshopper and Daffodil (each comes with literature on its namesake), have the most advanced yet unbelievably logical feature: a sensor that detects when the rooms are occupied and adjusts the temperature as necessary, using 15 percent less energy than most hotels. The shower water also goes through a filtration system that drains into the courtyard's pond, and a copy of Al Gore's book *An Inconvenient Truth* is tucked into every nightstand, alongside the Bible and Buddha's teachings, for whatever sort of enlightenment you're seeking. *JD*

Lavender

2020 Webber Ave, Yountville
944.1388
www.lavendernapa.com
$$

Sprinkled with lavender plants, golden feverfew, purple sage, and black-eyed Susans, this cozy inn looks more like Grandma's house than a Wine Country destination. During late afternoons, the wheelchair-accessible wraparound porch is speckled with smug couples drinking gratis wine and rekindling romance. Little rows of cabinlike rooms, each with its own private vine-covered veranda, hem in the original structure, a classic craftsman-style bungalow.

The woman at the desk, Marion, greeted me jovially, pushing extra scented bath salts on me and encouraging me to use the pool and hot tub at nearby Maison Fleurie, a sister hotel. The retreatlike aspect of the private outdoor space made it hard to leave—two lounge chairs, a fountain, and full, fragrant wine barrels lulled me into long reading and writing sessions. With a complimentary wine tasting and a filling breakfast buffet, plus amenities like light-switch fireplaces and huge tiled baths, Lavender is a complete Yountville experience. *SB*

The Bordeaux House

$$$
6600 Washington St, Yountville
944.2855

www.bordeauxhouse.com

Keeping with Napa's ever-present theme, the Bordeaux House is perched at the midpoint between good eating and good drinking. Its warm brick structure immediately invited me in, and I got distracted sitting by the courtyard fountain before I could find my way to my room. Simple, old-school designs with updated perks make each varietal-named room sing with homey comfort. Retreating back to Gerwurtz (which is equipped with a private hot tub) after eating far too much at a string of star-studded eateries makes it not quite so bad that we decided to go for dessert. *SB*

Starr Mansion Bed & Breakfast

503 Mclane St, Vallejo
645.8164
www.starrmansionbb.com
$$

This is one of the reviews I wish I didn't have to write. I want to keep this place a secret, keep it to myself, but alas, my duty is to share my finds, so listen up. The restoration of this 1896 Victorian, just 5 miles from Napa and its attractions, has eight unique rooms at a fraction of the cost of places on the other side of the county line. Palm trees, bay views, and double-down comforters, plus free wine, cheese, and hot bevvies make Starr Mansion Bed & Breakfast just as comfortably luxurious as its neighbors, but more historically rich and much less expensive. Personal service includes in-room massages (schedule in advance) and a full breakfast, including all the extras like homemade jam and unsalted fresh cream butter. The powder-blue building is lit up at night, welcoming me even when I arrived a little later than expected. *SB*

Less Expensive Stays

Courtyard Marriott

1000 Fairgrounds Dr, Vallejo
644.1200

Best Western Inn

1596 Fairgrounds Dr, Vallejo
100 Soscol Ave, Napa
877.846.3729

Fairfield Inn by Marriott

315 Pittman Rd, Fairfield
864.6672

Motel 6 Vallejo

1455 Marine World Pkwy and 597 Sandy Beach Rd, Vallejo
642.7781

Camping in Napa and Suisun Valleys

Skyline Wilderness Park

2201 Imola Ave, Napa
252.0481
There's room for 20 tents and 40 camper vans or RVs in a shrub-lined parking area. For only $15 a night you can take in the beautiful hiking trails and rest your head close to the Napa action.

Spanish Flat Resort

4290 Knoxville Rd, Napa
966.7700
Just to the west of Lake Berryessa, Spanish Flat is ideal for a more rural Napa experience, loaded with paddling, fishing, and s'mores at sundown.

Bothe Napa Valley State Park

3801 N St. Helena Hwy, Calistoga
942.4575

A full-service state park, Bothe Napa is always busy with annual celebrations, bocce players, day hikers, and camping groups. There's a creek and a pool, trees to climb and shaded picnic benches—all that you'd want in a centrally located park.

Twin Sisters Park

1875 Twin Sisters Rd, Suisun City
425.1298

Pretend this area of California is still the Wild West, as you sleep under the stars and warm breeze, the discoverer of gold, grapes, and green gold—olives!

Resources

Helpful things

Wine Library TV

http://tv.winelibrary.com

Belligerence was never so good. I love this fearless, funny, lighthearted take on drinking wine, and if you don't already know about Wine Library TV, get on the boat. A chalkboard behind host Gary Vaynerchuk (pronounced "vay-ner-chuk") tells the theme of each episode (for a recent classic Chianti show, it was "Family Is Everything"), and fun guests make this quirky show even quirkier. While his best buddy films, Gary directs us toward value vintages with a good QPR (quality-price ratio), and he also goes off on non-wine-related tangents: one episode you may hear about his vast baseball knowledge (a bonus for me, a lifelong Phillies fan), be entertained by his comedic blathering, or listen to anecdotes from his life and family. Watching this vlog will make you happy to enjoy wine casually. Gary spits into his bucket, which is covered with Jets stickers, and always gives his two cents while reminding us to follow our own opinions and "listen to nothing [he] says." *SB*

St. Helena Shipping Company

1241 Adams St, St. Helena
963.0141
www.sthelenashippingcompany.com

With increased airport security measures and policies, it is harder than ever to transport your drinkable souvenirs back home. Avoid high shipping costs at wineries by using this resource, which will package and ship any number of bottles to your home or friends' homes. Easy.

Nouveau Highlands Calendar

January

Napa Valley Mustard Festival

Last weekend of January through the end of March
Various locations
944.1133
www.mustardfestival.com

February

Dinner Is Served

Last weekend in February
Various restaurants, Napa
738.3178

June

Auction Napa Valley

First weekend in June
963.3388

It's June Thing

First weekend in June
Suisun City
www.suisun.com

July

Fourth of July

July 4
Suisun City, Napa, and Yountville

Napa Valley Classic

Third weekend in July
Napa Valley Fair Grounds, Calistoga
942.4222

Wine Country Film Festival

Last week in July
Various theaters and venues, Napa and Sonoma
996.2536
www.winecountryfilmfest.com

Napa Valley Shakespeare Festival

July through August
Various locations, Napa
www.napashakespeare.org

August

August Fest

Second weekend in August
Suisun City
www.suisun.com

Napa Town and County Fair

Third weekend in August
Napa Valley Exposition Center
253.4900

September

Napa River Festival

Throughout September
257.0322

Suscol Intertribal Powwow

Last weekend in September
Veterans Home of California-Yountville
Picnic Grounds

October

Wine Flights at Wineries of Napa Valley

First weekend in October
1285 Napa Town Center
253.9450

Waterfront Festival

First weekend in October
Suisun City
www.suisun.com

Fire Department Open House

Second weekend in October
Suisun City
www.suisun.com

Fun Family Farm Days

Third weekend in October
Suisun Valley
www.suisunvalley.com

Annual Benefit Art Auction

Third weekend in October
Di Rosa Preserve, 5200 Carneros Hwy,
Napa
226.5991

Halloween Parade

Evening of October 31
Suisun City
www.suisun.com

Halloween Spooktacular

Last week in October
V Marketplace, 6525 Washington St,
Yountville
944.2451

November

Napa County Farm Bureau Barn Dance

First weekend in November
Napa Valley Expo Chardonnay Hall,
575 Third St, Napa
224.5403

Napa Valley Viticultural Fair

First weekend in November
944.8311

December

West Coast Gingerbread House Contest

First weekend in December
Cedar Gables Inn, 486 Coombs St, Napa
224.7969
www.cedargablesinn.com

Suisun Valley Grape Growers Association Winemakers Dinner

Last weekend in December
www.suisunvalley.com

SUBURBAN COWBOYS

About Livermore Valley and Beyond

Livermore's quickly growing agricultural industry has a nice and pretty face. Let me explain: first off, the valley looks like Tuscany as soon as you veer off Interstate 580 and get lost on Isabel or Wetmore Road. Also, the 40-some winemakers here aren't exactly just messing around with a hobby. Bigger producers Concannon and Wente have even taken some of the smaller producers under their wing, chatting about tricks of the trade in between planting new acres of vineyards. Since 1994, the Tri-Valley Conservancy has protected the land from exponential suburban sprawl by mandating acre-for-acre development/intensive agriculture, which equates to acres and acres of olive trees and grapes for every couple of ticky-tacky houses put up.

The Tri-Valley, consisting of towns in the Amador, Livermore, and San Ramon valleys, has a sandy-colored, rolling landscape, similar to that of the aforementioned Tuscan countryside, with year-round sunshine and bristling cypress trees running alongside old olive trees and corduroy vineyards. Right off the highway you can escape the big-box stores and see this beautiful place through its locally owned shops and family wineries. But you might also notice the many opulent homes in the area, particularly in Danville and Pleasanton, which vie for the title of "richest midsized town" in the nation with a median household income of over 100 grand. A major reason for this wealth is the infamous Lawrence Livermore National Laboratory, set up by the University of California over 50 years ago. During the Cold War, this 700-acre site was where nuclear weapons were conceived of, created, and tested, and a long list of them, from the W27 Regulus cruise missile to the Navy's Polaris missile, are still safely housed here, continually monitored. Now that nuclear warfare has gone out of fashion (thankfully), the lab has shifted into laser tech, how to store dangerous and complicated chemicals like plutonium (did you know it has nine different solid states alone?), groovy magnetic transportation (which will revolutionize mass transit in the not-so-distant future), and how to accurately model the climates, and thus climate changes, which fetched Nobel recognition in 2007.

"Science in the name of national security" has employed a large population of brainiacs in the area, and some of them have retired from chemistry at the lab to chemistry of the soil with a winery of their own. Scientific pursuits and farming existing side by side isn't new—olive and pear trees were planted here in the mid-1800s around the same time the area became known for film production, and the area still produces some of the tastiest fruits and oils in all of California.

But the rolling hills of the Tri-Valley are home to more than bulbs and bombs. There are also lovely beasts roaming around: horses! Livermore is known for the "quickest rodeo," with more horses and bulls hitting the dirt each hour than anywhere else in the world. And there's no shortage of cowboy boots and stylin' hats either. Other highlights? The world's longest-burning light bulb is housed in the Livermore Firehouse, and the Bay Area's largest Hindu temple sits on Livermore's hills. This dynamic area is one of the best undiscovered gems of California. Although it's often passed over for Napa and Sonoma counties, there's no way I could write a Wine Country book without including this bountiful and interesting area.

Getting Around
Helpful tips to get from point A to point B

Dublin Cyclery

7001 Dublin Blvd, Dublin

925.828.8676

www.dublincyclery.com

More than just a place to rent a bike for a day, Dublin Cyclery is nuts about all the other biking bells and whistles. Try a recumbent for a new challenge; it is fun sitting back while your legs go round and round in front of you. You can also find bike stands to turn your cycle into an indoor machine, so you can bike without going anywhere when it is too soggy for a long ride outside. Tune your bike up or just stop it here to get a new water bottle and some trail tips for the Tri-Valley area. *SB*

BART (Bay Area Rapid Transit)

510.464.7134
www.bart.gov

BART is the award-winning rapid transit system serving the East Bay, San Francisco, and parts of the Peninsula. BART has several stops in San Francisco, but it's mostly an East Bay thing. BART is the best way to get to and from Oakland International Airport (with a free shuttle to the Coliseum BART station) or from San Francisco International Airport direct to Oakland. BART cards, available from vending machines in each station, can be purchased in any amount for a single trip or multiple trips; fare charts are posted. You can carry your bike on BART provided you're not traveling during rush hour (7:05–8:50am and 4:25–6:45pm).

BART has Tri-Valley stops in Fremont, Pleasanton, Dublin, and Walnut Creek—just check the system map online for all the stops out that way. *SB*

Livermore Amador Valley Transit Authority

925.455.7500
www.wheelsbus.com

The main transit center for handy Wheels buses is at Livermore's Railroad Court, which is close to local shopping and near the weekly farmers market. Find detailed routes and schedules online so you can get around the area sans car and easily between BART and your final destination in the Tri-Valley. *SB*

Transbay Blog

http://transbayblog.com

Out in the blogosphere, the best place to get under the skin of Bay Area transit is the Transbay Blog, which gives daily updates on the newest routes, schedule changes, and other transportation news. Find all the info you could wish for about public transit in this neck of the woods. *SB*

Local Banking

Tri Valley Bank

1756 First St, Livermore; 925.791.4360

Valley Community Bank

1986 Second St, Livermore; 925.243.9600

Bank of Walnut Creek (Livermore branch)
211 S J St, Livermore; 925.373.3811

Even though Livermore is dotted with big-box stores and multinational chains, the town's local banks have a strong community ethic and serve a large percentage of individuals, and many locally owned businesses choose to bank locally and keep the money circulating (and benefiting) the community. All three of these banks have ATMs that charge less than the $2–$3 fee Bank of America or Wells Fargo will hit you with around the corner. *SB*

Explore
Places where the wide world is explained and adventure is waiting to be had

Hindu Community and Cultural Center
1232 Arrowhead Ave, Livermore
925.455.0404
http://livermoretemple.org

The biggest temple for Hindus in the Bay Area, this cultural and religious center hosts unique musical events and art shows throughout the year, in addition to the more traditional celebrations. The community is very welcoming, even if you know little about the culture, and it is not a high-pressure environment. People can come as they are, with whatever beliefs they hold dear, as long as they respect a few ground rules: namely, don't be insanely rude, maintain a peaceful manner, don't show up after a two-week backpacking trip with no shower first, don't smoke or chat away on your cell phone, and don't photograph the deities. Artist Day is usually in mid-July, and Basava Jayanthi is celebrated in early May. *SB*

Antique Shops of Niles

Niles Antiques and Collectibles
37759 Niles Blvd, Niles; 510.744.1602

Bite and Browse
37565 Niles Blvd, Niles; 510.796.4537

Lost in the Attic
37663 Niles Blvd, Niles; 510.791.2420

My Friends and I

37521 Niles Blvd, Niles; 510.792.0118

Morning Glory

37372 Niles Blvd, Niles; 510.790.3374

Tyme for Tea

37501 Niles Blvd, Niles; 510.790.0944

Alan Ginsberg told the world that Kansas was the central vortex of these United States. Did we listen to his holler? Now I tell you that Niles is the belly-button vortex of the antique world. On this stretch of seemingly dusty, corral-style conveyance as street I have found many of the best shops for high-quality collectables and antiques. It is a hoot and a half to stroll from shop to shop, as you feel you have gone back in time, into this area's actual history. Step across the threshold of the dusty brick façade of Dan Grimes's Niles Antiques and Collectibles and then roam in either direction. *IB*

Niles Essanay Silent Film Museum

37417 Niles Blvd, Fremont
510.494.1411
www.nilesfilmmuseum.org
Sat–Sun 12–4p

Would you want to leave the Chicago winters to find a place where you could make movies all year long? In 1912 the start-up Essanay Company traveled to the Fremont area, which boasted glorious apricot and other fruit and nut trees as far as the leaves met the sky. The *S* and the *A* of Essanay, Spoor and Anderson built a moviemaking home along the dusty trails in the wilds of Niles. The cowboys had to evacuate the hotel for the easterners to occupy it. You still get the western feel in the cavernous wooden theater with folding chairs for screenings of silent and old-timey flicks.

It is worth the ride to the Niles Edison Theater for one of its special events, which often include an expert panel from old Hollywood. I went to a Charlie Chaplin two-film extravaganza there, at which relatives of the original Essanay Company actors and players attended. The event exploded into a party between films, with a hot dog barbecue that included locally made coleslaw and sweet baked beans. *IB*

Livermore Heritage Guild

2155 Third St, Livermore
925.449.9927
www.livermorehistory.com
Wed–Sun 11:30a–4p

Growing up in Livermore since I was 7, I spent time in Carnegie Park, sitting on the edge of the central fountain. But embarrassingly, although I consider myself a "Livermoron," or so the kids say, I had never stepped foot into the Carnegie Building itself to visit the town museum or art gallery (did I miss the field trip that day or what?).

Originally the Carnegie Library in 1911, this well-preserved yellow building, surrounded by late-nineteenth-century Queen Anne cottages, reminds you of a time when life in Livermore was much simpler. Now home of the Livermore Heritage Guild, which was formed in 1973 by a group of citizens

concerned with preserving and encapsulating Livermore's past, the Carnegie Building is the stop for visitors. One half of the building is an art gallery with rotating exhibits and pieces by local artists for sale. The other half is a history center, where you can see Native American artifacts discovered by the Guild and view documents dating back as far as 1869, the year Livermore began. I recommend picking up the brochure titled "A Self-Guided Walking Tour to Historic Downtown Livermore," which contains a map and a brief history of 32 city buildings and private homes; it can tell you all you'd ever want to know in just an afternoon stroll. *JD*

Niles Canyon Railway

Boarding Stations: Sunol Depot, 6 Kilkare Rd, Sunol; Niles Station, 37001 Mission Blvd, Fremont
925.862.9063
www.ncry.org
Jan–Oct, select Saturdays; Train of Lights Fundraiser Nov–Dec (evenings only)

OK, I've figured it out—this is the best place for an East Bay wedding. Guests assemble in the Niles district of Fremont in the morning and they have an hour or two to shop for wedding gifts, which is easy since downtown Niles has more antique shops per block than any downtown on the planet. Then everyone boards the historic Niles Canyon Railway (you can rent the whole train or a single car, depending on how many guests you've invited). The ceremony takes place just before the train pulls out of the Niles depot. You pop the champagne, pass the hors d'oeuvres, and then party as the train chugs through the beautiful wilderness of Niles Canyon, following Alameda Creek, and then passes an old brick kiln and other ruins on this historic route. You don't have to disembark when you arrive in the charming little town of Sunol thirty minutes later. You can arrange for the band and the cake to be set up at the Sunol depot and end the trip by throwing the bouquet from the train window. How cool is that? *CHERYL KOEHLER*

Studio 7 Fine Arts

77 W Angela St, Pleasanton
925.846.4322
www.studio7finearts.com

Although I have to say my taste in art differs from many of the jazzy, landscape-oriented pieces on display at Studio 7 Fine Arts, there is no better place

in the valley to see the work of local artists like Livermore's Debbie Wardrope or Robin Purcell. Sort through the kitschy nature of the many interior design objets d'art and you'll be delighted by the exquisite handblown glass, soulful oil paintings, and rare portraits of this wine valley. *SB*

Buy Me

A unique take on shopping, from artichokes to zippers

 Baughman's Western Outfitters

2029 First St, Livermore

925.447.5767

Mon–Fri 9a–6p (Thurs 9a–9p), Sat 10a–6p

Oh, that horse! That brown, life-size plastic horse that no matter how many times you travel past Baughman's Western Outfitters, you always take a quick glance at, like maybe someday that pony will come alive. However, it's certainly no pony; that horse has been silently greeting customers for years, though not the entire 128 years Livermore's longest-running business has been selling western wear to the valley's real cowboys.

Although I was never much of a cowgirl myself, Baughman's inventory of large belt buckles, Wrangler jeans, western shirts, and even cap guns for the kiddies makes me wish I knew more about Livermore's rich western culture and maybe even hopped on a horse at some point. Then again, taking a stroll through the store, whose walls are lined with black-and-white photos of the downtown area in earlier years as well as rodeo plaques and trophies (Baughman's is one of the biggest sponsors of the annual Livermore rodeo), I almost feel it's not too late for me to sport a "Save a Horse, Ride a Cowboy" T-shirt or American eagle belt buckle. *JD*

Fantasy Books & Games

2247 First St, Livermore
925.449.5233

Don't dig comic books, role-playing games, or sports cards? No worries. Just enjoy the sensory overload of brightly colored bobblehead dolls, classic action figures, and fantasy novels. Sure, chances are that if you are of the female persuasion, you may be the only woman in the store, but Bob Borden, owner of Fantasy Books & Games for the last 30 years, says the number of women customers has increased. It's more common to wander past young men in black Sandman T-shirts hunched over the comic book rack fiddling through to find their desired issue. This store attracts both the hard-core collectors and the casually curious—be whomever you like, young Jedi. *JD*

Juju's Nature Foods

4359 First St, Livermore
925.960.9134

Although new and lightly stocked, Juju's Nature Foods has a sunshiny vibe rare for the Tri-Valley. This boutique-style health-food store specializes in natural, organic, and healthy products from Asia, the South Pacific, and the Americas. The store boasts an eclectic variety of snacks, supplements, sauces, and seasonings, and Juju herself will enthusiastically attempt to treat whatever ails you with holistic remedies she personally uses regularly. One of the most popular products she'll tell you about is coconut oil, which can be used for cooking, reducing bad cholesterol, and conditioning your hair. Despite the fact that it is located in a Safeway shopping center, Juju's inviting Polynesian decor, personal service, and exotic products will make you wonder whether perhaps you should go all out. *JD*

Outside
Relish the fresh air and open spaces

Iron Horse Regional Trail

www.ebparks.org/parks/trails/iron_horse

Biking and horsing around the Italianesque landscapes of the Tri-Valley are the best ways to take in the scene. Try the Iron Horse Regional Trail, which runs from Concord all the way to San Ramon, winds through Danville and parts of Dublin and Pleasanton, and is ideal for either activity. Pass the ticky-tacky houses and bountiful vistas, and imagine Squirrel Nutkin coming to join you on your trek. If you conquer the whole loop, an afternoon's bike ride or an easy horse ride in a little less time, you'll rack up 24½ miles. *SB*

Sycamore Grove Park

Arroyo Rd across from the Restaurant at Wente Vineyards, and also Wetmore Rd near where it intersects Holmes Road (there's signage here)

www.larpd.dst.ca.us (look under "Parks" for a downloadable map)

Take in the natural beauty of Livermore on the Sycamore Grove Park trail. Sycamore Grove is a well-trodden trail around preserved open space and up the Sycamore Grove peak, just beyond Wente's swank golf course. Across the street from Wente's restaurant and main tasting room is the entrance to the Sycamore Grove Park trail, past the gate leading to Charles Crohare's Olivina Ranch and just in front of the Veteran's Memorial Hospital. Pass over a short bridge to the trailhead for a flattish jaunt around the bluffs, sometimes by a creek, sometimes among crooked trees. Head uphill after following the water for one of the best views in the valley. The trails are bikeable if you have mountain bike tires, and dogs are welcome on the trail as long as you pick up their you-know-what and keep them on leash. If you start at the Wente end of the trail, you can continue your loop onto Hansen Road, which then curves left toward Marina Avenue, so you get more walking in—and with the glorious climate and atmosphere along the trail, trust me, you'll want to. *SB*

Del Valle Regional Park

7000 Del Valle Rd, Livermore
888.327.2757
www.ebparks.org/parks/del_valle
Daily 6a–9p
Admission: $6

I spent my teenage years going on lots of camping trips with friends' families to places like Lake Tahoe and Capitola, but honestly, the best campfires were held at Del Valle Regional Park. Only about three miles outside of downtown Livermore, Del Valle has more than 100 inexpensive campground sites, the best and roomiest of which are situated along the gentle creek. May I recommend campsite number 34—it brings back many memories of sing-alongs, Natural Ice beer, and summer flings.

And I highly recommend renting a motorboat for a few hours before the sun goes down, and cruising Del Valle Lake. Even if you don't fish—which seems pointless, anyway, since I've never seen anyone catch anything there worth keeping—there's nothing like soaking up the sun in a drifting boat. A boat is also the best way to explore the hidden coves of the lake, places often unreachable by land. *JD*

Farm to Table

Edible bounties direct to your tavola

 Joan's Farm and Pumpkin Patch

4351 Mines Rd, Livermore
925.455.6623
www.joansfarm.com

This place typifies the classic "day at the farm" experience with a small petting zoo, harvest pumpkin patch, u-picks throughout the year, and a barn-housed shop with farm produce, house-made jams, and apple butter. Get back in touch with old-school American foodways—after a trip here you'll want to learn to can your own preserves and churn your own butter. I especially recommend visiting during the harvest season, when hayrides and storytelling around the farm are in full swing. *SB*

Foothill Worm Ranch

Pleasanton (call to visit)
925.484.4192
www.foothillwormranch.com
Mon–Fri 8a–6p

It doesn't sound like the tastiest adventure, but without the helpful inverte-brates raised at this ranch, gardens around here wouldn't be as plentiful. The ultimate waste processing is done by worms, and Foothill Worm Ranch is where most of the Wine Country worms come from. Visit the farm or go online to learn about an entirely sustainable way to compost many kinds of refuse. Then again, I would love this kind of adventure since I was the one dissecting fish eyes on the playground (and making loads of friends in the process), but seriously, vermiculture is a crucial part of the green movement, a natural solution, and totally intriguing to a buggy girl like me. *SB*

U-Pick Cherries in Brentwood

Bacchini's Fruit Tree
Walnut and Concord aves, Brentwood; 925.634.3645

Freitas Cherry Ranch
555 Hoffman Ln, Brentwood; 925.634.5461

DC's Extraordinary Cherries
Marsh Creek Rd, Brentwood; 925.516.4495

Peter Wolfe Ranch
700 Creek Rd, Brentwood; 925.634.1308

There's no disagreement: cherries like it here in Contra Costa County. There are loads of farms where you can pick your own or swipe some from the stand at great prices compared to the stores. Do me a favor and eat fruit in season direct from the farm—at least when you are out here, there's no reason not to, plus I've even seen some grocery stores located just miles from these bountiful farms shipping manipulated and pesticide-farmed cherries from Chile at the height of cherry season (May–July). Shocking! Here's a guide to some of my favorite u-picks of the cherry variety. Bacchini's Fruit Tree is one of the larger family operations. It isn't certified organic, but the family that runs this place takes great pains to keep the soil healthy. Freitas Cherry Ranch is one of the best places to pick your own fruit, with all the gear provided to make a great

harvest. Be prepared for a postpicking cherry-pit spitting contest or canning session to start chipping down your newfound treasure. DC's Extraordinary Cherries grows shorter trees and eliminates the ladder in the cherry picking (I kind of like the ladder, but anyway . . .). There are more varieties here than at some of the other farms. The sweet, light-yellow-fleshed Rainiers are tops, but Royal Anns are a rarer, treasured snack with a bright flavor. Peter Wolfe Ranch has Van cherries in addition to bakeable bings and sugary Rainiers, and picking fruit on this farm has a special feel. A shady, lush atmosphere with an air of magic keeps this farm giving through most of the year. *SB*

Gliedt Family Farm

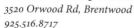 *3520 Orwood Rd, Brentwood*
 925.516.8717

Journey to Brentwood to pick apricots at the Gliedt Family Farm. Never sprayed or otherwise altered, these fuzzy balls of joy are the reason for many glowing, smiley faces. Just don't forget to bring your own buckets—you can pick up cheap ones at the nearby thrift stores (there's a Goodwill in Oakley at 2047 Main Street, 925.679.2824, and in Dublin at 7232 Regional

Street, 925.833.8610)—so you can truck off your gatherings for immediate eating or making into gooey apricot preserves. *SB*

Forest Home Farms
19953 San Ramon Valley Rd, San Ramon
925.973.3284
www.srhf.org

Bringing the beauty of old-time inefficiency to life, I choose many of the techniques taught here rather than their modern-day automated alternatives. Quality over quantity is a way of life at historic Forest Home Farms, where you can learn how to make real lemonade, wash your clothes without using a single watt of energy, or shear sheep and learn all the steps to turn the oily fluff into a sweater. Take a tour and learn about the area's rich history from a household perspective. *SB*

Danville Farmers' Market
Railroad and Prospect sts, Danville
www.pcfma.com
Year-round, Sat 9a–1p

Everything at the Danville Farmers' Market is certified organic and brought fresh from the farm. This is the most certified market in the area. Though the Thursday market is smaller than the big Saturday event, it is nonetheless worth shopping to bring this quality bounty to your table. I am always interested in what is available at the North Bay Quality Seafood stall, as all the fish sold there is sustainable and of the best quality. North Bay Quality Seafood also has a store in Cotati, another interesting town in the North Bay. *IB*

Rancho Alegre
Sunol (call to visit)
877.586.3748
www.ranchoalegre-lavender.com

Lavender is not just a sweet-smelling purplish flower associated with southern France—it has also been shown to have an aphrodisiac effect! Come visit this huge lavender farm, which harvests primarily for producing essential oil. Call ahead and the new owners will be happy to show (and smell) you around. *SB*

Terra Bella Family Farm

7637 Foothill Rd, Pleasanton

925.462.3569

Community Supported Agriculture (CSA) is a great solution for feeding your family produce directly from a nearby family farm. But if you can't pick up weekly bushels, you can visit the farm and buy a meal or two worth of gorgeous organic goodies. *SB*

The Olivina Ranch

4555 Arroyo Rd, Livermore

925.455.8710

www.theolivina.com

Long before wine tourism and overall beautification transformed the town, Livermore was planted with olive trees—some 2,000 acres of them. The Crohares, heirs to the olive oil throne in this county, still trim the 120-year-old trees and produce Century Mission olive oil from them. But more than that, they've created a family business that gives back in more ways than one, and that is just what I am always looking for.

Arbequina, frantoio, lucca, Mission, and picholine olive trees, all evenly spaced (when there's not a horse, rusted antique plow, or solar panel in the way), dance in the breeze, each branch surrounded by ample light and air so the olives get nice and happy. Charles B., the third of four generations of Crohares to run the Olivina Ranch, in his crisp purple dress shirt (he's an olive guy-cum-banker-cum-rotary member-cum-veteran's foundation member), teaches us everything about olives, from the composting to the growing to the harvesting to the pressing to the storing and, finally, the tasting.

After getting lost at the Olivina for an hour longer than was planned, we ate at the Restaurant at Wente Vineyards, where his oils are on display all over the menu (but just in case Charles finds himself in a spot with no olive oil, he always has a flask of his own oil on his person). You can even see some of his trees from the patio dining room at the vineyard. Talk about slow food—you'd have to walk only about 100 yards from the Crohares' press to sous chef Eric's lunchtime kitchen.

You can find the Olivina's oils online, at several restaurants, or at the Livermore Farmers' Market each week. *SB*

Livermore Farmers' Market

Third St, Livermore
925.825.9090
www.pcfma.com

The abundance of the Livermore Valley is collected from the Tri-Valley reaches and brought to town Thursdays, May–October, and Sundays, November–April. Inspired by a recent read in *Edible East Bay Magazine*, I started a collection of local olive oils and decided it will be the consistent gift I give myself when I travel to the olive-growing regions of the world. Livermore is blessed with an olive-growing tradition more than 100 years old, with trees dating back to 1881. As I walk under the golden green slivers of leaves, I imagine discovering this valley and being born into it before Lawrence Livermore National Laboratory, the infamous Ruby Hill development project, and the little rows of ticky-tacky houses were built. Now the land is protected by some strict conservancy ordinances, including the mandate that every home built requires 1 acre of farmland to be conserved and planted by the responsible party. Farms are often organic in the valley, relying on time-honored planting practices that combine beneficial species of flora to reduce the harmful pests and increase the good ones. Talk to the honey guy about that, or the egg guy about his angle, or the lavender lady—they all know their stuff. This is truly America's Tuscany. *SB*

Do Lunch

Outstanding midday eating of every sort

Tommie's Deli & Sandwiches

2152 Second St, Livermore
925.456.3354
www.tommiesdeli.com
Mon–Fri 10a–7p, Sat 10a–6p, Sun 11a–5p

While most of downtown Livermore is going through an extreme gentrification process, in which historic structures are being replaced with obscenely large buildings that will house numerous short-lived restaurants and boutiques, Tommie's Deli & Sandwiches goes back to the basics of a good ol' sandwich and friendly neighborhood deli. Of course, prepare for some "big" with your basic—a large-sized sandwich, aptly titled Big-n-Messy, is nearly 2 pounds of hormone-free meat. But if you aren't one to eat all that extra meat (and that may be best), for mere pocket change Tommie's sell scraps for dogs. You can also get picnic baskets to go, if you'd prefer to lunch in the sun at nearby Carnegie Park, and since sodas are only available in old-timey glass bottles (who has black cherry soda anymore?), there's a recycling bin right in front of the garbage. Waste not, want not, says Tommie's. *JD*

$$ Casa Orozco

325 S L St, Livermore
925.449.3045
www.casaorozco.com
Mon–Thurs 11a–9p, Fri–Sat 11a–10p

Livermore has a decent-sized Hispanic population and therefore a nice selection of hole-in-the-wall taquerias that offer quick, tasty burritos much larger in size than your stomach can comfortably accommodate. But the sit-down Mexican food experience is Casa Orozco, always. Never mind that I've never had a bad meal here (or a weak margarita, for that matter), but you could waste the day away on the semi-enclosed outdoor patio listening to the sounds of contemporary Mexican pop music. Seriously, as the sun goes down and the patio gets loud and the twinkling lights get kind of tequila-blurry, you'd swear you were on holiday in a Mexican resort. *JD*

$ Railroad Cafe

2041 Railroad Ave, Livermore
925.447.0235
Daily 7a–2p

Imagine a grandma's house—yellow wallpaper with bunches of grapes printed on it, shelves with ceramic roosters and a variety of baskets, maybe a salt-and-pepper-shaker collection—and you have the Railroad Cafe. Despite the overactive country kitsch, you can't help but appreciate the modest women that happily serve heaping mounds of ham-and-potato pancakes with a grandmalike sincerity. As breakfast is served until 2pm, most dishes blur into the brunch category, so strolling in late morning sporting sunglasses is a common practice. And while there's a wait on weekends, at least there's always a hot coffee station outside. Isn't that thoughtful? *JD*

⚑ **Terra Mia**

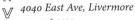

4040 East Ave, Livermore
925.456.3333
www.terramiarestaurant.com
Daily 11a–2:30p and 5–9:30p

As an old high school friend and I sat down at a corner table of the bustling Terra Mia restaurant, our slightly awkward conversation turned into laughs about past adventures over a delicious bottle of Italian cabernet sauvignon. It was like an Olive Garden commercial except with authentic Italian food, prepared and served by real Italians, and no one was paid to act like they were having a good time. The waiters offered recommendations of wine and food pairings, our conversation carried on, the food kept coming, and before we knew it, it was nearly two hours later, and both the restaurant and wine bottle were empty. *JD*

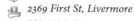 Firehouse Bistro & Books

2369 First St, Livermore

925.449.3473

www.bistrobooks.com

Daily 11a–3p, Tues–Sun 5–9:30p

My mother and my boyfriend's mother met for the first time at Firehouse Bistro & Books. It's a great place for nerve-racking first-time meetings, since you always have a conversation starter: books. With new releases and local travel guides in front, and used romance and children's books in the back, this is the last locally owned bookstore in town. The bistro menu is simple, with constantly changing gourmet sandwiches (mine was smothered in a white dressing—strange, but yum!), and the decor follows the downtown gentrification code of replacing historical architecture with a modern industrial look. But when staring out of the two gigantic front windows, you can't help but be reminded that once upon a time, early-twentieth-century fire trucks used to go blaring in and out of the building. *JD*

Jim's Country Style Restaurant

5400 Sunol Blvd #1, Pleasanton

925.426.7019

Daily 6a–4p

I knew Jim's Country Style Restaurant was going to be good right when I walked in because it's not just country—it's trailer. The restaurant, whose booths are a thrift-store rose pink, is adorned with toy-sized tractor models, retired agricultural tools, cow clocks, and beer-can mobiles—a decor so hideous and authentic that I knew I was going to be getting a rockin' meal, most likely covered in gravy. As it turns out, for lunch I had one of Jim's famous foot-long omelets—all of which have names like Sue or Marti (the same you'll see engraved on your servers' name tags) and accompanied by a side of country potatoes, the equivalent of about five large spuds in their natural state. To-go box, please? *JD*

Vines

Don't listen to anything but your own taste buds to discern your likes and dislikes when it comes to Wine Country's namesake

Fenestra Winery

 83 Vallecitos Rd, Livermore
 925.447.5246
www.fenestrawinery.com
 Fri–Sun 12–5p

One of the first wineries in the Tri-Valley to go solar, this family-owned operation actually puts power back into the grid from its efficient power system. The bright rays also grace the rows of vines, giving sun-drenched flavor to each and every vintage. *SB*

La Rochelle Winery

 5443 Tesla Rd, Livermore
 925.243.6442
www.lrwine.com
 Daily 12–4:30p

From a long line of area winegrowing greats comes Steven Mirassou at the helm of La Rochelle Winery, one classy place to experience a Livermore tradition. But this winery is actually known for its pinot noir, which means the grapes come from elsewhere in California, as Livermore is too hot for this varietal. The estate-grown vintages are not too shabby, but I come for the pinot, even though it's from another family-run farm. Come in and taste a flight of La Rochelle's best bottles together with local cheeses in a sit-down setting. You'll be lucky if Steven himself is there—he is one knowledgeable guy who tells a good story. *SB*

Wente Vineyards

 5050 Arroyo Rd, Livermore
 925.456.2400
www.wentevineyards.com
 My travel-writing-group friends recently returned from a winemaker dinner in Livermore. Suzie Rodriguez, author, sent me photographs showing a slew of journalists seated around a table laden with gourmet food at Blackhawk

Grill, with 29-year-old winemaking heir Carl Wente strumming away on his acoustic guitar as his winery's latest cabernet sauvignon is being poured. This is the guy who makes wine at Livermore's largest winery, which has vines dating back to the valley's first plantings, a place known as much for fantastic concerts and elegant yet rustic dining as for its wines.

With five or six tiers of wine, the newest member of the family being Carl's classy Nth Degree, Wente Vineyard's thousands of cases a year make it more of an empire than the locally owned businesses I usually love. I don't know whether it's Carl's refreshing touch or what, but Wente goes the extra mile to make the winery experience the best it can be, even incorporating a few sustainable practices into the operation. Fava beans, chocolate mint, Chinese mustard greens, and fish peppers sprout up along the winery's driveway as a demonstration of the larger garden where chef Arthur Wall gets some of his ingredients. Nitrogen-enriching clover blossoms between rows of vines, and as few chemicals as possible are used in the production, even though the sulfates in some Wente wines are as high as 150ppm. Reuse is also big around Wente—you'll find repurposed wine boxes popping up as all kinds of new and useful things around both the original property (which now houses Wente's Tamas Estates tasting room; see page 91) and the cavern and restaurant that are the current core of Wente.

The whole experience of wine is portrayed as multisensory: one day you may eat line-caught salmon with the haricot verts grown next to the vineyard while Chris Isaac hypnotizes you with his songs, and another day you may be with a group of friends in the Wente cavern at an aroma tasting of two chardonnays, where everything from yeast to pineapple to butter is placed in goblets for your comparative satisfaction. Be prepared to spend $30 for a good bottle of Wente wine and no less than $80 for two at the restaurant, but both are worth the trip to this large, small, big, little, beautiful winery.

Wente clone chardonnay, made by a previous generation of the Wente clan, is used widely across the globe, so if you're open to white wine, talk to these guys about their chardonnay. I sure learned a thing or two. *SB*

Concannon Vineyard

 4590 Tesla Rd, Livermore

 925.456.2505

www.concannonvineyard.com

Famous for being the first to bring petite syrah to California in 1883, this vineyard produces many of the bottles you'll see in the aisles of chain grocers. But quickly upon visiting the gorgeous property, waltzing under the vines heavy with table grapes, and wriggling through the warehouse of barrels, you'll want to go for a taste despite this fact. And you should. Unlike the huge bottlers in Napa that serve a similar demographic, Concannon Vineyard makes some delicious wines, my favorite of which is the hard-to-find 100 percent grenache, which does very well in Livermore Valley's Tuscanesque sun. Winemakers Jim (a Concannon himself) and Adam keep a careful eye on all the operations here, ensuring that their children and grandchildren will be able to continue growing on this fertile soil. Cover crops and strict energy-use policies are among some of the tricks used to ensure sustainability, in addition to what Jim calls the "UN of winemaking," his sought-after bottling setup consisting of the highest-end machinery gathered from around the globe. Pass by a certain famous football player's Victorian mansion (which has actually been transported around the property, but never left it) toward the tasting room, and keep your mind open to this unexpected delight. *SB*

 Elliston Vineyards

 463 Kilkare Rd, Sunol

925.862.2377

www.elliston.com

 Daily 10a–4p, office; Sat–Sun 11a–5p, tasting room

Coming up the gravel driveway, I was struck by the charm of Elliston Vineyards. Part of the Livermore Valley Wine Association, this 3-acre property pumps out only 3,000 cases per year of pinot blanc and chardonnay, but visitors will be grateful to discover this historical secret simply because of the perfectly restored blue sandstone mansion that now serves as a tasting room. Built in 1890 by the last elected San Francisco official, Henry Hiram Ellis, this European-style family home still has some original furniture, and in the men's parlor, history speaks through burns on the wooden fireplace mantel where gentlemen would rest their lit cigars. *JD*

Tamas Estates

5489 Tesla Rd, Livermore
925.456.2380
www.tamasestates.com
Daily 11a–4:30p

I always thought wine tasting was for yuppie wine snobs willing to pay $10 for tastes of a handful of overly expensive wines that don't even give you a buzz. But I really like the Tamas Estates wine-tasting room: it's simple and unpretentious, and the staff pours wines even the most out-of-the-loop wine drinkers have heard of (e.g., pinot grigio, zinfandel). Part of Wente's sustainable farming family—who creates living soils, monitors water usage, and instead of using pesticides includes special plants in the vineyards that draw pests helpful to the crop—Tamas Estates uses bottles that have an often taboo feature: a screw cap. Although the screw cap is often unjustly associated with cheap wine, Tamas Estates national sales manager Kris Hillstrom says it ensures quality closure and keeps the wine just as well as cork. Besides, she notes, who said corking was the only way to go? *JD*

Murrieta's Well

3005 Mines Rd, Livermore
925.456.2390
www.murrietaswell.com
Wed–Sun 11a–4p

History tells us that Joaquin Murrieta used to ride through the Livermore Valley with his fellow thieves and stop to let the horses drink from the very water well located just feet away from what now is the winery tasting room. It's rumored that he considered the water the best in the country, and it's this small piece of history—a well that's now decorated with colorful tiles and a flurry of flowers—that makes this vineyard so special. Scratch that—it's also the wine. Not much of a wine taster (drinker, sure, but taster, no), I found that the Murrieta's Well tasting room offers a unique blend of varietals (for those who are not familiar with wines, like me, think spicy, bold reds made with grapes commonly used for port wines). The pourer, Bill, was a colorful character well-educated on the history of the building, which he says was built like a log cabin: five planks stacked upon each other, reinforced by huge steel rods, and filled with bottles, sticks, and whatever else was laying around. Even though visitors can see daylight coming through the cracks in the wall behind the wine bar, Bill insists he'd rather be nowhere else during an earthquake. *JD*

Les Chênes Estate Vineyards

 5562 Victoria Ln, Livermore
925.373.1662
www.leschenesvine.com
Sat–Sun 12–4:30p (tasting room)

Once upon a time there was a couple who were chemists and weekend wine drinkers. Then they got smart and got vines, and now they plant their own backyard with a variety of berries, awaiting their careful crush. I wish the owners of Les Chênes Estate Vineyards were my grandparents—their sweet and knowledgeable nature is so endearing! I tasted several wonderful vintages and also learned about how Lincoln's Monticello rose gardens were irrigated; the same complex gravity drip system is employed at the perfect picnic grounds here. This winery is a real treasure, tiny and undiscovered. I give it my vote for most romantic Tri-Valley winery. *SB*

Cedar Mountain Winery

 7000 Tesla Rd, Livermore
925.373.6636
www.cedarmountainwinery.com
 Daily 12–4p (tasting room)

I was touring the new Ruby Hill Events Center when I met one half of the couple behind Cedar Mountain Winery (it is a husband-and-wife operation, and they ensure every part of the process is as green as can be). Before I had even tried her wines, which I have since grown to love, I had learned how the woman used her background in physics and chemistry to build on an impressive estate library as well as how to maintain a mother of vinegar. If you are ready to get serious and learn about Tri-Valley wines, there's no better spot to do so than Cedar Mountain, which also hosts live jazz performances in the tasting room now and again. *SB*

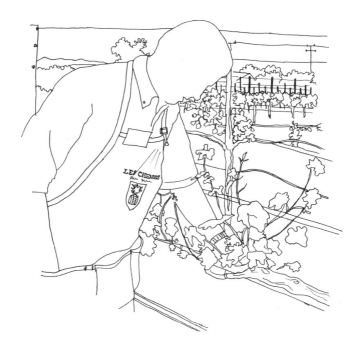

 Retzlaff Estate Wines

 1356 S Livermore Ave, Livermore
925.447.8941
www.retzlaffwinery.com
Tues–Fri 12–2p, Sat–Sun 12–4:30p

Incredible grapes make incredible wines, and that truth can be tasted in Retzlaff Estate Wines' accessible berry-bold vintages, all created in small batches from organic fruit. The family mentality equates to environmental stewardship, which shows in the way the winery uses water and carefully protects soil health. It is confusing that so many wineries use "estate" in their name when they rely on a slew of vineyards for their grapes, but Retzlaff wines are all estate grown—what you see when you visit is what you taste in the bottle. The picnic grounds are gracious and welcoming, and the 2-year-old oaky merlot is an easy favorite for a summertime dinner. *SB*

Tesla Vintners

5143 Tesla Rd, Livermore
925.606.9463
www.teslavintners.com
Wed–Sun 12–5p

The Livermore Art Association was so enamored at the effort of this first community tasting room in the Tri-Valley that they asked to use the space to showcase their up-and-coming artists. Come here to taste the secret talents of Livermore's wine community, like Marr Cellars and Ryhan Vineyards, and hear a singing winemaker strum away while you sip and swill. Tesla Vintners is also one of the only tasting rooms that is totally kid-friendly, with a separate tasting section and a big backyard for children with too much energy. SB

Pamper

Shelters from the hustle and bustle, simple enjoyments, and all things feel-good

Spa Bella

6680 Regional St, Dublin
925.556.5459
www.spabelladayspa.com
Sun–Mon 11:30a–5:30p, Tues–Fri 10a–8p, Sat 10a–6p, 55-plus specials every Tuesday

Healing touch is the name of the game at this locally owned spa housed in a Radisson Hotel. Take an hour off from adventuring for a classic Swedish massage with all-natural essential oils—your skin and your spirit will be radiant afterward. Waxing and facial services are also available, but I say massage is the standout here. SB

Purple Orchid Inn Resort & Spa

4549 Cross Rd, Livermore
925.606.8855
www.purpleorchid.com

Jane greets me at the log-cabin-like entrance of the Purple Orchid Inn and leads me into an orchid-filled sitting room; through French doors and past a pool with waterfalls and no right angles; through a garden with redwood mulch and yellow, orange, pink, and purple roses; beyond an upward-sweeping vineyard and a linear grove of 100-year-old olive trees to her spa room. I already feel like I've had a spa treatment and I haven't even hopped on the table yet.

A room-temperature (easier for your body to process) cucumber-infused glass of water later, I get ready and lie face down on the table in Jane's corner of the six-room spa facility. I abhor easy-listening music, and she graciously turns it off even when I timidly suggested she just turn it down. An intuitive! She carefully tailors my scheduled 60-minute Swedish massage to my immediate needs: a strained neck and right shoulder. She uses a cross-section of her skills in cranial-sacral, deep tissue, reiki, and other techniques to get my blood flowing, minimize headaches, and get me back in gear.

But I leave with more than a healing glow: Jane taught me about reflexology (did you know your toe and toe knuckle represent your head and neck as foot pressure points?), getting a good night's rest (if you're sleeping on your side, place a pillow between your knees to keep your spine relaxed), and stretching (every half hour or so when working on the computer, you should get up briefly, reach your left hand to the ceiling, and your right palm to the floor, and then reverse for several rotations). She uses medicinal arnica as massage oil, so that healing glow I spoke of lasts for a nice long time. The spa also offers facials, waxing, and other fun beauty treatments for fairly reasonable prices.

If you're too woozy from your massage, or you want to torture yourself by watching smug newlyweds traipse around the rose garden, stay the night at one of the best (and few) locally owned lodging options in the Tri-Valley (see page 112). Let the healing begin, whether it's the kind you get at the spa or the racier Marvin Gaye type. SB

The Pleasanton Spa

6155 Stoneridge Dr, Suite 150, Pleasanton
925.463.1572
www.pleasantonspa.com
Tues–Sat 9a–7p, Sun–Mon 10a–5p

Two rosy-cheeked couples own this ideal spa, which completes every treatment with ample lingering time in and out of the sauna and steam rooms in cozy bathrobes and fluffy slippers. Slip into black lava mud (without the trafficky trek to Calistoga), or go the whole nine yards with a Javanese Beauty Ritual, with a foot soak, body scrub, and scalp treatment for the betterment of your entire self. Deep-tissue massages here are addictive—once one of the highly skilled masseuses works out an impossible knot, you'll yo-yo back the minute you feel another one develop. *SB*

Lily Ann's Lingerie

350 Main St, Suite B, Pleasanton
925.846.1950
www.lilyannslingerie.com
Sun–Mon 12:30–5p, Tues–Sat 10:30a–6p

You never know what will happen when you are totally beautiful as well as comfortable in your intimate apparel. This is *the* place to stop and shop before turning in to the Rose Hotel. Carol DiSalvi and Kelly Cruz fit you with the certain touches of a truly family-owned and -run apparel shop—all the best brands from around the world are right in town. Lily Ann's Lingerie has a selection of lotions and candles to further frame and materialize your dream image of an adult nighttime adventure. The store also offers special events, including bridal showers and girls'-night-out parties. *IB*

Bibiane Bakery

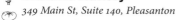

349 Main St, Suite 140, Pleasanton
925.931.0626
www.bibianebakery.com

I am always surprised by the smells as I trot down the street and step into this truly terrific bread and pastry shop. I know there is a slice of chocolate-raspberry cake freshly made and ready for my decadent desire. My mother always contradicted other parents, saying that it was healthier to eat dessert first—but whether you agree or not it is difficult to skip the sweets at Bibiane. For your first course grab a quiche, some ratatouille, or pastries. There's a selection of pizzas to round out this delightful shop. Go ahead, try eating dessert first. *IB*

Hang Out

The best chill-out spaces

Earl Anthony's Dublin Bowl

 6750 Regional St, Dublin

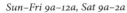 *925.828.7550*

www.earlanthonysdublinbowl.com

Sun–Fri 9a–12a, Sat 9a–2a

America has many sporting styles, from sweat-inducing paddling in a small, enclosed box (racquetball), to swinging a chunk of wood at a speeding piece of cork and cotton (my favorite spectator sport, baseball). But perhaps the most lighthearted of all is hurling a 14-pound ball of purple plastic down a wooden lane, with the aim of knocking down some bottle-shaped pins. For an evening of fun and an atmosphere full of locals getting their bowl on, head to Dublin Bowl. *SB*

Cafe Main

 401 Main St, Pleasanton

 925.425.9708

 Daily, hours vary

Pleasanton can get a little busy for me at times. Not busy in the city sense, but the mood of many shops in a small area gives me the urge to just sit and stew for a minute, out of sight. When I get this feeling, I tuck into Cafe Main for a cup of soup and a toasty avocado sandwich with a good book. My last trip here I was in the middle of Thomas Friedman's *Hot, Flat, and Crowded*, which went down easier in the comfy atmosphere. Not that I want to shy away from the realities of the planet, but eating at a family-run spot like this and drinking a steaming cup of coffee makes it easier to face the challenges ahead. *SB*

Campo di Bocce

 175 E Vineyard Ave, Livermore

 925.249.9800

www.campodibocce.com/Livermore

Daily 9a–close (Bocce), 11a–close (restaurant)

Not all of the bocce courts around Northern California Wine Country offer the same winery-side experience, where you toast with a bottle of the estate red and hop on the rocky course to make a fool of yourself learning the fine-line rules of the game. At Campo di Bocce, the game is elevated to something more precise and sophisticated, which actually makes it more fun and more worth playing. Since there are semipro bocce teams that practice and play here, the people who care for the courts know every in and out and are happy to teach novices a few handy tips. Rent a court in the early hours to beat the crowd, and share a scrumptious breakfast and a mimosa with bubbles from nearby Battaion Cellars winery. Make sure to call ahead and reserve a spot on these smooth courts. This is a game you'll want to share with your whole gaggle—it is that accessible and that fun. *SB*

First Street Alehouse

2086 First St, Livermore
925.371.6588
www.firststreetalehouse.com
Mon–Wed 11a–10:30p, Thurs–Sat 11a–12a, Sun 11a–10p

The First Street Alehouse's half-pound Angus burgers could make any burger connoisseur's taste buds go mad with satisfaction (and don't forget the garlic fries!). Pair the meal with locally made beer and wine (no liquor) and some good conversation on one of two outdoor patios, and lounge in the sun at this modern-day English pub. I've battled the crowd on all-day happy-hour Tuesdays and pint-night Thursdays, and I can tell you that it was totally worth it. *JD*

Panama Red Coffee Co.

2115 First St, Livermore
925.245.1700
www.panamaredcoffee.com
Mon–Thurs 5:50a–10p, Fri 5:30a–11p, Sat 6a–11p, Sun 7a–8p

No place allows you to better experience Livermore culture than this popular hangout in the heart of downtown. Panama offers individual "we don't brew it until you order it" rare coffee blends (with organic options available) and a refreshing variety of fruit smoothies to locals basking in the sun on the streetside patio with a book or friend (often of the K-9 variety). When the weather is warm the wall-length windows slide open, diminishing the boundaries between the indoors and out, which makes it easier to hear acoustic sets permeating the air on Friday and Saturday evenings. *JD*

Redcoats British Pub & Restaurant

336 Saint Mary St, Pleasanton
925.462.6600
www.redcoatspub.com
Mon–Thurs 11:30a–11:30p, Fri–Sat 11:30a–1a, Sun 11:30a–11p

Redcoats is a rather zipped-up version of the British original, but since the weather is ideal and the beer menu echoes European roots, I can make an afternoon or evening of it here. Guzzle and gorge with buddies at the bar, or take a pint and a notebook to the outdoor patio for a little suds-inspired poetry writing. Bass and Guinness come together for a filling black and tan, or try a bit of lime cordial in your Stella—a lager and lime, as it is called here. This is a major after-work place for locals, but you can find solace in the afternoon at an outside table. *SB*

The Hopyard American Alehouse & Grill

3015 Hopyard Rd, Pleasanton
925.426.9600
www.hopyard.com
Tues–Fri 11:30a–11p, Sat 1p–1a

This warm-weathered area of California used to be hung with thousands of acres of golden hops, trellised up on 10- or 12-foot poles with twine connecting the wooden posts. The Hopyard American Alehouse & Grill is located right on top of one of California's greatest hop farms, which shut down from a combination of prohibition pressures, a lost right to nearby water resources, and the need to increase other forms of production during World War I. Even though local hops are still grown at far-and-few-between family hop farms, as discovered by California Gold's loveable if hokey host Huell Howser, Hopyard keeps the local brewing tradition alive, with everything from cider to IPA to stout on the menu. Livermore Brewery makes some great beers, and they're nowhere as well showcased than at this locally owned pub. *SB*

Sunol Jazz Cafe

11882 Main St, Sunol
925.862.2000
www.sunol.net/jazzcafe
Daily 7:30a–3p

On a weekday afternoon, Sunol isn't a really hopping place. But if you're looking just to browse antique stores, sit at the community park, or sip a

vanilla latte (essentially, if you enjoy a life of leisure), it's a great place to be, as long as you don't mind a train thundering through every 15 minutes. The Sunol Jazz Cafe, a new addition to this one-horse town, is a blend of modern comfort and old Sunol charm: coffee bean sacks and impressionist paintings on the walls and many mirrors and stained-glass grapes hanging on the windows give the place a light and relaxing vibe. My favorite piece, however, was the gigantic brown couch that I sunk so far down into I don't even think my head was visible. As I doodled on my notepad, I was beginning to be thrown off by the elevator jazz music, but the owner quickly made me feel at home by throwing on some Amy Winehouse. This was the one time my tattoos gave the right impression. JD

$ Donut Wheel

2017 First St, Livermore
925.447.8190
Always open!

Mmm . . . doughnuts. There's nothing like ending a barhopping evening on First Street with a stop at the Donut Wheel for a glazed old-fashioned and a cup of joe. The only 24-hour walk-in eatery in town, this glowing, blue sugar palace, which sports original 1950s space-age architecture, is always there to soak up the alcohol (or for the early-morning crowd, a pink-boxed dozen gets the day started). Don't expect anything extraordinary—this dinosaur has survived simply on traditional sugar and caffeine, and those elements will keep it alive through to the next ice age. If you don't have my kind of sweet tooth, a ham and cheese croissant is a yummy alternative. Tell them to warm it up to get the cheese all melted, of course. *JD*

$ Livermore Public Library (Civic Center Branch)

1188 S Livermore Ave, Livermore
925.373.5500
www.livermore.lib.ca.us
Mon–Thurs 10a–9p, Fri 10a–6p, Sat 10a–5p, Sun 12–6p

When the new Livermore Public Library opened in May 2004, only yards away from the old library building just on the other side of the police station, the grand, long-awaited 52,715-square-foot building made newspaper headlines, but not because of its extensive reference section or its cafe run by AID employment, which provides job opportunities for the developmentally disabled. No, Livermore's new library became national news when it was revealed that its tile mosaic in the entry plaza titled "The Doors" tragically boasted misspelled names of famous people in world history such as Shakespeare and Einstein. Although the Miami artist, Maria Alquilar, originally refused to return and make corrections, the seven misspellings were quietly fixed the following year.

But don't let first impressions fool you. The Civic Center branch feels like walking into a Borders bookstore or a university campus library: quiet, spacious, cool, and clean. It's a place where you could happily spend a hot summer afternoon lounging on comfy couches in one of the many reading areas. If you are the type to associate libraries with places you had to go when a book report was due, let it go, will you? Research and reading is fun now, with more than 30 Internet-accessible computers (get there early, as they are *always* occupied) and the Bunshah Index, a detailed index of local newspapers (e.g., the *Tri-Valley Herald*, *Valley Times*, and the *Independent*) that allows visitors to peruse articles from 1899 to 2002. There's also a display of photography by Bill Owens, who documented the suburban migration to Livermore in the 1970s. Find his book *Suburbia* in nonfiction, 770 OWE, to learn how relaxing Tri-Valley life was without commuter traffic. *JD*

Volunteer

Fun, quick, and easy ways to give back to the community

Taylor Family Foundation and Camp Arroyo

5555 Arroyo Rd, Livermore
925.455.5118
www.ttff.org
Kids get the chance to have a weeklong excursion to this playful camp, where "disabilities are checked at the door." Get hands-on training to make this place special for every camper, or volunteer for the Day in the Park auction fundraiser to ensure this place stays around for many years to come. *SB*

Tri-Valley Conservancy

1736 Holmes St, Livermore
925.449.8706
http://trivalleyconservancy.org/volunteer
Give a few hours of your time to maintain trails, enliven exhibits and events, keep the offices up to snuff, or with the Stewardship program, visit properties to see how they are doing. The Tri-Valley Conservancy is responsible for hedging unlimited development in favor of keeping open space and healthy agriculture at the valley's fore. It is a great group, with lots of fun ways to give back. Fill out the online form to get set up. *SB*

Dublin Senior Center

7600 Amador Valley Blvd, Dublin
925.556.4511
Mon–Fri 9a–4p (Wed 4–8p)

There's always a lot going on at this vibrant senior center, such as creative writing groups and dance classes. Take part in serving a meal or helping out with one of the programs and meet some great locals in the process. *SB*

Valley Humane Society

3670 Nevada St, Pleasanton
925.426.8656
www.valleyhumane.org

For some 20 years this group has been supported by large numbers of volunteers, all aiming to keep our furry friends happy and to prevent unnecessary euthanasia. There are pet training classes for prospective owners and lots of duties around the grounds to keep the organization running smoothly. Join a monthly volunteer orientation so you can get in the know about the various jobs around the center. *SB*

Tri-City Ecology Center and Fremont Creek Watershed

3375 Country Dr, Fremont
510.793.6222
www.tricityecology.org
Thurs 11a–2p, but call anytime for volunteer opportunities throughout the week

Salmon isn't just an Alaskan specialty—salmon live, and used to thrive, in Bay Area creeks, too. With the help of the Fremont Creek Watershed group, the population of salmon in the Bay Area is on the increase once more, along with that of other vital fish in the ecosystem. Help keep the watershed safe and clean, or volunteer to aid in wildlife preservation classes and advocacy programs. The group puts on a big fundraiser in July that could always use a hand, and the local folks who make up this group are a joy to work with. *SB*

StopWaste

1537 Webster St, Oakland (volunteer and resource projects at various locations throughout the Tri-Valley)
510.891.6500
www.stopwaste.org

Alameda County is the seat of this nationally recognized waste reduction force, which prints a complete how-to guide for residents wondering what to do with their old leaking batteries or their broken boom box from the good old 1980s. Advocating for long-term sustainability in many areas, both industrial and residential, the program has many facets, some of which you can take part in on a broader scale by pitching in your time. If you can't find an applicable position, at least order the guide—or better yet, download the paperless PDF—and get busy keeping an eye on your own waste. *SB*

Casual Night Out
Dining and delighting in a relaxed atmosphere

El Balazo

5331 Hopyard Rd, Pleasanton
925.737.1300
www.elbalazo.net

In 1993, Marino Sandolva opened his first restaurant using his own family recipes. Now he serves thousands of people a day at El Balazo, and in my opinion, everything on the menu is good. His family business uses high-quality local produce always with an eye toward perfection. Pick up a rewards card and collect points redeemable for various menu items, El Balazo hats, and catering events. I am holding on to my card until I reach 2,000 points so I can bring home a big appetizer party. My favorite order is perfectly cooked octopus with all the traditionally bright colors and flavors over spicy rice. The vegetarian menu is comprehensive, with a unique cactus selection as well as traditional mixed veggies, plus the restaurant's famous rellenos. *IB*

Oasis Grille

780 Main St, #101, Pleasanton
925.417.8438
www.oasisgrille.com
Daily 11:30a–9:30p

There may be fusion going on at Livermore Labs, but the kind of fusion at Oasis Grille is more about world flavors and fabulous drinks. Leave the chemistry to the experts! I delight in taking my taste buds on a tour. The combination of expansive Saharan spice and the clarity of Mediterranean crisp flavors enters every dish, even the mix of greens with healthy local produce. Step out of your usual culinary experience by ordering dishes named aushak, mantoo, and sabzi. Taste the ageless nomadic travel scooped up with your California fork, and then continue the adventure after your meal with a visit to the visually amazing Hindu Community and Cultural Center (see page 72) on Arrowhead Avenue. *IB*

Essanay Café

37533 Niles Blvd, Fremont
510.792.0112
www.essanaycafe.com
Tues 5–9p, Wed–Fri 11a–2:30p, 5–9p, Sat–Sun 9a–3p, 5–9p

Cheryl, the editor of *Edible East Bay*, and I were on a mission to raise money for our cause of the night: the annual Dine Out for Life fundraiser to benefit AIDS centers in the East Bay. Who insisted on being a part? Essanay Café, the gem of the Niles dining scene. One of the owners uses old bits and pieces of housing to decorate his beautiful spot. You'd never guess the tomato-covered hanging planters were made of historic wooden gutters, and when you see the way he uses old windows you'll want to go home and spiff up your house with his inspiration. Sit on the back patio or in the cozy dining room to swirl and sip local wines while savoring mouthwatering steak or the pasta of the season (in the fall it is divine pumpkin ravioli with a sage-butter sauce). Cherry demi-glace douses the famous duck confit made with local free-range birds. The people behind this place could easily be the mayors of the town—cumulatively they volunteer on several boards, from watershed preservation to historic renovation, and even help out at the nearby private nursery that aims to maintain rare plant species under threat in the current environmental conditions. Eat up and enjoy—this place is a unique treasure in an unlikely spot, the sleepy village of Niles. *SB*

Sansar Indian Cuisine

2220 First St, Livermore
925.606.6191
www.sansarindiancuisine.com
Mon–Fri 11a–2:30p, 5–10p; Sat–Sun 12–3p, 5–10p

Most of my friends are die-hard ethnic foodies, and if it weren't for them I wouldn't know so many secrets—like the best Vietnamese food in the Bay Area is in San Jose and the best Indian food is in Fremont and Livermore. Trekking into these communities is the best way to get a truly authentic meal, without froufrou Californication. I used to take a drive to Pleasanton for Gold India, the apple of my eye when it came to fresh Indian food, but now the family has moved to Livermore, with the same family chefs behind the tandoor grill at Sansar Indian Cuisine. My faves are on the Tandoori Delight section of Sansar's menu. The chicken, served whole, is supreme for poultry lovers, and the rack of lamb complements crispy papadum dipped in zesty raita, the spiced-up yogurt sauce that is a must-have with whatever you order. Ask your server about the favorites of the day and you'll get a real answer, not just the typical responses that speak to the most Americanized or expensive items on the menu. The chai is unstoppable—the ultimate cold-killer if you aren't in tip-top shape. (P.S. The web site has coupons, so print them out and take them with you to get a discount!) *SB*

Gay Nineties Pizza Company

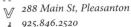

288 Main St, Pleasanton
925.846.2520
www.gayninetiespizza.com

Nothing gets me going like a good ghost story, and Gay Nineties Pizza Company has plenty of them. Like the mysterious woman in a blue Victorian dress peering out of an upstairs window or the word "Boo" owner Rob Earnest and his dog watched being inscribed on a dining room mirror by a phantom hand. This place is a tourist attraction that keeps curious visitors coming.

Originally a 10-room Wells Fargo stop and brothel in 1864, the pizza parlor has a turn-of-the-century ice cream parlor look, like a barber shop quartet should be performing and kiddies should be slurping root beer floats. But

Gay Nineties has been serving award-winning pizza for more than 50 years, and in addition to its ghostly strangeness, it also serves a monster pizza with a strange purpose: the Frank's Special, loaded with five different meats, has been known to induce labor. *JD*

Dress Up

Don your shiny shoes and head out to one of these fancy places

Blackhawk Grille
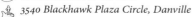
3540 Blackhawk Plaza Circle, Danville

925.736.4295
www.blackhawkgrille.com
$$ *Mon–Sat 11:30a–3p, 5–10:30p; Sun 11a–3p, 5–9p*

Ryan Jackson wants to make you giddy over food. And in this big American eatery, nothing is easier than getting sucked into the nouveau opulence and the fancy flavors. Goat cheese fondue with 25-year-old balsamic vinegar, white corn soup with vanilla oil and lump crab, New York steak that comes from happy, grass-fed cows served in brandy cream—don't you get hungry just thinking about the possibilities of a meal here? I put my repulsion of the manicured 'burbs aside. When local winemakers work with a local chef, and when seasonal produce purchased from surrounding farms is showcased, then why not disappear into the rotunda of the restaurant with my honey by my side and an impatient belly? Skip the salmon and the tiger shrimp (both of which aren't sustainable), but otherwise indulge in this ideal special-occasion menu. I challenge you to save room for dessert. *SB*

Faz

5121 Hopyard Rd, Pleasanton
925.460.0444
www.fazrestaurants.com
$$$ *Mon–Fri 6:30–10:30a, 11:30a–3p, 5–10p; Sat–Sun 7–10:30a, 11:30a–2p, 5–10p*

Faz is one of the most conscientious local chains in the area, composting or recycling everything and maintaining close relationships with the nearby farms to ensure the best stuff makes it to the table. I had a five-course tasting menu here with a slew of local food and wine heroes. Steven Mirassou, the man behind La Rochelle Winery (see page 107) and a Livermore winemaking legend, gave us gut laughs throughout the meal with his tales of mishaps, valley lore, and winemaking fun. We started with filo-wrapped brie, a luxury for the mouth, with the creamy flavors punctuated by sour cherries dappled atop this pretty dish. Tantalizing calamari and perfectly prepared seafood (some are marine-stewardship certified; just heed my precautions on page xiv) are my favorite things to order, but veggies and salads are what bring out the flavors in the fish, so order them side by side. Dress like a million bucks and relax in this comfortable atmosphere where your every whim is catered to by Faz Poursohi and his handpicked staff. *SB*

 Bridges Restaurant and Bar
44 Church St, Danville
925.820.7200
www.bridgesdanville.com
Mon–Fri 11:30a–2:30p, 5:30–close; Sat–Sun 5p–close

Wow-wee! While Bridges Restaurant and Bar may make your wallet shake in horror, if you really want to make a night out with someone special memorable, break out the plastic and do it right. Not only is the food here exquisite, but this East-meets-West cuisine is best enjoyed on the patio, which is so romantic that the general manager says she witnesses at least one marriage proposal per week. Tables 64 and 91 are the most popular patio seats—with a trickling granite fountain and vine-covered coves, it's a private party for two.

If price is still a fear factor, Thursday's happy hour offers discounted drinks as well as $5 small plates. And did you know that Bridges was the setting for Robin Williams's unmasking in *Mrs. Doubtfire*? *JD*

 **Aura Nightclub**
4825 Hopyard Rd, #10, Pleasanton
925.416.0777
www.nightclubaura.com
Wed–Fri 10p–2a, Sat 9:30a–2a

To relive my days frolicking in Lake Tahoe after a long day on the mountain, I go to frivolous Aura Nightclub, where the 'burbs get glitzy and beats are booming. Wednesdays are cover-charge-free, with cheap mixed drinks through 10:30pm and poppy dance hits spun by DJ David. It is a grooving party like none other in the area, but it is a bit of a showdown, if you catch my drift. Don't expect a heart-to-heart with anyone you meet—just a buzzy night of recklessness and dancing. *SB*

Listen
Any auditory experience you can imagine

Livermore-Amador Symphony
Livermore, various concert locations
925.373.6824
The Livermore-Amador Symphony has been successfully staging four concerts per year, featuring classical music from baroque to modern, in the sanctuary of the Presbyterian church for over 45 years. Its dedication and cooperative spirit of the area have supported adult musical education as well as a youth orchestra and a dance theater group, choral groups, the Livermore Valley Opera, and a woodwind quintet with all-volunteer musicians. The orchestra conductor is Dr. Arthur P. Barnes, who has conducted for 44 years, since his doctoral days at Stanford University, and the concertmistress is Sally Dalke. She and Dr. Barnes, and the principal cellist and violist, are the only paid members of the mass of music makers; the rest are enthusiastic volunteers. This local group supports young musical competition and study with annual scholarships. Membership in the guild is stimulated by being open to all who share its values and live in the area. *IB*

Live Music in the Tri-Valley
Pine Street Sports Bar & Grill
875 Rincon Ave, Livermore; 925.606.8266

Downtown Ollie's Saloon
2128 Railroad Ave, Livermore; 925.443.6507

Main Street Brewery
830 Main St, Pleasanton; 925.462.8218

Pleasanton Hotel
855 Main St, Pleasanton; 925.846.8106

Bosco's Bones & Brew
11922 Main St, Sunol; 925.862.0821

Polomoni's

1845 First St, Livermore; 925.447.5311

The Tri-Valley, despite its outwardly yuppie appearance, has many venues in which to boogie down, shake your groove thang, or just plain rock out. Unfortunately, the weekdays don't offer much live music—you're more likely to find comedy or trivia game nights. But the Pine Street Sports Bar & Grill has live music every Friday and Saturday, mostly alternative and hard rock, with an open mic night on Tuesdays. Ollie's (a country bar that's my personal fave for karaoke) and the Main Street Brewery both have weekend bar blues, if you like Van Morrison and renditions of "Mustang Sally."

If you want to try something different, Bosco's Bones & Brew has live rock music Friday and Saturday nights. From what I hear, it's usually a packed house! And if you're in Livermore on a weekend, stop by Polomoni's. Although the shows are far and few between, you may catch a locally organized punk rock or rockabilly show at no charge. Other nights Polomoni's is a chilled-out local dive, but the drinks are always strong and cheap. *JD*

Livermore Performing Arts Center, Bankhead Theater

2400 First St, Livermore
925.373.6800
www.livermoreperformingarts.org

Think you have to travel to New York City to see a full-scale production of *Miss Saigon*? To Florence to see *The Barber of Seville*? To Vienna to see a dynamic Chopin concert? Not so—look no further than the newish Bankhead Theater, where the world of performing arts comes to the Tri-Valley in surprising quality. Bankhead offers affordable tickets for a diverse season of shows, all catering to a discerning audience of classical music junkies (like myself) and regular Broadway lovers (not like myself). The Regional Theater and Bothwell Theater are two other nearby venues, so sort through the offerings on the Livermore Performing Arts Center web site so you can head to the right venue for your concert of choice. I love the Bankhead for its stately opulence. During intermission I gather with fellow listeners on the broad front entrance and smell the lavender-scented breeze while reminiscing about the chords I've just enjoyed. *SB*

Livermore Valley Opera

2400 First St, Livermore
925.960.9210
www.livermorevalleyopera.com

One of the prestigious groups of performers to take the Bankhead Theater stage, Livermore Valley Opera is a community-based operatic troupe. *La Traviata, Die Fledermaus, Don Giovanni,* and *Tosca* have all been highlights since the group's start in the early 1990s. For a recent *Barber of Seville* production, Daniel Helgot, the producer, put together a special web site with clips with arias from the opera sung by Maria Callas and Thomas Hampson, and the famous overture acted out by one of America's favorite cartoon characters, Bugs Bunny. As much as I may dislike the idea of cartooning an opera (I'm a classical music junkie and don't even like when movements are left out of a symphony on the radio), it is great that this group is reaching out so that future generations catch the buzz of this amazing art form. No matter which performance you've chosen, head to the web site first to get the gist of the story and the history behind it. You'll be that much more enthused when you are listening in person, no matter what your age or musical background. *SB*

Pleasanton Playhouse

1048 Serpentine Ln, #307, Pleasanton
925.462.2121
www.pleasantonplayhouse.com

Want to see a local winemaker dressed up in frilly Victorian attire? How about a bocce ball coach dressed head to toe in leather gear from the 1950s for *Grease*? This is the place—a theater company that involves the community while maintaining high production standards and perfect picks for musicals. Even as someone who isn't a huge fan of the genre, I've been happily surprised by a telling incarnation of *Thoroughly Modern Millie* with Morgan Breedveld playing the lead and Joan Evans as Mrs. Meers. Come join the fun without the pricey flight across the country for a serious dose of musical action. *SB*

Lodge
Great places to rest your noggin

The Rose Hotel

807 Main St, Pleasanton
925.846.8802
www.rosehotel.net

This is a boutique-pretty place to stay in Pleasanton, with waterfall wrap-around stairs over the hearth-centered lobby—you'll be set whether you're there for a quick drink or a weeklong stay. Step from the plush California gold rush interiors, where the complimentary continental breakfast is served daily, out into a city bustling with contemporary vitality. Whirlpool baths and glass-enclosed showers, a choice of bathroom amenities, and a fresh rose to heighten your senses are just a few of the niceties here. Everything you might need or have forgotten is available for your use during your stay. All of the rooms and suites are luxurious and range from $255 to $710 a night, with room 302 ($510) created for a special romantic encounter. Shopping at the companion lingerie store (Lily Ann's Lingerie; see page 96) before crossing the threshold is de rigueur. *IB*

Purple Orchid Inn Resort & Spa

4549 Cross Rd, Livermore
925.606.8855
www.purpleorchid.com

The largest log cabin in California, this beautiful, romantic inn is ideal for a long night's snuggle, with waterfall pools and rose gardens to enjoy during your stay. The spa is a definite highlight (see page 94)—the massages are worth the trek whether you are staying here or not. The wooden inn abuts an olive tree–lined vineyard that rolls back into the sunset, giving every room a view. Rooms range in price from a reasonable $150 to $375 a night, and the honeymoon suite should be booked in advance. *SB*

Marriott Pleasanton

11950 Dublin Canyon Rd, Pleasanton
925.847.6000
www.marriottpleasanton.com

After the sensuous retrofit that Marriott went through in 2008, this was the first location I stayed at to enjoy the changes: new doubled-up down comforters on the luxe mattresses; gold, green, and orange glamour in the lobby spaces; and improved tech for writers like me and business travelers who are always looking for their next plug-in. I applaud the upgrades, and paired with the courteous staff, it is a winning combination. If you can't find a reservation at a locally owned spot, this should be your next step. *SB*

Evergreen B&B

9104 Longview Dr, Pleasanton
925.426.0901

With only four bedrooms, this cozy love nest represents for me a true getaway from it all. Here I find a wonderful bed-and-breakfast right in the Pleasanton foothills, just a short distance from the Sports and Recreation Park. Evergreen B&B is ready for the most discriminating traveler looking for an environmentally sensitive place within a beautiful natural setting to rest, recharge, and recover. Reflective of the environmentally conscious attitude here, I'm comforted by simple quality and efficiency. *IB*

Suburban Cowboys Calendar

February

Romantic Horse-Drawn Carriage Rides

February 14
Downtown Livermore
www.elivermore.com

New Orleans Bash

Fat Tuesday
Bothwell Arts Center
www.livermoreperformingarts.org

April

California Independent Film Festival

Second week in April
Various locations
http://caindiefilmfest.org

May

Livermore Wine Country Festival

First weekend in May
First St to P St, Livermore

Livermore Scottish Games and Celtic Celebration

Third weekend in May
Robertson Park, Livermore
www.livermoregames.com

Art in the Vineyard

Last weekend in May
Wente Vineyards (see page 88)
www.wente.com

June

Livermore Rodeo

Second week in June
925.455.1550
www.livermorerodeo.org

Sommerfest

Last Saturday in June
Bankhead Theater
925.373.6800

July

Livermore Old-Fashioned Fourth of July

July 4
Robertson Park, Livermore
925.373.5700

Pleasanton Fourth of July

July 4
Lions Wayside Park, Pleasanton
www.pleasantondowntown.net

Art Under the Oaks

Second weekend in July
Alden Lane Nursery, 981 Alden Ln, Livermore

Wine Stroll

Third Thursday in July
www.pleasantondowntown.net

August

Tri-Valley Shakespeare Festival

First weekend in August
www.trivalleycvb.com

September

Harvest Wine Celebration

Labor Day weekend
925.447.9463
www.lvwine.org

Livermore Children's Fair

Second weekend in September
925.373.5700
www.larpd.dst.ca.us

Harvest Festival Original Art & Craft Show

Second weekend in September
415.447.3205
www.harvestfestival.com

Pleasanton Art and Heritage Festival

Second weekend in September
www.pleasantondowntown.net

October

Hops and Vines Fall Fest

First Sunday in October
Pleasanton Downtown Association
925.484.2199, ext 4

Del Valle Dog Show

Second Sunday in October
Robertson Park and other locations
925.455.4158
www.dvdc.org

Gem Faire

Last weekend in October
3131 Pacific Ave at S Livermore Blvd
503.252.8300
www.gemfaire.com

Haunted Barn and Livermore Trick-or-Treating

www.larpd.dst.ca.us
www.livermoredowntown.com

November

Hula Festival

First weekend of November
Location varies between years
www.kumuhulaassociation.com

Country Folk Art Craft Show

Second weekend in November
Location varies between years
www.countryfolkart.com

Magical Evening in Pleasanton

Friday before Thanksgiving
Downtown Pleasanton
www.pleasantondowntown.net

The Great Train Expo

Last weekend in November
www.greattrainexpo.com

December

Holidays in the Vineyards
First weekend in December
www.lvwine.org

Big Fat Year-End Kiss-Off
Comedy Show
December 26
www.livermoreperformingarts.org

New Year's Labyrinth Walk
December 31
First Presbyterian Church, Fourth and L
sts, Livermore
www.elivermore.com

GRAPES AND GREEN THUMBS

About Inland Sonoma County

The name Sonoma could have been derived from one of several native languages. According to the Coast Miwok and Pomo Indians, the earliest human settlers of the region, Sonoma translates to "valley of the moon," as it was told in legends. There is also the common occurrence of the word *tsonoma* in the native languages of the area, literally meaning "earth village." The most amusing possible derivation is that from the Wintun word for nose, *sonom*. One theory purports that Spanish settlers met an Indian chief who had a big schnoz and decided to nickname the territory "Chief Nose." Another theory claims that the name was given for a geographic feature resembling a nose. Whatever the origin may be, one thing's for sure: you'll find plenty of good noses in the county's local wineries.

Long before Sonoma became known for its rich agriculture, the Coast Miwok, Pomo, and Wappo tribes lived for centuries within the carrying capacity of the land. European settlement in the nineteenth century would spell the end of this way of life, beginning with the arrival of the Russian-American Company. In 1812 the Russian settlers established Fort Ross on the Sonoma coast, where it still stands today. Other historical monuments include the Mission San Francisco Solano, established in 1823 and the last and northernmost of the California missions, and El Presidio de Sonoma, built by Comandante General Mariano Guadalupe Vallejo in 1836 to pacify the native tribes and oversee the Russian traders.

In 1846 American settlers in the town of Sonoma were warned by U.S. Army Major John C. Fremont of impending action against them by the Mexican government. Reaction came from a small band of 33 men, who raised the iconic Bear Flag of the California Republic, claiming their independence from Mexico. That same day, Comandante General Vallejo was captured, and the events became known as the Bear Flag Revolt. News of war being declared between the United States and Mexico later reached the Bear Flaggers, who in turn abandoned the idea of the Republic, electing to support California's adoption into the United States. The Republic's first and only president, William B. Ide, was in office a mere 25 days.

Despite being the seat of one of the original counties formed when California was admitted into the United States, the town of Sonoma soon saw its significance decline in terms of commerce and population while other areas experienced a surge. The newer towns of Petaluma, Santa Rosa, and Healdsburg began to vie for the county seat, and in 1854 it was Santa Rosa that took the prize for its more central location and booming agriculture.

Although Sonoma has changed drastically from a place where people once lived within the land's carrying capacity to a region of monocultural use, the people of Sonoma have since supported funding for the preservation of forests and coastal habitats. With the high number of endangered plants and animals in Sonoma County, the need for more sustainable land use practices and general environmental conscientiousness has never been more crucial. Fortunately, many Sonoma business owners and residents are answering the call. As visitors, out of great respect for the land and all of its inhabitants, we should do the same. *DL*

Getting Around
Helpful tips to get from point A to point B

Sonoma Segway

524 Broadway, Sonoma
938.2080
www.sonomasegway.com

Getting around on an electric vehicle doesn't always have to be the same-old same-old. Segways are electric, and their internal gyroscope makes them loads of fun. Rent one of these two-wheeled contraptions or try out an electric skateboard (I have yet to venture out on this one) for another take on getting around electrically. Segways are the perfect way to see the town of Sonoma. Whizzing along Broadway and around the town square on one of these machines is unforgettable. *SB*

Wine Country Biodiesel

888.8811

www.winecountrybiodiesel.com

With a quick phone call or e-mail to this place, the owner or one of his compadres will deliver American-made biodiesel to your diesel vehicle at a competitive price. Don't assume that a green vehicle is out of your reach—yours can be one with the help of this eco-friendly company, which has provided many of the winegrowers and tour buses with biodiesel since before it was the new cool thing to go green. Gas prices and biodiesel prices aren't even that different, and running clean is the coolest way to go. *SB*

West County Revolution Bike Shop

6731 Sebastopol Ave, #130, Sebastopol

829.2192

www.westcountyrevolution.com

Mon–Fri 10a–6p, Sat 9:30a–6p, Sun 10a–4p

Direct your bike questions and concerns to the knowledgeable staff at West County Revolution, one of the most informative bike shops I've set foot in. The store carries all the gear you could possibly need, plus the staff will tell you about which routes to choose and which to avoid. *SB*

Sonoma Bicycle Company

264 Petaluma Blvd, Petaluma

776.0606

www.sonomabicyclecompany.com

Mon–Fri 10a–6p, Sat 10a–5p, Sun 12–5p

If you're one of those bikers with a slinky neon costume or a brilliant windbreaker and bags of bike-packing gear strapped to your saddle, you've met your match with the gearheads fiddling with wrenches at the back of this shop. If you are a cautious biker like me, more comfortable with your arms out in front of you and a smooth and safe ride, you're also in luck. Because the Sonoma Bicycle Company shop is so big, it can cater to us both, and with the especially good array of commuter bikes, it definitely gets my nod of approval. Peruse the bike maps and talk up the salespeople to find the right route for you, or plan a future trip where you can carry your luggage with you on your bike. That's green transit, baby! *SB*

Biking to Grapes and Green Thumbs Country

From San Francisco, the way to go is first by Baylink Ferry and then by bike lane. Boarding a Vallejo-bound ferry is an ideal way to travel to Northern California Wine Country, taking a route not all too dissimilar from that of Sonoma County's first residents. They went by steam and "paddle boat" up the rivulets of the bay waters to the Napa River, where they would travel due west to the rolling hills of Sonoma and its various microclimates. I take my bike on the Soscol-bound ferry if I don't have time for Mare Island and Vallejo—the route of which I don't like to miss. Vallejo is the behind-the-scenes backbone of Wine Country, a historic yet lesser-known town responsible for getting a lot of the proverbial wheels turning in the more publicized neighboring counties.

From the ferry landing at Vallejo, heading due north along the water the road soon turns to a separate, newly planted bike trail. You have to weave along the water, bypassing the 37 to stay on a safe route. Follow the signs to 37 San Rafael, and then continue straight at the on-ramp. You'll soon meet up with the 29 via the back roads. The 29 is fast paced, so bike cautiously to the side and veer left at the grape-crusher statue. At the first light, which you'll follow the traffic to the left and then make a right at Napa Road, follow for less than a mile; you'll find an ideal place where you can take a rest and get some orange juice at the small Vine Grocery shop.

A right on Broadway sends you straight into the town of Sonoma, and it's a good opportunity to take a detour by biking around the square before continuing to the left on West Napa Road. You'll go under a wrought-iron arch and follow the separate path out of the town of Sonoma. West Napa Road is also the 12, and it's eventually called Arnold Road and Sonoma Highway. It's a little like the streets of London, where you continue straight and watch the street signs keep changing names.

As the names change, follow on the small shoulder with caution; there are several spots where it is necessary to dismount if there is traffic coming and going at once. As a bike accident survivor, I urge you to be safe and ask yourself where you really need to go in such a hurry. Err on the side of caution—it's the journey that counts anyway, right?

Kenwood Inn and Spa is the ideal resting spot for a complete respite and reward for the long ride, but Valley of the Moon and Aqua Caliente also have a number of bed-and-breakfasts that are often available the night of (Kenwood must be booked in advance), but they aren't cheap. Santa Rosa, another 10-mile ride, is full of hotels, motels, and camping, and is really the largest town in of all Wine Country, where you'll be able to find whatever cherry you want to top your sundae-of-a-bike-ride. Once you're in Kenwood or Santa Rosa, you are poised for exploration in any direction—the grapes and green thumbs area is at your beck and call. *SB*

Up Early
Early-bird specials and morning treats

Sonoma Bagel and Deli
515 Hahman Dr, Santa Rosa
526.1631
Mon–Fri 7a–6p, Sat–Sun 9a–5p

When I'm circling around Santa Rosa in the morning, the last place I'd look for a delish bagel is a strip mall. But lo and behold, the best family-owned bagel shop in Sonoma is located in Montgomery Plaza, which is very much a strip mall. These bagels (onion and Asiago are my two top choices) are boiled the old-fashioned way, firm but not gooey like most California versions. Sonoma Bagel and Deli also makes bagel dogs, which are good for picnics with kids. *SB*

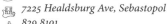

Village Bakery

7225 Healdsburg Ave, Sebastopol

829.8101

Mon–Sat 7a–5:30p, Sun 8a–2p

To me, being a fan of spices means being a fan of all things Scandinavian. Whole spices go into every dish, from cured fish to cardamom cookies (I guess being Vikings made it possible to bring the stuff back to the king's table up north). But most cardamom cookies are just sugar cookies with a sprinkle of now easy-to-come-by cardamom, doing damage to my pure vision of this classic treat. Not so at Village Bakery, which would be more aptly named "Authentic Spicy Bakery" if I had my way. Deep, dark smørrebrød, linzer torte, and both cardamom rolls and cookies are all mainstays here, and much of the dough for the pastries contains locally made almond flour, so it tastes like marzipan, one of the holiest things on the planet, I'll have you know. There's no better way to spice up your morning than with some sweets (or cardamom rolls)—just make sure to get some for your friends who are still in bed, or they'll never forgive you. *sb*

 ## Hank's Creekside Restaurant

 2800 Fourth St, Santa Rosa

575.8839

Mon–Fri 7a–7p, Sat–Sun 9a–9p

Lest you forget you are in America while touring the Mediterranean-feeling Wine Country hills and valleys, one stop at Hank's Creekside Restaurant will remind you. This all-American breakfast hut is a splendid respite from all the fancy-pants eateries around town, and the simple eggs Florentine or a heaping bowl of oatmeal will fill you up and allow the slow wakers to ease into the day. Coffee is always bottomless, and regulars are the main clientele. *sb*

 ## Wild Flour Bakery

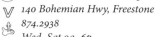

140 Bohemian Hwy, Freestone

874.2938

Wed–Sat 9a–6p

What does the perfect loaf of bread have to do with exquisite stained glass? They both require timing and creative sensitivity. I'd say they also require a great deal of passion, sprinkled with patience and diligence, and to master either one is a tremendous undertaking. But not for the owner of Wild

Flour Bakery, where—make no mistake—the perfect loaf of bread is served. Some of the flour is actually harvested locally, ground from heritage wheat varieties that used to cover the Bay Area near the time of the gold rush. Bite into one of the book-sized sticky buns or "egyptians" (made with seasonal fruits like pears and figs) and you'll want this kind of whole wheat from now on. The bakery is most famous for its hearty loaves, but the snack-time breads are tempting when you're standing at the counter, gazing off toward the oven as they come out still steaming. Local goat cheese–filled flatbreads and fougasse with rosemary and onions can be eaten on large tables while watching the grasses blow in the wind outside. The morning rush is around 9am, though many of the chefs from nearby eateries get there earlier to plan for their evening menus. Look carefully for the stained glass (and I'm not just talking about the kaleidoscope of flavors in the baked goods): there's a pretty piece of glass art in an unexpected place. *SB*

Sonoma Plaza in the Morning

A walk around the historic Sonoma Plaza is ideal in the early morning, before the town is fully awake and while the dew still drapes the greenery. I start outside General Vallejo's home in Sonoma Historical State Park, imagining what life was like under his rule, and walk south toward Sonoma Highway on Third Street West. At Sonoma Highway (there's a sidewalk, so even though it is called a highway, it is easily walkable), turn left toward Sonoma Plaza. After a couple of long blocks you'll see the wooded plaza. Walk around the square's interior and then travel around the sidewalk on the outside to find a cup of joe or a breakfast spot to finish off your morning walk. *SB*

Coffee Time

Coffee beans: roasted, ground, pressed, steeped, and served

Barking Dog Coffee Roasters

201 W Napa St, Sonoma
996.7446
www.barkingdogcoffee.com
Mon–Fri 6a–8p, Sat–Sun 7a–8p

Barking Dog Coffee Roasters is just a few blocks from my old job, and I always like stopping in for an iced vanilla latte, simply because it reminds me of college: 20-something baristas with black tribal tattoos on their forearms and modern rock music pumping through the cafe that's littered with people on laptops. But don't get me wrong, this isn't a college hangout. All ages come down to plug in, get caffeinated, and actually keep to themselves and their work. *JD*

Sawyer's News

733 Fourth St, Santa Rosa
542.1311
Daily 6a–6p

Sawyer's News isn't so much a coffee shop as it is a glorified newsstand: here you can find nearly every magazine and newspaper imaginable, including a large selection of free local publications and flyers; buy a candy bar; and then get a mocha from the indoor espresso cart. I could sit at one of the outdoor tables all afternoon, as many customers do, just watching the people wander by (especially the rowdy patrons of the brewery next door). Seriously, eat your heart out, Barnes & Noble. *JD*

Petaluma Coffee & Tea Company

212 Second St, Petaluma
763.2727
www.petalumacoffee.com
Daily 7a–6p

It is rare that a coffee shop can tell you which farm the green, unroasted beans came from, much less tell you about the farmer who grew them. At Petaluma Coffee & Tea Company, coffee is treated like wine is in the rest of the county—in fact, the roastmaster, Brian, used to work in the wine industry. Coffee here doesn't insult your intelligence. Each roast is sold by the country or origin, and fair trade varieties come from Bolivia, two different Ethiopian mountain regions, Mexico, and New Guinea. Since I don't drink coffee every day, I like the macadamia rooibos tea, which is full of healthy antioxidants and is as tasty as it is warming. *SB*

Café Newsstand (part of the Hotel Healdsburg)

301 Healdsburg Ave, Healdsburg
922.5233
www.hotelhealdsburg.com
Daily 7a–10p

In the midst of the small-town charm, sometimes I just need to know what's going on in the rest of the world. Café Newsstand has a well-stocked magazine and periodical library, two flat-screen TVs above the counter, and free Wi-Fi to satisfy my daily dose of news intake. With a stretch of one's imagination, the wraparound ceiling display could resemble one of those excessively elaborate TV news sets. What better way to catch up with this crazy world than with a flaxseed and oat biscotti the size of a brick and an energizing coffee. Baked goods, sandwiches, and all the standard cafe fare can be enjoyed quietly during the winter months, and with the whole town during the busy summers, when the cafe doors break down and the coffee crowd pours out into the street. *DL*

Flying Goat Coffee

324 Center St, Santa Rosa (other locations in Healdsburg)
575.1202
www.flyinggoatcoffee.com
Daily 7a–7p

Forget the coffee shops of the past—Flying Goat Coffee is the future of the espresso elite. Located right next to the tracks of Railroad Square, this modtastic, ultra-hip coffee joint feels like it should have a cover charge. You won't find any soccer moms here or even any loitering teenagers asking for change—just physically fit dog owners and well-dressed urbanites on their cell phones. Paris, JLo, and Britney would all wander in with their little dogs, Ugg boots, and big sunglasses if only Santa Rosa had a celeb scene. *JD*

Coffee Catz

6761 Sebastopol Ave, #300, Sebastopol
829.6600
Sun–Tues 7a–6p, Wed 7a–10p, Thurs–Sat 7a–9p

On a Thursday morning at Coffee Catz, it's the blue-haired crowd: older women sitting in groups of four, chatting over iced tea on the sunny patio. But it's totally understandable—when I hit my golden years, I will so be looking to hang out at a charming Victorian teahouse such as Coffee Catz. With a grand piano, chandeliers, and stylishly pulled-back curtains giving certain tables the extreme privacy of a ladies' boudoir, this Gravenstein Station coffeehouse gives a feeling of home and serenity. While I wait for my mocha and breakfast burrito, I enjoy glancing over the extremely large bulletin board across from the espresso machine at flyers for community events, photos of patrons and employees, and, you guessed it, lots of kitty cats just doing the darndest adorable things. *JD*

Roasters Espresso Bar

992 Gravenstein Hwy S, Sebastopol
829.3882
http://roastersespressobar.com
Mon–Fri 6a–6p, Sat–Sun 7a–6p

If you blink you'll miss Roasters Espresso Bar. In an old shopping center off the Gravenstein Highway, this tiny to-go coffee shop, which serves organic coffee and espresso products, can seat only about two comfortably, so either come to hang out alone or plan to order and go. Even in this extremely small space, Roasters still manages a local jewelry display. And not cheesy, craft-like jewelry either—more like really neat bone and imitation ivory tribal earrings. *JD*

Explore
Places where the wide world is explained and adventure is waiting to be had

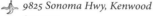 Kunde Family Estate Sustainable Winegrowing Hikes

9825 Sonoma Hwy, Kenwood
833.5501
www.kunde.com/sustainable_winegrowing/winegrowing_hikes.asp
About once a month
Cost: $15 under 21; $25 otherwise

Want to take a step (or many uphill steps) to see sustainable winegrowing in action? Go on this docent-led hike around the beautiful Kunde Family Estate and get the full scoop on all that goes into a healthy winery. Water, waste, soil, pests, harvest, employment, and processing all have a wide range of sustainable solutions involved, and there's no better way to understand it all than to see it firsthand. You can take what you learn here on all your Wine Country travels, ask insightful questions, and see which wineries are talking the talk and which are walking the walk. *SB*

Petaluma Adobe State Historic Park

3325 Adobe Rd, Petaluma
762.4871
www.petalumaadobe.com
Daily, sunrise to sunset

Visit the 1830s structure where Mexican landowners used to celebrate the fandango each year—dancing, eating, and singing after the ranch harvest. Exploring the barracks takes you back to the good old days, before California was the Bear Republic or even a part of the United States. The grounds are a fun place to learn about history and celebrate nature in one fell swoop. *DL*

Helen Putnam Regional Park

411 Chileno Valley Rd, Petaluma

433.1625

www.sonoma-county.org/parks/pk_helen.htm

Daily, sunrise to sunset

This regional park on the tip of the Sonoma-Marin border is my favorite all-in-one park in Wine Country. It isn't too showy and it's usually not crowded, but the amenities are a perfect combo of all you'd want in a park. Picnic in the sun or find shade under the pretty wooden gazebo; bike on the paved trails and hike on unpaved ones; ride horseback through the meadows, viewing the countryside panoramas; fish for bluegill in the lake; or just hang by the playground and watch the smiles on children's faces multiply. You can find easy-to-download maps of all the trails on the main web site. *SB*

Jack London State Historic Park

2400 London Ranch Rd, Glen Ellen

938.5216

www.parks.sonoma.net/JLPark.html

Daily, 9:30a–5p

This expansive park, which Jack London called Beauty Ranch, is a crucial part of any Wine Country trip. Not only is it the site of London's and his wife Charmian's graves, but also the sweeping views and historic buildings make it one of the most picturesque places to adventure. I recommend taking a docent-led tour so you can really get to know the place and many details about the couple who lived and loved there, including the location of the manure pit for the English shire horses. Jack London was way into preserving the land and finding ways to propagate healthy crops, animals, and people on it. *SB*

Sugarloaf Ridge State Park

2605 Adobe Canyon Rd, Kenwood

833.5712

www.parks.ca.gov/?page_id=481

Campsites open year-round

Cost: $20 and up for campsites, $6 parking fee

There's nothing better than getting the best site at a campground: spacious, private, with a creek running through the back, and completely engulfed in trees. I patted myself on the back for choosing number 26, and my friends applauded my decision as well, but it's not like there were many choices: Sugarloaf Ridge State Park has only 50 campsites, all located in a valley surrounded by majestic mountains.

Now, if you're a water baby or you like to haul the boat along on camping trips, then lakeless Sugarloaf isn't for you. However, if you love nature or horseback riding, then you've come to the right place. With 25 miles of trails, some that take a few hours to traverse and others that take only a few minutes, nature is plentiful. And don't come planning to party late into the night—only 20 minutes past the quiet time of 10pm the friendly ranger asked our group of five to keep it down. *JD*

Get Inspired

Museums, tours, and awe-inspiring exhibits—anything that aims to enthuse

UC Davis Cooperative Extension, Sonoma County

 133 Aviation Blvd, Ste 109, Santa Rosa
 565.2621
http://cesonoma.ucdavis.edu/vitic/Index.htm

Not too far away from Sonoma, the University of California, Davis, viticulture and horticulture programs are among the most prestigious in the world. People cross oceans to study soil and clone specifics at UC Davis, and its outpost in Sonoma is a local extension of the program, smack-dab in the middle of Wine Country, where all the studying is applied. Olive-harvesting efficiency trials, organic olive oil production, orchard floor management for fruit trees, irrigation issues, and nonchemical weed and pest control are all examples of the studies going on here, and you can take part in many of the classes as a resident of the area or even as a traveler. Take a healthy gardening class one afternoon, learn the good bugs and the bad bugs on another, or bring the whole family for a county harvest event, where the season is both celebrated and explained. *SB*

Santa Rosa Junior College

1501 Mendocino Ave, Santa Rosa (main campus); 527.4011
6225 Eastside Rd, Forestville (Shone Farm); 887.1187
www.santarosa.edu

Hailed as one of the best community colleges in the state, Santa Rosa Junior College is a powerhouse of cheffing and nursing, running and reading, offering classes to suit various studying styles and a slew of interests for students young and old. Download a course catalog and become a part of the student body, if only for a short quarter, or take a peek at the daylong seminars and productions that require a shorter time commitment but are just as educational and inspiring. Shone Farm is an exhibit of the horticulture, farming, and viticulture courses, where you can learn how to start a goat cheese business or how to graft vines. *SB*

Sonoma Compost Company

550 Mecham Rd, Petaluma
664.9113
www.sonomacompost.com
Mon–Fri 7a–4p, Sat–Sun 8a–4p

As you drive beyond the Sonoma County dump, the rotten garbage smell dissipates as you see new kinds of waste piles, including 3-story-high mounds of yard scraps and piles of wood pieces—300 tons of it delivered daily, to be exact. All of it will be sorted through by hand, reduced to organic composts and mulches, or fashioned into new pieces of lumber. The Sonoma Compost Company offers environmentally conscious customers—including about 200 vineyards, landscapers, and, most often, homeowners looking to improve their gardens—recycled products that it claims cost one-third the price of new materials, yet produce priceless results. And this private company, which offers the largest selection of organic compost mulches in Northern California, can prove its results: every year it plants a seasonal vegetable in five wine-barrel planters, four of which are in the company's own compost blends, such as the mallard mix enhanced with duck dung. The remaining plant, most recently tomato, is planted in a store-bought organic compost. It's no surprise which one comes up, well, short. *JD*

Buy Me

A unique take on shopping, from artichokes to zippers

Artists and Farmers

237 Center Street, Healdsburg

431.4704

www.artistsandfarmers.com

Next door to Barndiva (see page 168) is a large room full of carefully placed treasures. Many are made by local artisans, each designed with an air or balance or a splash of color that makes the store stand apart from other boutique shops around town. The items here are also sustainable to the best degree they can be: mohair scarves are hand-woven with local wool; ornaments and jewelry are made from repurposed metal and found objects. The sculptures are created to inspire a nature enthusiast as much as city slickers with a woodsy look in mind. Find fig jelly and rosehip jam made for Barndiva, or schedule a party and use their backyard—it's a beautiful smattering of unique landscaping and practical gardening scattered with treasured sculptures large and small. *SB*

Hand Goods

3627 Main Street, Occidental

874.2161

Daily 10a–6p

If you want a new mug, come to Hand Goods as there's no better place in Sonoma for locally made pottery. All colors of glaze and zillions of shapes and styles are affordable, especially when you consider how each piece is unique and often comes from locally procured clay. Other than the vases, mugs, and teapots that set this place apart, there is a dynamic jewelry collection as well as fair-trade gifts from South America and Asia. Head next door to Renga (874.9407; Fri–Mon 11a–5p) too, where everything is made from recycled or found objects, to get another eyeful of local artistry. *SB*

Powell's Sweets

322 Center Street, Healdsburg
431.2784
www.powellssweetshoppe.com
Mon–Sat 10a–8p, Sun 10a–7p

Powell's is the corner store of yore. Candy from all around the world—like hard-to-find Austria Mozartkugeln and Japanese licorice candies—finds its place among the walls of gummies, multicolored Jelly Bellys, and a rusted wagon toppled over with Abba-Zaba bars and bubble-gum cigarettes. There are at least seven different Elvis mint tins, plus loads of sugar-free or low-sugar delights. For me it is always down to the long strands of black licorice rope and a gag gift for my mother: last time I found a plastic platypus that remains in her car to this day as a token of the sweet memories found at Powell's. *sb*

Gardens
Blossoming bounties and picnic places

Garden Valley Ranch

498 Pepper Rd, Petaluma
795.0919
www.gardenvalley.com
Wed–Sun 10a–4p

I adore flowers—few things give me such a sense of joyful awe. And being a flower nerd, I've learned the ins and outs of growing my favorites: hydrangeas, tulips, lilacs, freesias, gerbera daisies, irises, roses, and gardenias. Here at Garden Valley Ranch my most beautiful dreams come true; I am a kid in a candy store. These gardens are perfected, as neat and organized as the plant world can be, but sitting under the rose-covered gazebo or strolling under a boxwood- and wisteria-wound walkway shows an ideal meeting of man and nature. Perhaps the crowning jewels of this place are the roses: double varieties like gleaming white Swans or Winchester Cathedrals are mystifying, and I also love classic blush English Garden roses. Take a docent-led tour to learn all the details behind each bed, or guide yourself with Garden Valley's handy maps, and then take home a *macrophylla* 'Universal hydrangea' or an espaliered pear tree (groomed to grow flat, like edible fencing). *sb*

California Flora Nursery

2990 Somers St, Fulton
528.8813
www.calfloranursery.com
Mon–Fri 9a–5p, Sat–Sun 10a–4p

This nursery grows what it sells and focuses on native plants or Mediterranean varieties that like the climate and don't require oodles of watering. When you are poking around the beautiful gardens, the staff might come and ask you what your garden is like and where it is located, rather than what you are looking for. They are like gardening matchmakers, finding the right plants for your microclimate so the butterflies and bees are happy and attracted. I get mugwort here and make tea and tincture from it to help digestion, period cramps, and insomnia. My honey, who loves fuchsias, always eyes the chandelier fuchsias, which are native to the coastal California climate. California Flora Nursery has hundreds of varieties of plants, and none is more than $30, so it is as eco-friendly as it is affordable to build a garden from this amazing array of flora. *SB*

California Carnivores

2833 Old Gravenstein Hwy, Sebastopol
Thurs–Mon 10a–4p
www.californiacarnivores.com

Go back in time to the most fun and most natural bug repellent for indoors and out. Before those annoying buzzing bug-killers hanging in your neighbors' yards (all over the East Coast, anyway), there were natural bug traps. Locations with temperate climates, with humid summers and light-frost winters, such as New Jersey's Pine Barrens and the coasts of the Carolinas and northern Georgia, used to be covered with the perfect solution for houseflies, mosquitoes, fruit flies, and ants: carnivorous plants.

Talking with California Carnivores owner and Jersey transplant Peter D'Amato, I was filled in on the plants' history as a household staple in Victorian times. He began what is now the largest collection of carnivorous plants in the United States when he was just 11 years old, going full force into an extra-credit assignment and ordering a Venus flytrap by mail. Sadly, just about 5 percent of these plants are still remaining in their natural North American habitats (few are tropical), but one trip to his amazing greenhouse will get

you excited enough to take one to your abode. My honey and I picked out a reddish fuzzy sundew for our GrassRoutes fruit-fly problem. We named him Terrance, and he's happily eating up the compost bucket guests and banana groupies around the fruit bowl.

Peter encourages donating to the Nature Conservancy, which is the most productive organization working on protecting Eastern seaboard wetlands and their native flora. You can specify that your donation goes directly to saving the carnivores. *SB*

Vintage Gardens

4130 Gravenstein Hwy N, Sebastopol

829.2035

www.vintagegardens.com

Mon–Fri 9a–4p

Focusing on old-world and rare rose varieties, Vintage Gardens is the best place to get lost in history through flowers. If you have a specific rose in mind or are a particular gardener who requires attentive and intelligent answers to nitpicky questions, ask the staff here—it seems nothing stumps these guys when it comes to flowering bushes with thorns. What temperature should the soil be? Where did the rose originate and what is the story of this variety? Which kind of rose scent dominates in this type? Don't worry, all these questions are answered, and if you are interested in reading the backstories on the rose and forgot to get tips from the Vintage Garden staff, you can find this veritable encyclopedia of roses online. Don't miss creamy Focus or multiflowered Daphne, both of which smell like heaven itself. SB

Sonoma Horticultural Nursery

3970 Azalea Ave, Sebastopol

823.6832

www.rhododendron.org/display/sonoma1.htm

Thurs–Mon 9a–5p

Don't come here thinking you know everything about rhododendrons. Two docile Rhodesian ridgebacks will greet you at your car and lead you through acres of horticultural grounds and amazing plants, including varieties of rhodies you never dreamed existed. Alongside the 700-some rhododendron types are sweet-smelling *Daphne odora*, also in many varieties, which shouldn't be missed on your trip to this magical place. SB

Luther Burbank's Gold Ridge Experiment Farm

7781 Bodega Ave, Sebastopol

www.wschs-grf.pon.net/bef.html

Daily, dawn to dusk; plant sale Wed 9a–12p

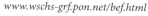

Since its beginning under the hand of Luther Burbank in 1885, this area of land has been privy to plant experiments whose results affect most Americans every day. This is where the Idaho potato was born, as well as the plums and prunes we know today, not to mention thornless blackberries and Shasta daisies. Start at Luther Burbank's cottage with a copy of the free map and guide yourself along the trails of edible history and biological creativity. *SB*

Farm to Table

Edible bounties direct to your tavola

Bodega Goat Ranch Artisan Cheese

 876.3483
www.bodegaartisancheese.com

Found only at select shops and farmers markets, this artisan cheese is made the way cheese has been produced for hundreds of years. Organic grain is grown on location for happy, free-running goats. The cheese-making equipment runs on solar power, and the helpers live by the garden in a yurt with a worm-bucket toilet. The cheese tastes as good as any I've ever had, and without animal rennet or any funny ingredients it is pure—the best way to eat dairy. *SB*

Saint Benoit Yogurt

 Bodega
 www.stbenoit.com

 In my opinion, this is how all yogurt should be. Delicious and healthy, and full of living cultures (digestive helpers), this pure yogurt is served in reusable jars and clay pots. Find it at the farmers market or at the best grocers around the Bay Area and beyond. *SB*

Occidental Friday Farmers Market

 *Downtown Occidental*
793.2159
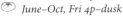 *www.occidentalfarmersmarket.com*
June–Oct, Fri 4p–dusk

Every Friday the streets of tiny Occidental come alive with people pacing around with baskets on their arms that are full of fresh fruit and vegetables fated for homemade meals all over the town. Rub shoulders with chefs on their day off or trade recipes with the growers themselves—I got a blissful roasted vegetable soup recipe from Star Mountain Gardens. Don't miss the

Bloomfield Bees honey and Sister Pot Pies stands if you are too hungry to wait until you're in the kitchen. *SB*

Spring Hill Dairy Cheese Tastings

 4235 Spring Hill Rd, Petaluma (farm)
 621 Western Ave, Petaluma (creamery and shop)
 762.3446
www.springhillcheese.com
Daily 10a–5p (shop)

Watch a full 25 different types of artisan cheeses being made while you sip a freshly made milkshake and eye the wobbly butter-churners. I know dairy isn't always the digestive tract's dream, but this is one great excuse to indulge in milky treats. Goat cheddar is one of my favorites. I like the crumbly plain version best, but Spring Hill also makes saltier-flavored versions with herbs like sage. The butter here is never salted and always golden yellow, and the shakes, well . . . you'll have to try one to realize its true glorious creaminess. Find the cheese at the Spring Hill shop and at many California farmers markets. *SB*

Laura Chenel Chèvre

Sebastopol

The sweet creamy goodness of chèvre is all over America thanks to Laura's Sebastopol goats. She began making the stuff in 1979, and with the help of a mention on Chez Panisse's menu a year later, she grew her herd and made goat cheese a popular thing in America. Even though the company is no longer locally owned, she still has some 500 goats grazing around Sebastopol, and her willful importation of chèvre, something many Americans would never have tasted if not for her, makes it fun to seek out these cute animals and hope you're looking at part of her legacy. The cheese bearing her name still tastes delicious, and with a careful eye when touring around Sonoma, you may just find a goat or two that is hers. Find Laura Chenel's chèvre at grocers nationwide. *SB*

Santa Rosa Farmers Market
Veteran's Building, Santa Rosa; year-round, Wed and Sat 8:30a–12p

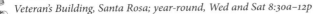

Sonoma Farmers Market
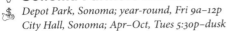
Depot Park, Sonoma; year-round, Fri 9a–12p
City Hall, Sonoma; Apr–Oct, Tues 5:30p–dusk

Most of the smaller farms, dairies, and flower growers come out of the wood-work in the most complete sense at these farmers markets. Decorate your suitcase, your friend's home, or your own place with a bountiful basket of veggies, fruits, herbs, bread, and garlic braids, and you'll be hard-pressed not to feel joyous. Being self-sufficient is one of the best side effects of shopping at a farmers market. (I call them "FM"s, and when I'm at one I say "I'm tuned to 24-7 FM," meaning I'm all about these community-centric markets.) Go find your own treasure, be it inspiration for a meal, a treat to add to your picnic basket, or an entire bushel of fruit for a day of canning with a clever neighbor. *SB*

Hardin Gardens
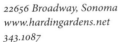
22656 Broadway, Sonoma
www.hardingardens.net
343.1087
June–Oct, Wed, Sat, and Sun 12–5p

Peter Cottontail, for those of us who remember the childhood fable, would have lived at Hardin Gardens. In fact, some of his family members do and sometimes feast on more than their fair share. Situated on 5 acres, the farm houses four generations of a family dedicated to sustainable growing. Amanda Schell's parents began the farm 25 years ago, an inheritance Amanda originally refused as a young woman. But now she embraces the life of mak-ing goat's milk soap and sharing her bountiful crop with quail and gophers. Tourists and locals alike enjoy the 48 varieties of heirloom hybrid toma-toes, and soon a chicken coop will be producing farm-fresh eggs. Amanda's daughter, who's in the fifth grade, declares that if she inherits the family farm, she's selling it on eBay. Like mother, like daughter. *JD*

Figone's
14301 Arnold Dr, Glen Ellen; 938.3164
www.figoneoliveoil.com

McEvoy Ranch
5935 Red Hill Rd, Petaluma; 778.2307
http://mcevoyranch.com

Olive Press
24724 Arnold Dr, Sonoma; 939.8900
www.theolivepress.com

My pet peeves: all-white sneakers, people who avoid saying please and thank you at all costs, most news anchors, and last but not least, Northern California Wine Country restaurants importing extra-virgin olive oil from Spain and Italy. It is not necessary, not at all. This region of California is ideal for growing top-notch olives of many varieties, and the people behind the various small-scale presses in the area are careful to ensure the product is as tasty as any flown in. Three main olive presses are located in this "grapes and green thumbs" region: Figone's, McEvoy Ranch, and Olive Press.

Figone's, in the tiny village of Eldridge, mills many of the smaller growers' olives for them in a state-of-the-art centrifuge press (all three presses use this method). The same family has been watching over the trees, Mission and manzanillo primarily, for generations and was a pioneer in the business before it was the new cool thing.

McEvoy Ranch is most attentive to sustainability, using ground cover mulch made from chicken poo and the by-products of the oil production process to fertilize the crop. McEvoy oil is sold at a chic booth in San Francisco's Ferry Building Marketplace, and this producer was one of the first to catch on to the EVOO craze.

Olive Press is the biggest of the three, with a tasting room in the Jacuzzi Winery. Though it is the oldest press, and the first to import a high-grade Italian press, Olive Press accommodates homeowners who've discovered they have a small olivina on their property. They also press for large producers like B. R. Cohn who want to sell the oil from their own olives in the tasting room, but don't want to reinvent the wheel. In the tasting room, avoid the flavored oils, which are the lesser-quality ones flavored with basil, garlic, or citrus to cover up the fact that they were picked too late or otherwise missed the boat compared to the pure blends.

Discount the fact that many of these oils are sold as "Tuscan blends"—that refers to only the variety of the olive, not the country of origin. Maybe if these producers marketed the fact that California olive oils have a wonderful character in their own right, aside from the European types, the restaurants wouldn't be so stubborn and buy from far, far away. *SB*

The Fruit Basket

24101 Arnold Dr, Sonoma
938.4332
Daily 7:30a–9p

Loosely enclosed in a huge, multicolored tent, the Fruit Basket is like the local produce big top—come see the colorful wonders of what California can produce, from 12 types of spicy peppers to yogurt-covered nut clusters and natural vegetable chips. OK, some work had to be done to create these yummy snacks, but I was happy to find bins of healthy goodies to fuel my road trip between sips of vino. *JD*

Oak Hill Farm

15101 Sonoma Hwy, Sonoma
996.6643
www.oakhillfarm.net
Wed–Sun 11a–6p

No, Sonoma isn't totally monoculture. Places like Oak Hill, a 45-acre farm set on 700-some acres of protected wetland, grow a great many things. Stroll through San Francisco's Ferry Building Marketplace and you can see the tip of the iceberg. Fresh-cut flowers are often a no-no for serious eco-geeks, but not here: Oak Hill's fresh bouquets, many of which are made of dried and long-lasting scented herbs and flowers, are taken from healthy, sustained soil. There's no better place to find a wreath for your door or a better-tasting peach than at Oak Hill. Visit the farm itself from April through December; at other times of year, you'll have to find the farm's produce at a local farmers market or at their books inside San Francisco's Ferry Building Marketplace. *SB*

Green String Farm

3571 Old Adobe Rd, Petaluma
778.7500
www.greenstringfarm.com
Mon–Sun 10a–6p

The warm winds gently shake the canopy shading the colorful sea of bins filled with ripe vegetables and fruits. But Bee, who spends her days outdoors organizing the Green String Farm produce, insists the farm stays away from the controversial *O* word. She says the biodiverse farm is better than organic: it has its own standards of quality, following the belief that the earth's soil, animals, and humans can live in harmony, right down to the beetles and ladybugs (the farm does not use pesticides). In fact, the sustainable Green String way of farming has become a standard many local vineyards seek to adopt. As you travel around Sonoma County, you'll see that some wineries sport wooden "Green String Certified" signs alongside the road. *JD*

Do Lunch

Outstanding midday eating of every sort

Rocker Oysterfeller's Kitchen and Saloon

14415 Coast Hwy 1, Valley Ford
876.1983
www.rockeroysterfellers.com
Wed–Sat 5–9p, Sun 10a–2p and 5–9p

The kitchen at Rocker Oysterfeller's has cheese plates and all the usual fare, but the real attraction for me is the Drakes Bay oysters done right. I have not found these oysters baked with cream cheese and a cornbread crust anywhere else! Rocker Oysterfeller's supports Sonoma fishermen, farms, and ranches. Fresh shucked oysters are $1 each every Thursday, and the awesome cooked oysters are only $1.50. Grub out! *IB*

Water Street Bistro

100 Petaluma Blvd, #106, Petaluma
763.9563
Mon–Thurs 7:30a–5p, Fri 7:30a–9p, Sat 7:30a–4p and 5–9p, Sun 8:30a–2:30p

I didn't know it, but crab chowder and pickled black-eyed peas were just what I wanted for lunch on my first trip to Water Street Bistro. On the side I had sweet potato, prune, and thyme salad, a sultry combination that excited my mouth. Prices are good for this restaurant's farm-to-table style of cuisine, and each meal served is both simple and complex, with interesting combinations of flavors that highlight the core ingredients. *SB*

$$ Willow Wood Market Cafe

9020 Graton Rd, Graton
823.0233
www.willowwoodgraton.com
Daily 8a–9:30p

I get tired traipsing around the lovely little towns and pockets of redwoods in Sonoma, and nothing beats a bowl of black bean soup with garlic bread, or creamy polenta and goat cheese at the Willow Wood Market Cafe. Strut through the shop and find a new book or a funny gag gift, and then settle down in front of a solid, energy-building lunch à la Graton. *SB*

Pho Vietnam

$
711 Stony Point Rd, Santa Rosa
571.7687
Daily 10a–9p

This family-run treasure is smack-dab in the middle of a strip mall, but the flavors are authentic (even though I'm not Vietnamese, I've been schooled by my good friend's granny, who makes the most famous pho in Orange County), and the prices are rock-bottom. Try hot noodles, cold noodles, fried noodles, or saucy ones. Each is served with fresh cilantro, cucumbers, and bean sprouts, and whatever meat or veggie is the highlight of the dish. Pho Tai Chin Nac is the best—it is classic all-beef pho, my favorite way to pamper myself on breezy or disappointing days. And, as always, I recommend the desserts, which I've talked up in every review I've done on Vietnamese restaurants from Seattle to Los Angeles. You'll be happily surprised with traditional dessert soup made from mung beans, coconut meat and juice, and sometimes fruit and tapioca. One taste and you'll be a dessert convert like me. *SB*

East West Cafe

128 N Main St, Sebastopol

829.2822

www.eastwestcafesebastopol.com

Daily 8a–9p

Some of Sonoma's best vegetarian dishes are served at this please-all place, where the organic tofu stir-fry is filling and the grilled tempeh is infused with smoky veggie broth. Your meat-eating friends will be satisfied, too, but the salads and huge braised veggie plate are tops in my view. *SB*

Martha's Old Mexico

305 N Main St, Sebastopol

823.4458

Wed–Mon 11a–3p and 5–9p (Sat–Sun 5–9p)

My idea of a quick, inexpensive, and tasty lunch is splitting a wet burrito with a friend at Martha's Old Mexico. Food is served fast, but it's prepared just for you, and burritos are what Martha's does best. Take your meal to go if you want to munch on a park bench nearby, and don't order two items for two people unless you have some special food-eating capacity that defies normal portion sizes. Also, this place is family-friendly and often full of children taking bites from their parents' huge plates. *SB*

Karma Indian Bistro

7530 Commerce Blvd, Cotati

795.1702

www.karmabistro.net

Tues–Sun 11:30a–2:30p, Tues–Thurs and Sun 5–9p

I still can't understand how Karma Indian Bistro does it—pardon the pun, but maybe good karma? For less than nine bones I get a full lunch buffet, and this is no heat-and-reheat heartburn fest, but a delicious and authentic set of Indian dishes made with local ingredients, including free-range chickens from Fulton Valley Farms, and never any MSG. Go nuts with Karma's house-made chutneys, which taste best sopped up with spinach and carrot pakoras or fresh-baked naan. It is amazing to have such a reasonably priced feast with local ingredients included. *SB*

Cafe Zazzle

121 Kentucky St, Petaluma
762.1700
www.zazzlecafe.com
Tues–Sat 11a–9p, Sun–Mon 11a–8p

For a light and healthy lunch without sacrificing flavor, order lettuce wraps or organic edamame with soy glaze from Cafe Zazzle. The restaurant goes out of its way to find organic soybeans, and since less than 2 percent of this huge crop is farmed sustainably, this is no small task. Spinach, tofu, and cucumber salad doused in sweet miso dressing is just how I make it at home and is a nutritious and filling meal that will get you ready for the rest of a big Wine Country exploration. *SB*

Sunflower Caffé

421 First St W, Sonoma
996.6645
www.sonomasunflower.com
Sun–Wed 7a–6p, Thurs–Sat 7a–9p

As my friend and I sat down in the back patio area, I knew the Sunflower Caffé was one of those places that, while there are a few tables indoors, is meant to be enjoyed outdoors in the lush garden with wooden arbors and a tranquil fountain. As I sipped my Spicy Maya Mocha (totally yum, even on a super-hot day) and discussed the cafe's biodegradable to-go cups and utensils, I felt totally at ease in the California sun. That is, of course, until my friend gave his sandwich recommendation: duck. I disguised my cringe with a smile, but my inner writer said, "C'mon, where's your adventurous side?" So the smoked duck breast sandwich it was, and now I'm a believer. Of course, when you smother a sandwich in melted Gruyère cheese and caramelized onions, who can say no? *JD*

Sweet Tooth

A convergence of sweet things—the best places to discover your soft spot for sugary treats

Fiorini's Truly Italian Bakery & Cafe

248 W Napa St, Sonoma
996.6119
www.fiorinisonoma.com
Tues–Sun 8a–6p

I first sampled Fiorini's authentic Italian cookies at the VinOlivo benefit at the Sonoma Mission Inn. Of all the delicacies there, these cookies were the standout, leaving a rich taste memory that has led me back time and time again. It is hard to find real *anginetti* and biscotti this side of the pond, but Fiorini's has re-created the originals with a touch of its own flair, like the rosemary cookies that I continually yearn for. *SB*

Wine Country Chocolates

14301 Arnold Dr, Glen Ellen
996.1010
www.winecountrychocolates.com
Daily 10a–5p

Wine Country Chocolates offers a tasting room for its fine, smooth sweets. Glen Ellen has enough olive oil–and–wine tasting rooms to make your head spin, but this is the prime spot for sampling chocolate. If you are in the mood for store-hopping around Jack London Village, there's ample parking and even electric car plug-ins. *IB*

Sift: A Cupcakery

7582 Commerce Blvd, Cotati
792.1681
www.siftcupcakery.com
Mon–Thurs 10a–6p, Fri–Sat 10a–7p, Sun 10a–5p

As I worked through the day, all I could think about was my last stop at Sift Cupcakery before I went home. However, I wouldn't recommend arriving late in the day if you can help it—Amanda's glass cases were nearly cleaned out. She says that since day one, people have been literally eating up her cupcakes. And I quickly found out why: they are a sweet trip to heaven and back.

Although I have still never even seen, let alone sampled, her infamous red velvet cake Ooh La Las, as they are quickly scooped up by the dozen in the morning, I did have quite a love affair with her Peanut Butter Ripple and got a kick out of her most unique cupcake creation, the Irish Car Bomb: chocolate Guinness Stout cake with Irish cream frosting decorated with green four-leaf-clover-shaped sprinkles. *JD*

Gandolf's Fine Chocolate

Forestville
874.3305
www.gandolfsfinechocolate.com

Gandolf the cat purrs. His owner, Guy Daniels, experimented until he discovered the unique secret of fine chocolates. The cat is glad that Mr. Daniels chose to use his name for the brand. Guy Daniels now markets Gandolf-brand delicacies Saturday mornings at the Santa Rosa Farmer's Market from 8:30am to 12:00pm and Sunday mornings at the Marin County Farmer's Market from 8:00am to 1:00pm. How different are these smooth chocolates from the run-of-the-mill? They are as different as fine wines are from the jug varieties! You can also order these delicacies online. *IB*

Snowbunny Organic Yogurt

312 Center Street, Healdsburg
431.7669

One of the newer additions to Healdsburg's town square is bright-white Snowbunny, a shop where coffee and frozen yogurt go hand in hand. If it's too hot out, grab an iced latte with a scoop of frosty vanilla yogurt, made with local, organic dairy products. When it's a rainy November day and you've got frozen cheeks, opt for a hot mocha with a matching scoop of mocha yogurt. Whatever the season, there is a sweet or caffeinated break waiting here, where you can chat about all your wine-country discoveries in comfort. *SB*

Vines

Don't listen to anything but your own taste buds to discern your likes and dislikes when it comes to Wine Country's namesake

Aroma Workshop at B. R. Cohn

15000 Sonoma Hwy, Sonoma
800.330.4064, ext. 124
www.brcohn.com/events
Two Sundays per month 10–11:30a

B. R. Cohn, the winery and olive oil company created by the manager of the Doobie Brothers, is always concerned with offering a complete experience and being true to its roots. I've made the trek down Sonoma Highway for quite a few benefit concerts where the Doobie Brothers brought out their guitars again. This time they're teaching me the ins and outs of aromatherapy in the hopes that it will help develop my nose for wine and olive oil, both of which are in large supply at this gorgeous property. Peach and vanilla, berries and herbs are all overtones of various vintages, after all. Reserve ahead to get a spot in the next series. *SB*

Viansa Winery & Marketplace

25200 Arnold Dr, Sonoma
800.995.4740
www.viansa.com
Daily 10a–5p

After driving around Sonoma all morning, my grumbling stomach directed me to my next stop for lunch. Sure, at Viansa Winery & Marketplace you can buy a barbecued pulled-pork sandwich at the stand outside the wine tasting room and scarf it down at a patio table while enjoying an outrageously beautiful 360-degree view of the valley, rolling vineyards, and Viansa's surrounding marshy wetlands, 90 acres of which the winery helped restore and protect. You can even taste wine if you'd like (it's a winery, after all). I, however, come for the free food. Viansa is where my friends and I have gone many times on a lazy Sunday afternoon when we just feel like, well, dipping. Viansa's Italian Marketplace is a bustling room full of just-off-the-bus tourists and many, many complimentary samples of wine-inspired gourmet finger foods. Now don't be shy, just grab a cracker or piece of French bread and push your way in there. Lemon aioli, garlic blue cheese butter, and green olive and orange tapenade are just some of the samples available. *JD*

Cline Cellars

24737 Arnold Dr, Sonoma
940.4000
www.clinecellars.com
Daily 10a–6p

While some of the historic features of Cline Cellars have been removed—the 350-acre estate used to house the last California mission, which is now located in downtown Sonoma—Fred and Nancy Cline are bringing back California's past one recycled bit at a time. No mission? How about a mission replica built with bricks from the Swiss Hotel? Better yet, how about creating a California Mission Museum out of recycled wood, with a ceiling-high stained glass window providing solar power, to house miniature replicas that get fourth graders jazzed about those notorious mission model projects? This isn't just a winery, it's a Neverland Ranch for wine enthusiasts and their children. I saw 5,000 rose bushes, 2,000 solar panels, 12 condominiums of exotic birds, 6 ponds with frogs and turtles, and 1 freaky, realistic-looking, Disneyland ride–quality bald guy on the porch. Oh, you'll see. *JD*

Jacuzzi Family Vineyards

24724 Arnold Dr, Sonoma
931.7575
www.jacuzziwines.com
Daily 10a–5:30p

The men of the Jacuzzi family were avid and continuous inventors—first the toothpick propeller, then the wine filter, and then when a 2-year-old Jacuzzi boy suffered from rheumatoid arthritis, the hydromassage machine. It's no wonder that this newcomer to the Sonoma Valley was designed as a big Italian family home and displays all of these accomplishments. Reclaimed eucalyptus wood doors and floors give a rustic look to the grandiose Italian fountain and sparkling imported chandelier that reportedly took two days to assemble. However, the best reason to visit Jacuzzi Family Vineyards is the Olive Press (see page 139), a portion of the vineyard that produces 4,000 types of olive oil, with flavors like blood orange and basil Parmesan, which visitors can watch being produced as they dip, dip, dip at the bar. *JD*

Ravenswood Winery

18701 Gehricke Rd, Sonoma
933.2332
www.ravenswood-wine.com
Daily 10a–4:30p

Two main factors make Ravenswood Winery's slogan "No Wimpy Wines" stand up: the zinfandel grape and native yeast (i.e., old-world winemaking techniques). Can you say "umph"? Ravenswood makes three types of zinfandel, all hand-crafted in medium-sized batches without sulfur or commercial yeast. At a recent wine function my honey picked up a new Ravenswood bumper sticker for me that now finds itself on my mother's busy bumper: *Kahn Nebishy Vahn* (the slogan in Yiddish). And the zin here is no *schlamazel*—it gets my vote for passionate vintage, year after year. *SB*

Wine Exchange of Sonoma

452 First St E, Ste C, Sonoma
938.1794
www.wineexsonoma.com
Mon–Thurs 10a–6p, Fri–Sat 10a–7p, Sun 11a–6p

Find yourself craving some comparison shopping in the midst of these single-family wineries that tout only their own products? Then you'll find the Wine Exchange of Sonoma refreshing. The Wine Exchange has a huge—and I mean *huge*—selection of Napa and Sonoma wines, many from tiny producers, plus more than 200 beers from around the world. It can be a little overwhelming to see so many wines at once, but you can find some great bargains, and you can talk with the more objective staff when comparing some of the wines you've spent your days tasting. *SB*

Gloria Ferrer Winery

23555 Carneros Hwy, Sonoma
996.7256
www.gloriaferrer.com
Daily 10a–5p

I love this stuff! Gloria Ferrer's sparkling wine may not be the most fancy of bubbles (in fact, it is only $20 for a bottle of their Blanc de Noirs or Sonoma Brut), but I just can't get over the fresh, champagne-style zing—it puts a skip in my step. Especially when the last bottle I had was in front of a cozy fire at a Kenwood Inn and Spa (see page 153) suite! I bring this stuff with me to any dinner party I get invited to, and everyone is pleasantly surprised. For the price point, this stuff is hard to top, and the quality instilled in each bottle is reflected in the way the winery treats its vines and soil, too. *SB*

Moon Mountain Vineyard

1700 Moon Mountain Dr, Sonoma
996.5870
www.moonmountainvineyard.com
Tues–Sat by appointment only

Moon Mountain Vineyard is the best and the worst. I'll start with the bad news to get it out of the way: it is owned by one of the largest wine and spirit groups in the world, which also owns the Guinness, Bailey's, Smirnoff, and Johnny Walker brands, among others. But the good news is the parent company lets the winemakers at Moon Mountain operate relatively independently, tilling the soil of one of the best plots of Sonoma turf and using strict organic practices to foster sustainability of the land and watershed and nuance in the quality estate wines. Why, you ask, am I writing about Moon Mountain, given that it's part of such a conglomerate, even if the winery is organic? I just can't ignore my love for the estate cabernet sauvignon, and the cabernet franc is one of the first I fell in love with. Visit the tasting room to try it for yourself—the estate wines here are really hard to top, at least from my taste buds' point of view. *SB*

Benziger Family Winery

1883 London Ranch Rd, Glen Ellen
888.490.2739
www.benziger.com
Cost: Biodynamic tram tours $15, vineyard tour with seated tasting $40

Perhaps the best example of sustainable winegrowing in Sonoma, Benziger Family Winery takes organic to another level, to biodynamic practices, which connect the life forces of the soil and the vineyard. Rather than stripping the minerals from the soil as typical farming does, the biodynamic method leaves the soil more vibrant and alive than it was before the grapes were planted. Not all the vintages here are certified biodynamic, but many are, and they taste like it figuratively and, I think, literally—the grapes sing a song in your mouth. Estate biodynamic vintages run from $29 for the

Paradiso de Maria sauvignon blanc to $80 for the flagship biodynamic blend called Tribute. *SB*

Kunde Family Estate

9825 Sonoma Hwy, Kenwood
www.kunde.com

Many believe that how humankind addresses environmental issues this coming decade will be the deciding factor in the life and health of our delicate planet. Luckily, Kunde Family Estate isn't waiting for the politicians to get it in gear and legislate sustainability. This winery has taken the lead and considered all the factors in maintaining the environment and a bountiful culture around its renowned wines. One sip of the estate sauvignon blanc and you'll be converted—or if you are an Italian red junkie like me, you'll go gaga for the sangiovese, barbera, and primitivo vintages, which are as zesty and complex as you'd dream of. *SB*

Valley of the Moon Winery

777 Madrone Rd, Glen Ellen
996.5809
www.valleyofthemoonwinery.com
Daily 10a–4:30p

Since the 1860s these acres have been planted with winemaking grapes, and each year another story gets bottled up and enjoyed. This big facility is modernized to include parts of the original century-old structures, but in every way it is a nouveau operation. Taste the fresh Glen Ellen whites and you'll see what makes the region special. Even with the size of this place, the winemakers and grape farmers do their best to maintain the nearby watershed, which is crucial to the entire region running to the Pacific, where the whales migrate. *SB*

Schug Carneros Estate

602 Bonneau Rd, Sonoma
939.9363
www.schugwinery.com
Daily 10a–5p

Chardonnay, pinot noir, chardonnay, pinot noir—this is the chant of Schug Carneros Estate, whose Bordeaux varietals are the backbone of the

Carneros estate vintages. The watershed-saving practices here have set an environmental standard in this appellation. It isn't just taste, it is also longevity that comes into consideration at this multi-award-winning winery. *SB*

Robledo Family Winery

21901 Bonness Rd, Sonoma
939.6903
www.robledofamilywinery.com
Mon–Sat 10a–5p, Sun 11a–4p

Whoever tried to pooh-pooh merlot obviously missed the Robledo Family Winery's version! This was an eye-opener for me, someone who admittedly wants to drink what's fashionable and savvy. Throw out the rule book and taste the grapy goodness. The lighter petite syrah and hard-to-find pinot blanc are two other surprises at this traditional Sonoma winery. *SB*

Sheldon Wines

 6761 Sebastopol Ave, Sebastopol (tasting room)
829.8100
www.sheldonwines.com
Daily 10:30a–4:30p

To test the authenticity of a family winery, I always ask to see the hands of the owners during the fall grape crush. Are they stained or clean as can be? At Sheldon Wines I always get the same reaction—when I can get the attention of the close-knit winemaking family, I can see their hands are nearly completely purple! Also, this family walks the walk when it comes to watershed and fish health, plus Sheldon shuns the "empire" status that many other nearby wineries seek out. Sheldon Wines is a self-described microwinery, and the young love of the owners is transcribed into the famous estate chardonnay. *SB*

Atascadero Creek Winery

 3541 Gravenstein Hwy N, Sebastopol
823.3040
www.atascaderocreek.com

The small Green Valley appellation is home to the even smaller Atascadero Creek Winery, which fulfills the need for a dry California rosé and single-block pinot noir with essential purity. The wines are available only at select restaurants and at the winery itself, so take the trip and add a bottle or two of this tried-and-true treasure to your stash. It'll be your favorite souvenir, I promise. *SB*

Pamper

Shelters from the hustle and bustle, simple enjoyments, and all things feel-good

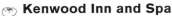 **Kenwood Inn and Spa**

 10400 Sonoma Hwy, Kenwood
800.353.6966
www.kenwoodinn.com/spa.php

Even weeks after my complete facial at the luxurious Kenwood Inn and Spa, my honey compliments me on my skin looking better than ever. For him to notice such a difference there must have been real results, and there were. I went in the spa after lounging around the saline pool for hours (the environmentally friendly pool and hot tub are free for you to use if you spend more than $250 at the spa; otherwise you pay an extra $25) and didn't know how much benefit a facial would give me. In the past my skin was pretty great, and I had never seen distinct benefits from a treatment. I've been pampered at Kenwood with amazing Arcona products, which are derived only from plant material. An 80-minute Wine Country Facial is all you'll need to feel the way I do, but you can tack on a couples massage or a soak in one of the vineyard-facing private tubs for an extra bit of relaxation. *SB*

 Osmosis Day Spa Sanctuary

209 Bohemian Hwy, Freestone
823.8231
www.osmosis.com
Daily 9a–8p

At Sonoma's premier green spa there are six easy steps toward becoming a better version of yourself. I feel like the benefits of a meditative spa journey are to not only shed the unwanted dead skin cells or what have you, but also restructure the personality, clearing the mind so that you can let go of unnecessary reactions or bad habits. It is with this in mind that I recommend Osmosis Day Spa Sanctuary, where it is near impossible to remain rigid, ego-focused, and stressed with an adventure of the outer and inner kind.

For the ultimate journey, start with the first of six steps: choose one of 25 herbal teas and sit in the Japanese organic tea garden, meditating or otherwise quieting your mind. Then enter the cedar bath, made of rice bran, plant enzymes, and finely ground cedar chips, which heat you up nicely and give you a feeling of weightlessness. Then settle into the bath, surrendering to this unique feeling and listening to your body so you know when you want out. When you've finished the bath, shower and get cozy in a resting room, ready for a massage. After the massage, enjoy a 75-minute facial with organic plant products that will release the tension in your face. Finish with a long sit in the meditation garden, with finely raked sand patterns like those you'd find in a Japanese Zen garden. You can skip the massage and the facial if you've got to jet back out into the world—any time spent here will reset your state of mind efficiently. *SB*

Infusions Teahouse

6988 McKinley St, Sebastopol
829.1181
www.infusionsteashop.com
Mon–Thurs 9a–5p, Fri 9a–9p, Sat 10a–10p, Sun 10a–6p

Drinking tea is a cultural celebration, an art form in some regions of the world, and a chance for us do-do-do and go-go-go types to slow down for a moment and instead just watch the steam rise out of the cup. Susan, the friendly owner of Infusions Teahouse, has 100 ways for you to do just that. With her *pu-erh* and organic oolong, you'll be transported in no time. If you are hungry, a few vegan snacks that go well with the teas are served, otherwise just center your focus on nothing in particular and give yourself a break from the stress of day-to-day life. *SB*

The Fairmont Sonoma Mission Inn & Spa

100 Boyes Blvd, Sonoma
866.540.4499
www.fairmont.com/sonoma

Located right on top of the hot spring British Captain H. E. Boyes called his own around 1900, the Sonoma Mission Inn & Spa has a direct connection to the naturally warm mineral water running below the earth's surface. Without any of the wonderful treatments this Fairmont-owned hotel offers, you can bathe in the exfoliating shower, sit in two different mineral baths, and experience the herbal steam room, dry sauna, and cool-down showers for a daily fee (which is reduced for hotel guests). Lounge chairs face outdoor thermal mineral pools and whirlpools in a luxurious setting, made all the more decadent with a hot stone massage or a reflexology treatment. *SB*

Healdsburg Soap

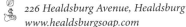

226 Healdsburg Avenue, Healdsburg
www.healdsburgsoap.com
Wed–Sun 12–5p
Healdsburg Farmer's Market
Saturdays 12–5 April-October

Delightful aromas fill the air in Jennifer's bricked-up Healdsburg soap factory. Her soaps are made from the highest-quality ingredients, including a few locals like Sonoma County lavender, Oak Hill Farm roses, and winery-influenced zinfandel bars. Without soapy residue, each pampering bar fills your shower with light and uplifting smells while healthfully cleaning your bod. Save money and paper by buying bars wrapper-free. *sb*

Imbibe
Where to sip and swill with a local feel

Third Street AleWorks

610 Third St, Santa Rosa
523.3060
www.thirdstreetaleworks.com
Sun–Tues 11:30a–12a, Wed–Sat 11:30a–11:30p

Brews, pool, sports, live music—this is a "working man's" pub in Wine Country. Although it's a bit snazzier than your run-of-the-mill bar, we're not complaining. Third Street AleWorks makes its own suds and does a good job of it. I like the Stonefly Oatmeal Stout when I'm famished and the Rye Special Bitter when it is on tap. *sb*

Russian River Pub

725 Fourth St, Santa Rosa
545.2337
www.russianriverbrewing.com

Zingy, hoppy beers are the tricks of the trade in this spacious brewpub with daylong happy hours on Sundays. There's live music to sweeten the deal and old-school American food, but on Sundays there is too much conversation and too many tunes to listen to for me to get hungry. *sb*

Hopmonk Tavern

230 Petaluma Ave, Sebastopol
829.7300
www.hopmonk.com

At Hopmonk Tavern you'll find all the good brews and none of the "This is a mic-ro-brew" (said in an annoying tone of voice) attitude. Both American and European beers are served here and are poured in the correct glasses. Don't order the same thing each round—you won't want to miss the diversity of ales, lagers, stouts, weisens, pilsners, IPAs, and other specially selected brews on the extensive menu. *sb*

Bear Republic Brewing Company
345 Healdsburg Ave, Healdsburg; 433.2337
www.bearrepublic.com

Lagunitas Brewing Company
1280 N McDowell Blvd, Petaluma; 769.4495
www.lagunitas.com

Bear Republic Brewing Company and Lagunitas Brewing Company vie for the outside world's attention as seminal California beers. They duel for the top spots in India pale ale competitions, and both do a good job of winning accolades. I'll admit that I don't adore IPA, but I don't mind being handed a bottle of either brew; both are made by righteous companies that take good care of their workers and also care about the communities in which they run their businesses. If you are loving IPA or want to see if it's your new BFF, try these beers out for yourself and maybe bring a gaggle of buddies to get the group vote. *SB*

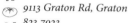

Underwood Bar and Bistro
9113 Graton Rd, Graton
823.7023
www.underwoodgraton.com
$$$ *Tues–Sun 11:30a–10p*

If you're lucky enough to have a friend ask if you want to go over to Underwood Bar and Bistro, give them the "Are you kidding me?" sarcastic face. Duh! You've been wanting to discover this place even if you didn't yet know it. Something about the maroon velvet seating and stylish wooden accents makes me feel like James Bond on a mission. Graton is a treasure trove for food and wine lovers—you'll be the best date bringing someone here for the first time or revisiting with a lovely someone. And food and wine are a happy pair at Underwood, an outcropping of nearby Willow Wood Market Cafe (see page 142). Order smoked trout and endive with Meyer lemon crème fraîche or white anchovy crostini with pressed Basque Country Idiazábal cheese, made from raw Lacha sheep milk. Oh yes, I think we like this place. *SB*

Stay In
The best take-out and take-home activities in town

King Hwa
636 Gravenstein Hwy N, Sebastopol; 823.1113

Peking Chef
7233 Healdsburg Ave, Sebastopol; 823.1566

Fried rice and spicy tofu and veggie dishes are best served direct to your house or hotel room. Plenty of great spicy reds go well with Chinese food in this area, so grab a phone, a good bottle, and a flick, and you're on your way to a Sebastopol-style chill fest. At King Hwa I remember my limited Chinese and say "No *mae ding*" so there's no MSG in my grub, and I order the beef and broccoli or chow fun noodles. Peking Chef gets my same request for no MSG, and the restaurant brings by the best vegetarian Chinese dishes, with tons of veggies and various tofu textures—some fried, some steamed, some stewed. Order at least an hour ahead of your planned mealtime, as delivery in the burbs is not like in New York. *SB*

Slice of Life
6970 McKinley Ave, Sebastopol
829.6627
www.thesliceoflife.com
Hours vary by day

Without using meat or eggs, Slice of Life caters to American and Italian-American tastes. Baked french fries and sweet potato fries; several types of meatless burgers made with tofu, nuts, or tempeh; and pasta primavera available with gluten-free spelt noodles are just some of the entrées served up every day. Easy take-out is available, so grab a healthy meal and steal away to a quiet picnic spot or a cozy indoor nook. *SB*

Willie Bird Turkeys
5350 Hwy 12, Santa Rosa
545.3308
www.williebird.com

Ordering a free-range Sonoma turkey from Willie Bird, smoked and ready for eating, was the heartiest delivery meal I've ever had. A whole smoked duck, raised humanely with lots of space and organic, whole-grain feed, is just $20. Pick up your goods and you'll save oodles on shipping. *SB*

Mombo's Pizza

560 Gravenstein Hwy N, Sebastopol; 823.7492
1880 Mendocino Ave #B, Santa Rosa; 528.3278
www.mombospizza.com

There's a spin on the East Coast mind-set here as I bite into the Lighten Up at Mombo's Pizza. Thin crust with just a loving taste of cheese and sauce and light on the quantities of add-ons, the Lighten Up is good for your gut and pocketbook. The cost of everything that makes a pie a pie has skyrocketed, so Fred Poulos, owner-operator of Mombo's, and his brother Mike have come to pizza lovers' rescue. Mike and Fred have kept costs down by not lowering quality but just the quantity of costly ingredients, which makes it possible for them to continue to deliver great-tasting pizza. *IB*

Oakville Grocery

Healdsburg (also Oakville/Rutherford location, see page 19)

When you just want to cuddle up and stay in for the night there's no need to skip the local goat cheese, handmade chocolates, and wines from Sonoma's vibrant vineyards. Find all the needed provisions for a romantic evening in at Oakville Groceries' Healdsburg outpost, right on the main square. *SB*

Casual Night Out
Dining and delighting in a relaxed atmosphere

Willi's Seafood and Raw Bar

403 Healdsburg Ave, Healdsburg
433.9191
www.willisseafood.net

With an unabashed East Coast flair imbued with a local personality, Willi's is not just another storefront on quaint Healdsburg's main drag. Rather, it is a neighborhood favorite, where the men and women who work around town are happy to gather at the end of a long night with beers and oysters to go around. I order the chef's *crudo* of the day, and if it is already sold out I am still satisfied with the daily seviche offering, as long as it isn't shrimp or tuna. Local Dungeness crab with homemade horseradish and succulent flash-fried calamari are two standbys when they are in season. You really can't go wrong with the staples of seafood eating here. *SB*

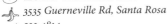 Zazu Restaurant

3535 Guerneville Rd, Santa Rosa
523.4814
www.zazurestaurant.com
$$ *Wed–Sun 5:30p–close*

I'd happily scram north to this little red barn to settle in with a crowd of excited diners awaiting seasonal delights. The winter menu is my favorite, and after coming here each season, I've been hard-pressed to find another place that tops Zazu's inspiration when it comes to using the more limited cold-weather crops. Tuscan bean soup with kale is a joy to behold, warm in the belly but not intoxicating or oversalted like so many other versions I've sampled. Roasted brussels sprouts with sherry chestnut cream are adored by my brussels sprout–hating honey. Braised meats and beet ravioli round things out, with each item built up with definitive, unique flavors, never trying to do too much on one plate, but rather celebrating the simple quality of sought-after ingredients with polished flair. Avoid the swordfish, tuna, and shrimp dishes, which frankly I am shocked to see repeated on the menu of a place that is so adamant about the farm-to-table relationship and sustainable cares. In the summer, Zucchini Three Ways is admirable and tasty, representing all forms of this bountiful squash in foam, flower, and gratin. Chefs Duskie and John have shared their sought-after duck recipe (from the spring menu), so if you are in the area, head to Liberty Farms to pick up a free-range duck for your kitchen foray. *SB*

Seared Duck *Farrotto* with Kumquat *Agrodolce* and Hazelnuts

1 shallot, sliced
1 teaspoon grated fresh ginger
½ teaspoon Chinese five-spice powder
¾ cup olive oil
½ cup kumquats, thinly sliced
½ cup viognier
2 tablespoons sugar

¼ cup sherry vinegar
Kosher salt and fresh ground black pepper
1 pound watercress, frisée, and other young lettuces, washed
2 legs duck confit, picked, off the bone

To make the vinaigrette, sauté the shallots, ginger, and Chinese five-spice powder in 2 tablespoons of the oil in a small saucepan over medium-high heat for a few minutes until fragrant.

Add the kumquats, viognier, and sugar and simmer until the kumquats are tender but still intact, about 12 minutes. Remove from the heat and place in a small mixing bowl.

Add the sherry vinegar and whisk in the remaining oil. Season with salt and pepper to taste.

In a large bowl, toss the greens and duck confit with the kumquat dressing to coat the leaves (you will have extra dressing for another time). Plate and serve with a chilled viognier.

The Girl and the Fig

110 W Spain St, Sonoma
938.3634
www.thegirlandthefig.com
Hours vary by day

The Girl and the Fig has been serving up magic for more than 10 years to discerning Bay Area eaters. Whisper in my ear poems from the book *Illuminated Heart: Love Songs of a Zen Romantic* as you devour the side of fig compote on the prix fixe plat du jour, $32, which changes every Thursday. Enjoy *cochon dehors*, a bona fide pig-out of duck confit with poached eggs, applewood-smoked bacon, and potato hash, or traditional pastis-scented steamed mussels with pommes frites to dip into the broth. This famous spot is good for lovers and families alike. Reserve one of the four cottages at the nearby Petite Maison so you can stay longer. *IB*

Jhanthong Banbua

2400 Mendocino Ave, Santa Rosa
528.8048
Tues–Fri 11a–8p, Sat 12–9p

Snooping around Santa Rosa I heard a bubbly conversation going on between two well-dressed ladies. I thought they were speaking Vietnamese, one of my favorite languages to listen to, so I asked them if they could point me to a fabulous pho spot for lunch. But I was very wrong—they were speaking Thai, which turned out to be lucky for me, because they sent me to one of the best Thai restaurants in the Bay Area. My order? Whole grilled fish with a vinegar-based sauce in a bright orangey-red hue. It was a perfect contrast to my creamy, mouthwatering plate of coconut milk squash, Gang Kiew Wan. The pad thai I took to go, brightened with thin-sliced cabbage and carrots and interspersed with a tangy sauce and nut fragments, didn't get too chewy even hours later. The Thai tea was too sweet for my taste, but a little Thai beer made up for the sugar shock. I love talking to strangers, and in this case I'm glad I interrupted my new friends' conversation to get the locals' tip on the best Thai in town. *SB*

 ## Wolf House Restaurant
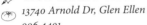

13740 Arnold Dr, Glen Ellen
996.4401
www.jacklondonlodge.com/rest.html
Mon–Fri 11:30a–3p, Mon–Sat 5:30–9p, Sat–Sun 11a–3p for brunch

This 1800s-era restaurant has a rustic Victorian interior. I take my time over a meal specially created by executive chef Jay Veregge. The air in Glen Ellen is refreshing and clean, whetting your appetite. To start, try the special cheese and fig crostini, or go easy with a salad of six market greens with pear dressing. Then savor the Roasted Liberty Farms Duck Breast Pecan and Dried Cherry Strudel with Sautéed "Cider" Cabbage and Braised Kumquat Demi. Pasta lovers will adore the Local Dungeness Crab Ravioli with Truffle Cream. Reasonable prices for this elegant fare are a great surprise! The Wolf House serves dishes made from the freshest and most seasonal ingredients, and is committed to supporting local and organic farmers. *IB*

$$ Porter Street Barbecue

500 E Cotati Ave, Cotati

795.9652

Close to the grandeur of the Crane Canyon Regional Park is tantalizing tri-tip bliss. The sandwiches at Porter Street Barbecue are huge and tasty, and you can have all the finger-licking sauce you want. Chicken is succulent and soaked in a tomato-based sauce that complements the mac and cheese. Look for the place with the dark green umbrella or call ahead, as the restaurant accepts reservations. *IB*

Bodega Volunteer Fire Department Community Events

$

V

17184 Bodega Hwy, Bodega

876.9438

www.bodegafire.org

Ladder 37, otherwise known as the Bodega Volunteer Fire Department, is a busier hub than other spots in the tiny town of Bodega (not to be confused with Bodega Bay, which is farther to the west). And this is not because there are record numbers of fires in Bodega, but because the tri-tip, polenta, pancakes, and homegrown sounds of local bands light this meeting place up at least once a week. Follow your nose and the neighborhood families and farmers to the firehouse for the community event du jour. Check out the web site for an updated schedule of events, and don't miss the polenta and stew weekly dinners if you're on your way to the coast from Wine Country inland. *SB*

Mosaic Restaurant & Wine Lounge

6675 Front St, Forestville

887.7503

www.mosaiceats.com

$$

Daily, hours vary

You might easily pass by this low-to-the-ground restaurant, as I have many a time, but decipher the small, colorful sign and follow it to a truly inspiring meal. You'll enjoy mushrooms foraged from the redwood undergrowth, baby greens from nearby Kendall-Jackson's organic garden, and the redwood-plank fence made from a storm-felled tree, every detail captures the essence of the Sonoma environment. Chef-owner Tai Olesky is a bold flavor maker, pairing soft cheeses with pungent chanterelles and hard cheeses with crispy duck. He makes sure the ingredients in his meals come from places he knows, and from people he's met and with whom he shares common ground and a similar slow-paced attentiveness. Though this entire county (and the ones next door) is chock-full of epicurean bounties, this place has a small-town friendliness that makes a meal into something soothing, gentle, and organic, rather than a rushed, glitzy show. I visit on early spring afternoons and sit in the backyard on chairs made of reused wood, under the shade of a redwood, swilling a dry rosé and thinking to myself about the journey my plate of wild mushrooms went through to come to me. *SB*

Bovolo
106 Matheson St, Healdsburg; 431.2962
www.bovolorestaurant.com

Copperfields
104 Matheson St, Healdsburg; 433.9270
www.copperfields.net
Sun–Tues 9a–8p, Wed 9a–5p, Thurs–Sat 9a–9p

Bergman and Bogart, peas and carrots, Bovolo and Copperfields—combinations dreamed up on some ethereal plane. Copperfields, a treasure to any avid reader (see page 34), has banded together with an ideal eatery (from the owners of Zazu Restaurant, see page 160), where seasonal, local produce is transformed into hearty main dishes and lighter fare. I ordered a glorified grilled cheese, made of piping hot fontina and sautéed broccoli rabe, with a heaping side of Coo-Coo Fries, stuffed with salumi and mozzarella, to share. Salads are fabulous—quinoa with roasted grapes, butter lettuce, and sliced Black Pig salumi (made in-house) or try white beans and arugula pesto. Affordable, quick, and in the company of good books: there's no way I'd make it up to Healdsburg without stopping by this famous pair. *SB*

Dress Up
Don your shiny shoes and head out to one of these fancy places

$$$ Bistro Des Copains

3782 Bohemian Hwy, Occidental
874.2436
www.bistrodescopains.com
Daily 5–9p

Beautiful, classically prepared French food is a nightly affair at this warm little bistro. On a busy Wednesday night I was lulled with dollar oysters (sustainably harvested, of course) and a butter lettuce salad. Both were served with such delicate excellence that I was yearning for the next course. Although I stay away from a few dishes due to the limited natural resources, Bistro Des Copains has local lamb and sustainable scallops, which happen to be my two picks of the menu. The scallops are served au gratin with foraged mushrooms, and the lamb comes with the new American favorite, ratatouille, a staple my mother made my entire childhood. French-style comfort is hard to import without rickety translations, but this bistro seems to sail above it all. *SB*

$$ Syrah Bistro

205 Fifth St, Santa Rosa
568.4002
www.syrahbistro.com
Tues–Sat 11:30a–2p, daily 5:30–close

Although chef Josh Silvers's goal is to create sophisticated comfort food, I think his creatively plated entrées speak more to the romantic in me than anything else. Josh's food is inspired by the special Sonoma environment, a place where gardens grow throughout the year and tenderness is considered mandatory when growing crops or raising meat. He seeks out the best of the best for his meals, which you can order from the menu or by asking to be put in his hands. In fact, each table gets something slightly different when the tasting menu is ordered. Truffled herb salads and whiskey-creamed lobster vol-au-vent with crispy-soft polenta and glazed carrots made my head and heart volley back and forth just to grasp their culinary genius. As usual, I applaud the chef's use of small fish like anchovies, mackerel, and sardines. Grilled Sardine Ruben with garlic and breadcrumbs is the best of this fish outside Spain (or my bubba's kitchen). Play with the wine list and you'll start to think that eating was the reason we were put here on this crazy planet. *SB*

John Ash & Co.

 4330 Barnes Rd, Santa Rosa
 *527.7687*
http://vintnersinn.com/dining.asp
Fri–Sat 5–9:30p, Sun–Thurs 5–9p

I start my drive into Sonoma on a Saturday by listening to the Good Food Hour from 11am until noon on local radio station KSRO 1350 AM. I have my mind wrapped around chef John Ash's new cookbook, *From the Earth to the Table*, where you can get the full scoop on this nationally renowned wine and food educator and chef of John Ash & Co. His restaurant offers the great taste of farm-to-table fine dining with a vast view of the Ferrari-Carano Vineyards and Winery. I start with the Dungeness crab cake and a soupçon of sublime Meyer lemon crème fraîche plated on roasted beet and apple salad and paired with a clear, crisp sauvignon blanc. Move about the menu and order the main dish your heart desires, but save room for a sweet ending. In front of the restaurant is a great lounge for nibbles and a smart drink if you are unable to make a reservation. *IB*

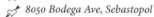 French Garden Restaurant and Bistro

 8050 Bodega Ave, Sebastopol
824.2030
www.frenchgardenrestaurant.com
Wed–Mon 11a–2p, 5–10p; Sun 10a–2p for brunch

"I've learned there are no straight paths in life," our host Dan Smith says, as he explains what he learned from growing up in a socialist community in the 1950s. "Opportunities come along. We seize them or we don't." He lives his motto: "Be a doer, not a talker." Just ask about the Tibetan monastery the restaurant is funding.

"Nothing on the menu has pesticide," Smith says. He should know—his garden produces most of the fruits and vegetables the restaurant serves. My sophisticated taste buds also tell me that none of the food arrived looking as though it should be in a coffin, as so much produce does after being shipped halfway around the globe. Nothing comes to this kitchen from a warehouse.

This is as fresh as it gets. Smith and his partner Joan Marler want to bring people together and to link all of us to the land through food and frolic and fun. In this spirit, the restaurant hosts music and movie nights (check the web site for the schedule).

Executive chef Didier Gerbi brings expertise to the extensive and continually changing menu. Start with a goat cheese purse with a hazelnut crust and honey reduction served with plum salad. Then enjoy either the luxurious lobster bisque or the salmon and seabass terrine. All the appetizers are $10, first courses are $15, and main dishes, which all come with vegetables from the garden, are $25. *IB*

Maxwell Village Cleaners

19131 Sonoma Hwy, Sonoma
996.1380
Mon–Fri 7a–7p, Sat 9a–5p

You want to look sharp for your snazzy dinner reservations, and you want your clothes clean, but in the process it isn't ideal to have a side dish of chemicals. Your skin is an organ after all, and it is receptive to the nasty agents used at most dry cleaners. Also, those chemicals go right into the groundwater, and that is where most residents of Napa and Sonoma counties get their tap water, not to mention the plants and wildlife. Maxwell helps us out by avoiding petroleum-based cleaners, instead using ones that break down into water, carbon dioxide, and sand when disposed of. You look really sharp now! *SB*

Barndiva

231 Center Street, Healdsburg
431.0100
www.barndiva.com
Wed–Thurs 5:30–11p, Fri–Sat 12p–12a, Sun 11a–12a

You might question your fancy digs when you walk up to this fancy dining spot—it is housed in a barnlike structure covered in vines and surrounded by stony paths. But whatever your attire, trust me, you'll be delighted once you sit down. Minimalist yet artsy sculptures and lighting spruce up the shed; the effect is a polished place, where slow food is given full attention. Shrimp from America and Mexico, farmed without detriment to the mangrove forests, is a highlight, as it is so hard to find sustainable shrimp. The preparations of chicken and game are the main draw for me—I like to order the 12-12 deal: $12 lunch in less than 12 minutes. On my last visit it was roasted chicken leg with savory bread pudding and wilted greens. Something about this carefully put together restaurant makes it great for long talks and the close, deep conversations you wouldn't want to have just anywhere or with just anyone. Eating here is a delight, especially in the colder months when the barn is less crowded and warmly glowing with good vibes. *SB*

Dry Creek Kitchen

317 Healdsburg Ave, Healdsburg
431.0330
www.charliepalmer.com
Daily, hours vary

Charlie Palmer is an American icon. I can remember when his Grand Central Station restaurant was going up in New York—each stride through the train terminal got me excited for Métrazur's opening. Palmer's food is lauded the world over, and though Dry Creek Kitchen isn't locally owned, it is a part of Healdsburg in a meaningful way. Continuing the county's tradition of fine food, Dry Creek is a smash hit, especially since it offers a local tasting menu Monday through Thursday for a mere $34, making it a bargain for the kind of haute plates you get. Plus, on Monday and Tuesday it hosts live local jazz. Whether or not you are staying at Hotel Healdsburg (25 Matheson St; 431.2800), connected to the restaurant, coming here is a romantic taste bud trip you'll remember for years. Artful desserts make it hard to leave the restaurant at all. Pear-and-honey cake with house-made yogurt looks too pretty to eat, candied butternut squash and carrot pecan gâteau with house-made caramel is seductive during the fall and winter months, and herb-infused cakes with frothy toppings brighten up a summer meal. Cheers to serious dining! *SB*

Listen

Any auditory experience you can imagine

Tradewinds Bar

8210 Old Redwood Hwy, Cotati
795.7878
www.tradewindsbar.com
Daily 11a–2a

A relaxed beer and live music, together with local company and a bar that doesn't close until the wee hours of the morning—what better way to relax and get in with the community? Sundays are block party nights, Thursdays bring out a resident DJ, and Mondays, Fridays, and Saturdays are a healthy mix of rockabilly, blues, funk, and soul. If you are like me, you'll come early, order a pint of Lagunitas, and do some writing in the quiet hours of Tradewinds, which reminds me of my pub writing days when I lived in London. *SB*

Santa Rosa Symphony

www.santarosasymphony.com

The Santa Rosa Symphony tosses fire, spinning from the baton of Bruno Ferrandis, who brings his stellar training from Guildhall, London, and Juilliard, New York, to the podium. This conductor and the professional musicians he leads are creating innovative programming that includes both traditional and contemporary concerts to bring all sorts of people, locals and others from the greater Bay Area, to the events. The Green Music Center at Sonoma State University, where the orchestra is in residence, is a magnet for education programs and cutting-edge composers, and organizes an over-the-top pop series each year to boot. *IB*

Wells Fargo Center for the Arts

50 Mark West Springs Rd, Santa Rosa
546.3600
http://wellsfargocenterarts.org

I'll forgive this theater its big-banking funding because it's the venue that brings national and international culture to Northern California Wine Country. On any given week Bill Maher, Joan Baez, or Margaret Cho might grace the stage. Music, comedy, theater—all the big-scale productions choose this spot, and locals pack in every time, when the world comes to them. *SB*

6th Street Playhouse

52 W Sixth St, Santa Rosa

523.4185

www.6thstreetplayhouse.com

Stroll around Railroad Square, sampling the bounty of the largest town in Sonoma County. I add to the drama of the day by getting a ticket to whatever is on stage at the 6th Street Playhouse. Call ahead for special educational programs and the full schedule of musical theater events. The local business owners are stars on this historic stage. *IB*

Sonoma County Repertory Theater

104 N Main St, Sebastopol

823.0177

www.the-rep.com

A woman who started a conversation with me in a parking lot on a fateful evening in 2003 took me, a few years later, to see her daughter and son-in-law in a play at the Sonoma County Repertory Theater. We entered through what seemed to be the back door. It was a surprise to be greeted by a warm hostess handing out programs. The staging was in muted grays and taupe, and the seating was intimate and comfortable, a double plus for comfort in culture crawling. I was delighted at the professional sets and sound, with good local actors giving riveting performances (the daughter was a Realtor). The Rep has been staging great live theater with 12 plays per season since 1993. The Rep also has a seminal young actor program where you can take a session or more to gain skills and use them on the Rep's stage. *IB*

Ledson Hotel Harmony Lounge

480 First St E, Sonoma

996.9779

www.ledsonhotel.com

Inside the historic Ledson Hotel, a wonderful inn in which to rest your noggin (see page 175), the Harmony Lounge is an ideal respite from the hubbub of Sonoma and its environs. Sit in a wingback chair and sip one of the Ledson family's own wines or a cocktail made just to your liking. I order the Let's Go Kid with Grey Goose vodka and Kahlúa when I need a bit of a jump start, but my more sophisticated companion chooses instead a martini, shaken, not stirred, with a splash of Kübler absinthe for extra fun. The light menu is an affordable way to eat without the whole restaurant to-do—beef carpaccio is a mere $11 and the chicken Caesar salad, with free-range breasts seared in aged balsamic, is the same price and pairs perfectly with the local cheese plate, which is served with exotic dried fruits. Lounge away, baby! *SB*

Lodge
Great places to rest your noggin

Bungalows 313
313 First St E, Sonoma
996.8091
www.bungalows313.com
$$$

I am a sucker for tucked-away, private luxury. It is just hard to get me up and out when I am immersed in such cozy environs and the company of my honey. We take our breakfast, choosing hot cocoa instead of caffeinated coffee, and head right back to our bungalow, not getting in much wine tasting outside of the cabin. These accommodations date back to the early 1900s, and the fine style honors history and modern amenities. I want for little else when I am situated in the Terra suite, with its vintage restored stove, or the Bella suite, which has the best bed ever and French doors facing the gardens. *SB*

Beltane Ranch

11775 Sonoma Hwy, Glen Ellen
996.6501
www.beltaneranch.com
$$

Hike, bike, hit around a tennis ball, and then stare deep into the eyes of some happy Cali cows. There's nothing more satisfying than staying in the middle of the Sonoma lifestyle at a historic bed-and-breakfast. Situated on a still-working ranch, Beltane Ranch is the perfect country setting for a romantic overnight. I go barefoot on the smooth stone paths that wind through iris and California poppy patches, slinking under shady oak trees or playing hide-and-seek on the white picket balcony. Anyone who's a returning Sonoma traveler is sure to tell you this place is everything you'd want from Wine Country. *SB*

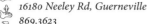

Creekside Inn & Resort

16180 Neeley Rd, Guerneville
869.3623
www.creeksideinn.com
$$

Your whole gaggle will be overjoyed to stay together at the Creekside Inn & Resort, which could also be called the Rare Albino Redwood Tree-side Inn. Just down the road and across from the babbling creek is one of a precious few albino redwoods, with bleach-colored leaves. On my way back from checking out this wild tree, I picked blackberries from the wild bushes and took them back to my stilted cabin, complete with a full kitchen, and baked up some cobbler. Smaller rooms are available for couples, and double-size private cabins are ready to sleep a family of six. Affordable weeklong rates make Creekside one of the most ideal jumping-off points for Sonoma explorations. Except for the main house, where breakfast is served daily and cool antiques abound, the accommodations leave no footprint: they use solar energy and are stilted to lessen impact on the soil. *SB*

Camellia Inn

211 North St, Healdsburg
800.727.8182
www.camelliainn.com

Just blocks away from the Healdsburg plaza, the appropriately named Camellia Inn stands surrounded by countless varieties of camellias. The large pink 1869 Victorian house provides an elegant vintage environment, upgraded with Wi-Fi and whirlpool tubs (available in Queen Deluxe suites). The Lewand family has owned and operated the inn for 25 years, also sharing their passion for fine wine with private tastings from their Camellia Cellars label. *DL*

Healdsburg Inn on the Plaza

112 Matheson St, Healdsburg
800.431.8663
www.healdsburginn.com

Perfectly located right on the Healdsburg Square, this exquisite inn has a romantic charm and vacation-y attitude that makes it stand out from the other bed-and-breakfasts around town. *SB*

Sonoma Orchid Inn

12850 River Rd, Guerneville
887.1033
www.sonomaorchidinn.com
$$

My first TiVo experience happened at the Sonoma Orchid Inn, the most relaxed bed-and-breakfast in the area, run by a fabulous orchid grower and an amazing lemon-curd maker. I fell in love with this spot as soon as I climbed up the driveway and sat under the lemon trees overlooking the orchards. A dip in the hot tub and a short search through the orchid-covered living room for a board game made my spirits soar even higher, but when I got to see back-to-back episodes of *The Colbert Report* stored on TiVo in my guest room, that's when I really fell in love. The fire blazed and kept me and my honey cozy as we rolled around in laughter. You see, we get about four channels on our tiny black-and-white TV at home and aren't accustomed to such television treatment.

The innkeeper's own lemon-curd recipe follows. To date, it is the tastiest version I've tried, but maybe that's because he picked the lemons off the Meyer trees a couple of hours before I was smearing the stuff on my fresh-baked scone. *SB*

Lemon Curd

Zest from 2 large lemons
¼–⅓ cup freshly squeezed lemon juice
6 tablespoons butter
1 cup sugar
3 eggs

Put all the ingredients in the top of a double boiler and stir occasionally until the butter melts and the sugar dissolves. Stir constantly until the curd is thick. Remove from heat and store until needed.

I always make a triple batch and use 1 cup plus a little lemon juice. I mix the eggs and the lemon juice and really beat them well. Then I strain the juice/egg mixture into the melted butter/zest/sugar mixture. I always use a microplane grater to make the zest as fine as possible. If you don't have a microplane, you could use a food processor to get a really fine zest. Straining the eggs/lemon juice gives a much smoother, finer texture to the curd, so I think it's an important step.

I also put the curd up in sterilized jars; I've found that it keeps in the refrigerator for months unopened that way. I always heat the curd until at least 175˚F (it has to hold at 175˚F for at least 30 seconds with an instant-read thermometer). But be careful—leave the curd on the stove too long and you'll get a grainy, scrambled-egg-like mixture that you'll have to toss. Remember, good curd requires patience.

Sebastopol Inn

6751 Sebastopol Ave, Sebastopol
800.653.1082
www.sebastopolinn.com
$$
I once entertained the idea of living in Sebastopol in a yurt. Suffice it to say, I have since decided that if I want to stay in a tent, I'll go camping, and if I want to visit Sebastopol, I'll choose the Jacuzzi suite at the Sebastopol Inn. I'm not desperate for luxury, but in this case I would choose to enjoy it for what it is and get used to the idea of a spa treatment at the New Dawn Day Spa, followed by a nice view from my private balcony with my special someone. I might revisit the yurt plan when I'm old and kooky; in the meantime I'll take this amalgamation of a bed-and-breakfast and boutique hotel. *DL*

Ledson Hotel

480 First St E, Sonoma

996.9779
www.ledsonhotel.com
$$
Exquisite—tell me about it! Six rooms, each as individual as the members of the Ledson family, with wonderful old-world qualities and modern luxuries. This is a wonderful place to take a step back in time to a grand era. In the Harmony Lounge (see page 171), I have a glass of wine, nibble delectables, and listen to top performers making music. Then I retire to a luxurious room with a view. *IB*

The Carneros Inn

4048 Sonoma Hwy, Napa

299.4900

www.thecarnerosinn.com

$$$

Mirroring the secluded nature of its surroundings, the Carneros Inn features 86 individual cottages, each with a private patio and set amid landscaped courtyards for the ultimate experience of exclusivity. Yet looking upon the row of humble cottages, you would think it was a real community. The spa treatments, based on ingredients from local farms and minerals abundant in the Carneros terroir, are not to be missed. Although the address is Napa, the Carneros Inn is located conveniently close to the town of Sonoma. *DL*

Birmingham Bed & Breakfast

8790 Hwy 12, Kenwood

800.819.1388

www.birminghambb.com

$$

The Birmingham Bed & Breakfast is just my style! This is a country estate with four guest rooms. The historic house has the feel of the old boarding houses I stayed at in Cape May, New Jersey, but all the rooms here have private baths and central air-conditioning and heat. The wraparound porch takes me back to another place, where there are three time periods in a day: before lunch, lunch, and after lunch. Every cell in my being slows down and slips into the beauty of the space and place. There is a cottage among the greenery for a private adventure or for the whole family in the heart of Sonoma. The breakfast menu is seasonal, with a monthly selection of fruits harvested from the estate grounds and local farms. You will be delighted and amazed at the mouthwatering selection.

After breakfast, take a walk around the neighborhood for a real human-scale experience. Wine Country seems overrun with contemporary experiences, which makes this step back in time a real treat. In the evening, you can settle on trying any one of the great local restaurants and walk back to your carefully appointed room. *IB*

 Gaige House

$$$

13540 Arnold Dr, Glen Ellen

935.6411

www.gaige.com

I want to bring home a granite soaking tub from the Gaige House playground for adults with time and means. Gaige House is advertised as a combination of vintage and contemporary, which makes this place truly Californian. This beautiful place offers a wide selection of rooms—just be sure to ask for a room not facing the highway if you want the simplicity of a retreatlike experience.

Amenities include tea, coffee, and a selection of soft drinks available around the clock in the lobby. A wide assortment of farmers market delectables cooked up in high Sonoma style, including home-smoked salmon with fresh figs and raspberries, await visitors' morning appetites. *IB*

$ Metro Hotel & Cafe

508 Petaluma Blvd S, Petaluma

773.4900

www.metrolodging.com

Without dropping big bucks on super-luxe accommodations deeper in the county, opt for the Metro Hotel & Cafe, which is just as pretty and clean as you could ask for, and colored red, blue, and yellow all over. With a nod to the Metro cars of Paris, this fun-loving lodge is an ideal jumping-off point. It offers cozy rooms and simple decor, including a mixed-use kitchen and lawn-side lounging. Drop the pretension at the door and dive into a comfy bed to get ready for your days of Wine Country exploration. *SB*

The Jack London Lodge

13740 Arnold Dr, Glen Ellen

938.8510

www.jacklondonlodge.com

The Jack London Lodge is part of the Wolf House restaurant and just a few miles from the verdant Jack London State Park and the public Sonoma Mission Inn Golf Course. Hikers and equestrians can enjoy the two other parks, beautiful Annadell State Park and Sugarloaf State Park, only minutes away. Wine tasting is just a hop away—Chateau St. Jean, Kunde Family Estate, Arrowood Vineyards & Winery, Benziger Family Winery, B.R. Cohn Winery,

Valley of the Moon Winery, Kenwood Vineyards, St. Francis Winery & Vineyards, and others are located in Glen Ellen and the immediate area. This is my sort of quiet place to leave the rigors of everyday life behind. *IB*

$$$ Kenwood Inn and Spa

10400 Sonoma Hwy, Kenwood
833.1293
www.kenwoodinn.com

In order to fully focus on your partner, it is sometimes necessary to escape from the hullabaloo of daily life. Kenwood Inn and Spa is the place for just such an escape; here it is effortless to forget the woes of the world and simply be in the moment with your partner. Ideally suited for a few nights (you won't want to leave after just one), this getaway is surrounded by native walnut trees and lush vineyards, and is secluded in a way that is earth-friendly but doesn't demand constant contemplation of anything other than yourself.

Take the time to refresh and rejuvenate in a series of saline hot tubs and mystical fountains that breathe life into the abundant plant life and also your own sensibilities. A jovial bartender will cater to your drink preferences at the guest-only wine bar, while cascading waterfalls and fountains enhance the atmosphere, and apples picked from the inn's own trees await your taste buds. In the high-ceilinged rooms, there are no distractions and no TV to take your attention away from your lover. Tuscan-style frescos and in-room fireplaces cozy the gracious spaces; jetted hot tubs greet weary, overworked bodies; and the chatter of squirrels bragging about a big walnut treasure chest is about the only commotion to be had.

At the spa, soaking tubs for couples, complete with hilly winery views and a trellised dual-massage space, make for a substantial contribution to your well-being and that of the apple of your eye. The winding gardens and secluded spaces are distinctly removed from the rest of Sonoma exploration, although if you wiggle through the main lobby (where port and a warm fire always await) or the spa reception area, you can get out into the wealth of fine dining, historical explorations, and natural wonders of the countryside.

I recommend saving up your pennies and indulging in a triple crown: three days of luxury accommodations with a spa treatment and unlimited access to chemical-free pools and unbeatable hospitality. You may think I'm gushing, but trust me, there is a reason for it. Go find out for yourself. *SB*

$$ Valley Ford Hotel

14415 Coast Hwy 1, Valley Ford

876.1983

www.vfordhotel.com

The rolling hills of west Sonoma County are the perfect locale for the quaint Valley Ford Hotel, with its oversize teak rockers on the large front porch and six charming guest rooms. It's worth a visit to the hotel, built way back in 1864, just to rock and enjoy the landscape while sipping a local tea. Finally, you can commemorate the experience by leaving your mark in the guest book, which is reproduced with page-turning animation on the hotel's web site. *DL*

Other Grapes and Green Thumbs
Bed-and-Breakfasts

Tons of quaint, craftsman, and Victorian bed-and-breakfasts are scattered around Sonoma, catering to romancing couples, reconnecting friends, or girls on a solo getaway (my bookish self desires alone time now and again). Here are the ones I've explored a little that are family owned and focused on creating a comfortable home-away-from-home experience for a variety of budgets.

$ Above the Clouds

3250 Trinity Rd, Glen Ellen

996.7371

www.abovethecloudsbb.com

Above the Clouds has the best views of the bunch, especially in the porch-equipped suite, and it looks a lot like what I imagine a typical American grandma's house to look like. *SB*

$ The Thistle Dew Inn

171 W Spain St, Sonoma

938.2909

www.thistledew.com

The Thistle Dew Inn is very affordable, and each unique room in the perfectly restored craftsman house has quilts that have been freshly dried in the sun for each guest. *SB*

$$ Donner Cottage

270 France St, Sonoma
996.2482
www.donnercottage.com

Donner Cottage is a single cottage, maintained in its historical beauty, that's perfect for a couple who wants absolute solitude, which is easy to get here since you are the only ones staying. There's even a private pool and a white wicker rocking chair, nestled under climbing wisteria and roses. *SB*

$$ Hidden Oak Bed & Breakfast Inn

214 E Napa St, Sonoma
996.9863
www.hiddenoakinn.com

Hidden Oak Bed & Breakfast Inn is a loftier choice, with a few more luxuries and a very cozy ambiance. Lace curtains and the most comfortable pillows make it one of the best night's sleeps in Sonoma. *SB*

$ Glenelly Inn & Cottages

5131 Warm Springs Rd, Glen Ellen
996.6720
www.glenelly.com

Glenelly Inn & Cottages is another affordable choice and offers distinct cottages to accommodate families. The rooms in the main house have copper bed frames and old-school wood furnaces. The cottages, situated around verdant gardens, have fireplaces and sofas on which to kick back and read a book, start to finish. *SB*

$ Ericksen's

851 Second St E, Sonoma
938.4654

Ericksen's is possibly the cheapest place to stay in the town of Sonoma, and the single studio makes it easy to stay affordable and private at the same time. The family who owns the studio lives next door and makes sure your every need is met in an efficient way, not in the typical slow-paced California fashion. *SB*

Rancho La Cuesta

 17000 Gehricke Rd, Sonoma

 935.1004

www.rancholacuestabnb.bizland.com

Want a whole house? For under $300 you can sleep eight at Rancho La Cuesta's Carriage House, an old barn that's been turned into an awesome vacation spot. *SB*

Sonoma Chalet

 18935 Fifth St W, Sonoma

 938.3129

www.sonomachalet.com

Although I don't think I like knickknacks as much as the family that runs Sonoma Chalet, I do love the lace canopy bed in Sophie's Room, which goes for $125 a night even during the high-season summer months. *SB*

The Gables Wine Country Inn

  4257 Petaluma Hill Rd, Santa Rosa

 585.7777

www.thegablesinn.com

The Gables Wine Country Inn is a welcoming spot with a variety of room sizes, shapes, and colors. It's furnished with the family's antique furniture collection, which includes comfortable wood-backed chairs for typing, lush wingbacks for reading, and rich wooden armoires for dressing. *SB*

Grapes and Green Thumbs Calendar

January

Cloverdale Old Time Fiddle Festival

Second weekend in January
Various locations
894.2067
www.cloverdalehistoricalsociety.org/fiddle

Russian River Winter Wineland

Third week in January
Various locations
800.723.6336
www.wineroad.com

Russian River Polar Bear Plunge

Last Sunday in January
Mud Island River Park
869.0691

February

Rohnert Park Crab Feed

First weekend in February
Dunham Elementary School
584.1415
www.rpchamber.org

Cloverdale Citrus Fair

Second weekend in February
Cloverdale Citrus Fairgrounds
894.3992
www.cloverdalecitrusfair.org

Santa Rosa Chinese New Year Celebration

Usually third weekend in February
Veteran's Memorial Building, Santa Rosa, following parade
576.0533
www.recacenter.org

Sonoma Valley Olive Festival

Third weekend in February
Various locations
996.1090
www.olivefestival.com

Amgen Tour of California Cycling Race

Third week in February
Through Santa Rosa
www.amgentourofcalifornia.com

March

Russian River Wine Road Barrel Tasting

First weekend in March
Various locations
800.723.6336
www.wineroad.com

Russian River Valley Winegrowers Crab & Fennel Fest

Second weekend in March
Sonoma County Fairgrounds
521.2535
www.rrvw.org

Battle of the Brews

Second Sunday in March
Sonoma County Fairgrounds
www.battleofthebrews.com

Savor Sonoma Valley

Third weekend in March
Sonoma County Fairgrounds
866.794.9463
www.heartofsonomavalley.com

Symphony of Food & Wine

Last weekend in March
Sonoma County Fairgrounds
546.8742
www.santarosasymphony.com

April

Bodega Bay Fisherman's Festival

875.3866
www.bodegabay.com

Sebastopol Apple Blossom Festival & Parade

877.828.4748
www.sebastopolappleblossom.org

Petaluma Butter & Eggs Day Parade

763.0344
www.butterandeggdays.com

Passport to Dry Creek Valley

433.3031
www.wdcv.com

Castles & Kites

Doran Regional Park
565.2267, 565.2041
www.sonoma-county.org/parks

Redwood Coast Whale & Jazz Festival

800.778.5252
www.whaleandjazzfestival.com

May

Cloverdale Spring Festival

894.4470
www.cloverdale.net

Windsor Festival & Parade

Windsor
838.7285
www.windsorchamber.com

Luther Burbank Rose Parade & Festival

Santa Rosa
542.7673
www.roseparadefestival.com

Living History Day

Petaluma
762.4871
www.visitpetaluma.com

Sonoma Jazz +

Sonoma Valley
866.468.8355
www.sonomajazz.org

Architectural Tour & Tasting

Redwood Coast
884.4343
www.simsc.org/tour.htm

June

Cotati Jazz, Blues & Arts Festival

795.5508
www.cotatijazz.com

Art at the Source

Sebastopol
829.4797
www.artatthesource.org

Harmony Festival

Santa Rosa
861.2035
www.harmonyfestival.com

Summer Nights on the Green

Windsor
838.5382
www.townofwindsor.com

Russian River Blues Festival

510.655.9471
www.omegaevents.com/russianriverblues

Taste of the Valley

Alexander Valley
888.289.4637
www.alexandervalley.org

July

Red, White & Boom!

July 4
www.sonoma.winecountry.com
Celebrate the Fourth of July Sonoma-style at this annual community get-together and fireworks show.

Fireworks and Old Time Celebration

July 4
838.1260
www.townofwindsor.com

Sonoma County Hot Air Balloon Classic

Second weekend in July
www.schabc.org

SSU Green Music Festival

Second week in July
http://greenmusicfestival.sonoma.edu

Wild Wild West Kids' Parade & Festival

Second weekend in July
765.3939
www.ci.cotati.ca.us

Sonoma County Fair
Third week in July through first week of August
www.sonomacountyfair.com

Shakespeare on the Green
Last weekend in July and first weekend in August
www.theatergreen.com

Philharmonic in the Park
July and August
www.sonoma.winecountry.com

Catalan Festival
Gloria Ferrer Winery
933.1999
www.gloriaferrer.com

August

Gravenstein Apple Fair
Second weekend in August
www.farmtrails.org/gravensteinapplefair/default.html

Grape to Glass Weekend
Third weekend in August
http://rrvw.org/grape-to-glass

Cotati Accordion Festival
Third weekend in August
www.cotatifest.com

Bodega Seafood, Art & Wine Festival
Last weekend in August
792.0288

September

Kendall-Jackson Heirloom Tomato Festival
First Saturday in September
www.kj.com/events/tomato-festival

Russian River Jazz Festival
First weekend in September
Johnson's Beach, Guerneville
www.omegaevents.com/jazzontheriver

Studio Discovery Tour
First weekend in September
http://studio-tours.com

Cajun Zydeco Music Festival
Second Saturday in September
Ives Park, Sebastopol

Valley of the Moon Vintage Festival
Second weekend in September
http://sonomavinfest.org

Sebastopol Celtic World Music Festival
Third weekend in September
823.1511
www.cumuluspresents.com/celtic

Russian River Food & Winefest
Last weekend in September
www.russianrivertravel.com

Sonoma County Book Festival

Last weekend in September
www.socobookfest.org

October

Harvest Fair

First weekend in October
www.harvestfair.org

ARTrails Sonoma County Open Studios

First and second weekends in October
www.artrails.org

Harvest Market Festival

Last weekend in October
Downtown Occidental
874.3279
www.occidental.org

Sculpture Jam

Sebastopol Center for the Arts
6680 Depot St, Sebastopol
829.4797
www.sculpturejam.org

Pinot on the River

922.1096
www.pinotfestival.com

November

Dia de los Muertos (Day of the Dead)

First weekend in November
Sonoma Valley Art Museum
996.9890
www.sonomamothersclub.org, www.svma.org

Wine & Food Affair

First weekend in November
Russian River Valley
www.wineroad.com

December

Healdsburg Holiday Stroll

First three Wednesday nights in December

THE QUIET COAST

About the Northern West Coast from Point Reyes to Westport, and Mendocino County

Once the native land of the Yuki, Pomo, and Wintun tribes, Mendocino County and the surrounding areas have remained relatively serene and isolated. Failed gold prospectors of the 1850s found it to be a suitable land to try their hand at something new and set out planting vineyards. The first wine to come out of Mendocino County was limited to a local customer base and continued its low profile even as the railroads expanded north. Mendocino County has since built a reputation for producing many superb varietals.

The quiet coast is not known for producing superstar celebrities (they probably wouldn't be too keen on the lack of cell phone and Internet service), but it had its own living legend in the late nineteenth century: Nathaniel Smith. Smith, who was of African-American descent, was perhaps the first nonindigenous person who lived in the area known as Cuffy's Cove and one of Mendocino County's first settlers. Coming from a slave state, his perseverance allowed him to create a new life for himself in California, where he hunted grizzly bear and elk, raced horses, and fished in the fashion of the neighboring Indian tribes. His doings were reported in local papers, elevating him to a status of one revered by all, much in the way we now glorify our pop icons.

Like the story of Nathaniel Smith, Mendocino County has managed to gain considerable clout in the world of winemaking yet maintain a sense of seclusion. *DL*

Getting Around

Helpful tips to get from point A to point B

Mendocino is known around California as being the greenest county, and the residents have certainly tried to contribute to the sustainability movement in any way they can. But let's face it, there isn't much to speak of in the way of mass transit in these parts, so what we're really talking about when we think of green ways to get around is either biking (which is actually pretty dangerous on many of the back roads around the coast) or alternative transit.

See Get Active (page 211) for bike tours and bike shops where you can get info on the biking scene around the county. For answers to your alternative transit queries, read on.

Natural Gas

A countywide report for residents details the latest improvements in sustainable transit, but it recognizes that one of the feasible alternatives for rural dwellers is the hybrid, which not only runs on regular gas but also has its share of debatable qualities, such as the chemicals required to make the battery and the efficiency of the engine. Compressed natural gas (CNG) is only for cars with CNG tanks or for those vehicles fitted with $1,000-plus conversion packages. You can rent a CNG vehicle in Santa Rosa, and there's a CNG station in Willits and another in Ukiah. For more on natural gas, contact the following:

American Gas Association
1515 Wilson Blvd
Arlington, VA
703.841.8574

Gas Research Institute
8600 W Bryn Mawr Ave
Chicago, IL
312.399.8176

Natural Gas Hotline
800.684.4648

Natural Gas Vehicles for America
202.824.7366
www.ngvc.org

Electricity

Electric vehicles (EVs) are a more convenient choice—in fact, many of the bed-and-breakfasts and locally owned inns I've stayed at in Mendocino would be happy to get out an extension cord to make it possible for you to "fill up" while you're staying.

The Real Goods Store/Solar Living Institute in Ukiah has the most obvious electric car plug-ins, and it is easier to rent an electric vehicle than any other alternative transit in Northern California. Here are some places to contact:

Green Motors
1500 San Pablo Ave, Berkeley
510.845.4743
www.gogreenmotors.com

Mendo Garden Center (scooters only)
44720 Main St, Mendocino
937.3459

Real Goods Store Plug-In
13771 S Hwy 101, Hopland
744.2017
www.solarliving.org

Revolution Moto
307 D St, Santa Rosa
523.2371

ZAP Headquarters
501 Fourth St, Santa Rosa
525.8658

Find out more about electric vehicles:

Alameda Bureau of Electricity
200 Grand St, Alameda
510.748.3901
Here you can get answers to questions of availability, updates on new vehicles, and usage on California roads.

California Energy Commission
1516 Ninth St, MS-41, Sacramento
916.657.1002
Get the scoop and all your questions answered on the policies behind EVs.

Electric Power Research Institute
Palo Alto, CA
415.855.2168
Ask about charging facilities.

Electric Transit Hotline (based in Southern California)
800.552.2334

Ford
23400 Michigan Ave, Ste 230
Dearborn, MI
313.390.5589
Contact: John Wallace

GM
515 Marin St, Ste 216
Thousand Oaks, CA
805.373.8492
Contact: Ray Buttacavoli
Bug the automakers themselves, and find out when and where you can get in on the EV revolution.

Fuel Cells

The best and, I think, most realistic alternative to gas-guzzling vehicles is hydrogen. Hydrogen has long been pooh-poohed as a dangerous way to get from point A to point B because of the misconceptions widely circulated about the *Hindenburg*. We should open our minds again to using hydrogen—safe ways do exist in using the stuff, even though it is a powerful element. And transit via hydrogen is something I strongly believe in, having dug my head into all the various solutions surfacing. So I suggest you take a moment to read up and consider fuel cells for yourself. California is the most forward-thinking state on the subject, and the following web site is a testament to that: www.fuelcellpartnership.org. Although it may be some time until there are fuel cells zipping all over the place, easily accessible for the mass market, they are becoming more and more a part of municipal fleets.

Several companies are making fuel cell passenger vehicles: models currently on the market are Daimler F-Cell, Ford Edge, GM Hydro-Gen3, Honda FCX Clarity, and Toyota FCHV. If you're lucky to have one of these vehicles, hydrogen fuel is available for purchase in kilograms, and for the industrial vehicles currently on the road, it costs about $4 a pop, which works out to approximately the same price as regular fuel. Though in the next several years, as more civilians are driving these babies, it is estimated that this fuel will be cheaper than gas! And remember, vehicles running on hydrogen fuel cells get on average twice the efficiency of diesel or regular gas cars and trucks.

You can currently fuel up at these spots, which are mostly south of Wine Country:

AC Transit Bus Yard
1100 Seminary Ave, Oakland
510.891.7244

Humbolt State University
Schatz Energy Research Center, Arcata
826.5100

UC Davis, Unitrans Bus Yard
Garrod Dr, Davis
530.754.4408

Biodiesel

What if you have a diesel car that also likes the taste of soy or veggie fuel, otherwise known as biodiesel? Well, you're in luck—here are several places to fuel up in the area:

Biofuel Oasis

1441 Ashby Street, Berkeley
510.665.5509
www.biofueloasis.com
Mon–Sat 10a–6p

Solar Living Institute

13771 S Hwy 101, Hopland
744.2017
www.solarliving.org/biodiesel
Mon–Sat 10a–6p

Yokayo Biofuels

150 Perry Street, Ukiah
472.0900
www.ybiofuels.org
Mon–Fri 8a–4p

If you are interested in making biodiesel or obtaining biodiesel equipment, contact the following:

Doctor Diesel

530.524.5020
www.doctordiesel.com

Doctor Diesel offers equipment leasing and a free, insightful biodiesel newsletter. Sign up online.

Home Biodiesel

888.424.6343
www.homebiodiesel.com

Use your cooking waste to make your own fuel, and it'll cost next to nothing.

Additional Resources

California Energy Commission
www.energy.ca.gov
This web site features California state reports on all kinds of energy efficiency programs for gearheads like me.

U.S. Department of Energy: Energy Efficiency and Renewable Energy, Vehicle Technologies Program
www1.eere.energy.gov/vehiclesandfuels
This site explains what new gadgets and solutions are on the table, and talks a lot about the infrastructure difficulties that make it so hard to transform America's auto usage. I go here to get the latest news. The site also features several tools to help you find out how to be a part of the movement, including where to get connected to alternative fuels around the country.

Up Early
Early-bird specials and morning treats

Anchor Bay
www.redwoodchamber.com/anchorbay.htm
On my first date with my honey, he mystified me with stories of his sand castles, beach explorations, and marine discoveries during summers at Anchor Bay. The microclimate here brings a warmer breeze, pushing away the fog to neighboring towns. In the early mornings, the beach and famous Fish Bay Rock are especially pleasant; my favorite time to make my own sand castles here is in the morning, when I can enjoy the solitude. Ocean undertow, which is a concern for swimmers in many coastal waters, isn't as much a factor here because of the sheltered cove, which keeps out the dangerous churning waters. Slip into a cool sea bath in the morning hours (I usually wear a cutoff wetsuit), before the divers, whale watchers, and kayakers even rise. Afterward, head inside for a hot rooibos tea at the historic village market. *SB*

Jackson State Forest

Off N Main St, Fort Bragg
www.jacksonforest.com
Daily, dawn to dusk

Like a little bit of activism with your morning cup of joe? Then get on your thinking cap and ponder the ups and downs of this state forest. Since back when a delegation was sent from San Francisco to discover a rumored Chinese shipwreck and instead found seemingly endless forests, the area has been under threat of deforestation, Jackson Forest in particular. In the last decade the saga has continued, and the question of whether certain private interests will be able to log this public forest is still not quite resolved, despite a powerful community effort. But headway has been made, and you can find out more on the park's web site or by checking out the 40,000 acres of trees for yourself. When the fog is still lingering and the wet air slides between the redwood branches, this epic monument of nature is at its best. *SB*

Garden Bakery

10450 Lansing St, Mendocino
937.3140
Mon–Fri, hours vary

On an early stroll around the sleepy streets of historic Mendocino, I have been known to get lost. Though the short blocks cover less than a square mile, somewhere between the morning fog and the tempting garden pathways I manage to lose track of where I am and where I am going. Getting caught up in the scenery and reimagined structures is a good thing, and losing my way is another plus. That's how I smelled my way to Garden Bakery, one of the first posts to open in the morning. Scented wafts of sweet baking bread, cinnamon, and sugar meet my nostrils and draw me in. A display of fresh rolls, croissants, and pies awakens my senses. I pick one to eat at home later, to share with those still tucked in bed. *SB*

Tomales Bakery

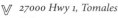

27000 Hwy 1, Tomales
878.2429
Thurs–Sun 7:30a–until they run out

If you envision yourself as a sugar daddy or a sugar mama, then you have to treat your special ones to a surprise from the Tomales Bakery. Sneak out in the early morning, as close to opening as possible, and create the ultimate goodie bag from the ovens of this epic spot, which many Bay Area foodies consider their top choice for baked goods. Cyclists huddle under the overhang on scattered benches, waiting their turn to order hot buns and lemon squares from the tiny counter to replenish their calories. I have trouble picking a reasonable number of things, but I always get a hot cider—much nicer, I think, than the typical morning cup of coffee. *SB*

Kortum Trail, Jenner

Sonoma Coast State Beach, off Coast Hwy 1

My favorite coastal walk is along this untouched slice of land between Shell Beach and Goat Rock State Park. Start with double-thickness sweatpants with pockets and you'll be comfortable and ready to pick up the odd shell or sea glass peeking at you from the rocky sand. Winding along the 2-plus-mile trail gives you a sense of absolute seclusion and a communion with nature, where land meets sea, that can't be matched. No one else seems to think of this spot for a pre-breakfast stroll, and I am left in blissful aloneness to take in the beautiful environment and release my negative thoughts with each outgoing wave. You'll find signs for the trail at the far end of Shell Beach, just to the south of Jenner, and it is a relatively easy hike into Goat Rock State Park, where you'll find more info on the park and its history. *SB*

Raven's Restaurant

Hwy 1 and Comptche Ukiah Rd, Mendocino

937.5615

www.ravensrestaurant.com

Mon–Fri 8–10:30a, Sat 8–11a, Sun 8a–12p

Ever done weightlifting with scones? Of all the baked goods, I think their heaviness would make them the ideal dumbbell if you only had baked goods to use as exercise equipment. That is, unless you were eating a Raven's Restaurant scone, the perfect flaky blend of nondairy ingredients that somehow work their magic to create a light, lovely morning pastry to shame all those *V*-word naysayers. I bet you won't have to proclaim its veganness to forewarn meat eaters—they'll probably never know the difference! *SB*

Raven's Restaurant's Vegan Scones

Makes 16 scones

9 tablespoons water
3 tablespoons egg substitute
2½ cups organic all-purpose flour
½ cup Sucanat (sugar), plus more for sprinkling
4 teaspoons baking powder
½ teaspoon salt
¾ cup Earth Balance spread, chilled and cut into small cubes
   (do not use the whipped version)
½ cup soy creamer (more if too dry)
1 tablespoon vanilla extract
1 cup fresh or frozen berries or currants
2 to 3 tablespoons soy milk, soy creamer, or hemp creamer

Preheat the oven to 350°F. In a food processor, whip the water and egg substitute for 1 minute. Set aside.

In a large bowl combine flour, Sucanat, baking powder, and salt. Cut in the Earth Balance spread with a knife or a pastry blender. (When you are finished, your mixture should look like small peas.)

In a small bowl combine the egg substitute mixture, soy creamer, and vanilla.

With swift, quick strokes, fold the wet mixture into the pastry mixture until the dough just comes together. Do not overmix.

Place the mixture on a lightly floured surface and press together without overworking the dough.

Flatten the dough with a rolling pin into a ½-inch-thick rectangle. Add the fruit of your choice by pushing it into the dough.

Fold the dough once and flatten again into a 1-inch-thick rectangle. Splash soy milk on top, brush evenly, and then sprinkle with Suncanat.

Cut into triangles and bake in the oven until golden brown, approximately 30 to 40 minutes.

Queenie's Roadhouse Cafe

6061 S Hwy 1, Elk

877.3285

Daily 8a–3p

In the midst of a morning daze, the sheer attention to detail and beautiful presentation of the breakfasts at Queenie's Roadhouse Cafe are enough to rekindle life in any tired body. As someone who is always striving for a breakfast of more than eggs, toast, and bacon to start my day, I can indulge in enormous plates of veggies, greens, and potatoes for breakfast at this accommodating roadside treasure. Every item, jam to bread, is made from scratch or sourced from within a short gallop. Just take a dining companion with you, even if he or she isn't into the whole morning thing, because you won't be able to finish what Queenie's dishes up without help. *SB*

Franny's Cup & Saucer

213 Main St, Point Arena

882.2500

Wed–Sat 8a–4p

Point Arena is the least touristy of the tiny towns dotting California's quiet coast, and the local feel is nowhere more apparent than on any given morning at Franny's Cup & Saucer. A newer addition to the area, the brightly colored façade and equally cozy bevvies and goodies inside have made it a fast favorite. On mornings before 10am crews of busy artists, nearby farmers, and the librarians from the community library down the street have their faces buried in deep mugs at Franny's. When I am in town, that's where my face is, too. *SB*

Egghead's Restaurant

326 N Main St, Fort Bragg

964.5005

www.eggheadsrestaurant.com

Thurs–Tues 7a–2p

Right across from Fort Bragg's Company Store, this hole-in-the-wall gives me the feel of a real working logging town. At times, I imagine sawdust drifting off the shoulders of the locals walking in for their morning meal. Attracting a mix of ages and professions, Egghead's Restaurant draws the town together and gives me the feeling I've stumbled on something truly unique. When my

Munchkin Marvel arrives, a pile of steaming veggies with poached eggs and an organic English muffin, I know that this is the right way to start off the day. Try any of Egghead's imaginative egg dishes or mushy oatmeal cooked just the way you like it. It seems like the restaurant creates a new omelet choice for each year it's been open—31 and counting! *SB*

Coffee Time
Coffee beans: roasted, ground, pressed, steeped, and served

 Thanksgiving Coffee
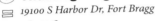 *19100 S Harbor Dr, Fort Bragg*
 964.0118
www.thanksgivingcoffee.com
Mon–Fri 8a–5p

This homegrown company gives a face to coffee beans. After touring the roastery and trying one of Thanksgiving Coffee's terrific cups, you won't be able to drink coffee without considering all the people and processes that go into each pot of the stuff. That doesn't mean you can't enjoy it—it is just that when you learn about how possible and beneficial fair-trade, shade-grown, organic practices are, and then taste how much better the flavors are, you'll want coffee this good all the time. And that's no problem, as Thanksgiving Coffee is distributed all over California and ships to wherever you are. In nearby hotels you'll see the one-serving packs, covered with the names and faces of the farmers who grew the beans you are about to brew. Drink up, you coffee lovers, you! *SB*

Moody's
 10450 Lansing St, Mendocino
937.4843
www.moodyscoffeebar.com
Daily 6a–8p

Moody's is reliable in three main areas. First, it has a solid Wi-Fi connection, a choice reason to visit in and of itself in a town where you're lucky to get a cell phone signal. Second, it offers peerless organic fair-trade coffee and fresh bran muffins. And third, you'll enjoy overhearing some new-age conversation. At Moody's I've heard men discuss how to evolve their sexual impulses and celebrate their manhood, and I've also heard yoga students asking deep questions of their turban-wearing teachers. In a world full of changes, this local treasure offers a surprising amount of stability. Check out the community bulletin board here—it's tops. *SB*

Headlands Coffeehouse

 120 Laurel St, Fort Bragg
964.1987
www.headlandscoffeehouse.com
Sun–Thurs 7a–10p, Fri–Sat 7a–11p

Outside Headlands Coffeehouse a traffic sign points the "One Way" to good coffee. But the real attraction is the overall relaxed atmosphere and the friendly staff. Even when the place seems to be bustling with people from all walks of life, the energy remains low-key. Sunday afternoons are alive with the sound of live jazz. *DL*

Explore

Places where the wide world is explained and adventure is waiting to be had

Fort Ross State Historic Park

 19005 Coast Hwy 1, Jenner
 *www.fortrossstatepark.org*
Daily 10a–4:30p (bookstore and visitors' center)

This land has roots in Russia, just like me. In fact, the very plots I camped on were settled by the Russians and their company of men in the early 1800s. Dig up more great views, hikes, and wildlife when you trip through the area's history with a visit to this special piece of California coastline. *SB*

Jug Handle State Natural Reserve

 Hwy 1, 1 mile north of Caspar, Mendocino
937.5804
www.parks.ca.gov/?page_id=441
Daily, dawn to dusk

The Ecological Staircase trail at the Jug Handle State Natural Reserve is a trek through time and earth movements. Head up the handle for one of the most enjoyable hikes in Mendocino County. Just under 3 miles in total, the trail sweeps out to coastal bluffs before winding in and up along the path of time. A free self-guided map is available online and at the reserve parking lot. *SB*

Van Damme State Park Pygmy Forest

Hwy 1, 3 miles south of the town of Mendocino
937.5804
www.parks.ca.gov/?page_id=433
Daily, dawn to dusk

Park at the free lot across Highway 1, right on the beach, and trek into the park to avoid day parking fees. You can camp here, too, but the biggest reason to squirrel around this state park (along the Fern Canyon trail) is the interesting pygmy forest—old, little trees that have been affected by natural chemical coercion, keeping them small and making the ecosystem unique. Stay on paths at all times and wind through a rare environment, all in the shade of the bigger redwoods. Van Damme has the best contrast on the coast: the tallest and the smallest of trees. *SB*

Russian Gulch State Park

Hwy 1, just north of Mendocino
937.5804
www.parks.ca.gov/?page_id=432
Daily, dawn to dusk

I love this park. Head a little way down the drive and you find yourself on a secluded beach framed by an old arched bridge and cluttered with sea glass and kelp fronds. Back at the campground are great little sites, many by the creek, that make ideal tent spots. Hike from the end of the campsite drive and you'll be gawking at a 36-foot waterfall; head the other direction and you'll be at Devil's Punch Bowl. No, not the alcoholic kind of punch—this sunken sea cave looks like a dream I once had of a giant washing machine. The water churns like it is washing the biggest pair of Carhartt overalls in the history of humankind. When you peer over the headlands you'll recognize Devil's Punch Bowl from its overhanging blowhole—every time a big wave hits the tunnel, a geyserlike plume shoots out. Whichever direction you head in this fabulous state park you'll find something breathtaking to behold. Russian Gulch gets my vote for the best place to camp, hike, and get sand in your toes in the Mendocino area, hands down. *SB*

Mendocino Botanic Garden

18220 N Hwy 1, Fort Bragg
964.4352
www.gardenbythesea.org
Daily 9a–5p Mar–Oct, 9a–4p Nov–Feb

In a world where being busy is often the norm, and tech gadgets sold to us to make our lives simpler actually add to our already stretched schedules, a waltz through these sprawling gardens is a breath of fresh air, figuratively and literally. Gazing at a collage of heather blossoms, the sage-colored big-leaved rhododendrons, and the mellifluous display of dahlia fireworks just around the corner from cormorant-scattered ocean bluffs is a soulful escape—a real dreamland. A complex pattern of paved and wood-chip-covered paths ensconced in a living museum of native flora gives my mind a rest, like I am in a safe place here on this ever-changing planet. Whether you are jogging during the park's early hours or simmering your passions over a coastal sunset, alive with the sights and smells that draw so many travelers to this quiet coast, it is impossible not to ooh and ahh at our world from the vantage point of this treasured garden. *SB*

Mendocino Historical Review Board

www.co.mendocino.ca.us/planning/MHRB/MHRBAgMn.htm

I am getting conflicting information here. On the one hand, Mendocino claims to be the greenest county; on the other, it's a place of historic preservation and small-town charm. And why these ideas can't coexist is beyond me. As I traipse around the short blocks of Mendocino proper, I see no solar panels. When I inquire at the Mendocino Garden Store, which bears a large Zap car sign, the staff says they are no longer allowed to rent electric vehicles. And why is this so? The Zap rental looked like an ugly used-car dealership, and solar panels take away from the original structures and make the skyline unsightly. That is, according to the Mendocino Historical Review Board. Apparently the board follows strict history-maintaining ordinances, which seem to do more harm than good to a town caught in the middle of global climate changes. All over town I hear whispers of the whale migration patterns shifting, of wicked weather, and of highly variable climate, yet the very system set up to preserve the town is a part of what makes it more vulnerable and less responsible. I appreciate the buildings remaining intact and also the history of the village, but just like anything, updating as we get new information is critical to survival (and this is also the definition of sanity—insanity being doing the same thing repeatedly and expecting a different result). My sincere hope is that this review board gets with the program, so we can come back and continue taking pictures here for generations to come. *SB*

Point Reyes Station
www.pointreyes.org/ptreyes.html

The year was 1890. Everything pivotal, memorable, or of any importance was built or established, was born or died, in 1890. This is not an exaggeration— just ask when the Old Western Saloon was built, or view the dates on the G Ranch cemetery tombstones. The year of Point Reyes Station was 1890.

This town, a perfect blend of history, art, and agriculture, is one of those places that you kick yourself for not discovering sooner. And after glancing through inn guest books, you learn that Point Reyes Station is a countryside retreat that many San Franciscans choose for weekend getaways. And why not? It's about an hour north of the city on scenic Highway 1, and it offers horseback riding, farm-fresh products, and a powerfully stunning stretch of coastline for the ultimate urbanite escape. Not to mention that the locals are surfers, equestrians, and artists, so if the scenery doesn't chill you out, the laid-back vibe certainly will. *JD*

"Road to the Edge" Route

If you're heading north on Highway 1, make a left turn on Sir Francis Drake Boulevard, less than a mile before you hit the town of Point Reyes Station. As you wind through the Point Reyes National Seashore, following the signs to the lighthouse as you pass historic ranches (apparently all established circa 1890—seems to be the peak year in development of the area), you'll certainly find enough aquatic and historic attractions minutes from the main road to fill an entire day trip. Just remember, it's not only about where you are going, but how you get there. *JD*

Drakes Bay Family Farms

  17171 *Sir Francis Drake Blvd, Inverness*

415.669.1149

http://drakesbayfamilyfarms.com

Daily 8a–4:30p

I don't like oysters. In fact, anything that you eat out of its home kind of creeps me out. But don't let my quirks distract you from this place. The only farm in California to harvest oysters year-round, this four-generation family-owned business practices an organic, sustainable growing technique, and much of its products end up on the menus of local restaurants, such as the Station House Cafe and Rocker Oysterfeller's. The leftover shells, which are piled in nearly 2-story-high mounds on the property, go through a recycling process that creates a micro-ecological habitat for other animals in Marin County's Drakes Estero.

I was happy to see that Drakes Bay Family Farms didn't put on a fancy façade to please tourists. For 70 years Drakes has produced hand-harvested, super-clean oysters, so why go changing? Oyster shells crunched under my feet in the parking lot as I approached the cracked and dirty market building, where you can purchase, shuck, and slurp an oyster right there or take a few pounds home for barbecuing. JD

G Ranch Cemetery

Look for signs along Point Reyes Rd

On the way out to the Point Reyes Lighthouse, this historic stop can easily be missed, despite how much it shouldn't be. Passersby will see many historic ranches along the way, beginning about midway through the alphabet and ending in, I believe, the B Ranch, unless I somehow missed A before I arrived at the seashore. Most of these ranches are still in full dairy operation. The G Ranch, although off-limits to visitors, does have one public attraction: the life-saving station cemetery. Pull into the parking lot built for two cars (apparently visitors are scarce) and take an easy hike up the hill to a patch of trees. This old yet not run-down cemetery doesn't have many inhabitants—only two sets of white picket fences house about a dozen life-saving station members, most of whom are grouped by family. What makes the place spectacular are the old trees whose limbs twist and turn into a fortress of grandeur and solitude. Although I had a companion with me on my visit, if I were solo I would climb to the highest point of the cemetery, sit on a rock with a journal or sketchpad, and enjoy the 360-degree views. JD

Point Reyes Lighthouse

End of Sir Francis Drake Blvd, Point Reyes National Seashore

415.669.1534

Thurs–Mon 10a–4:30p

I have driven from downtown Point Reyes Station out to the famous, historic Point Reyes Lighthouse twice. However, I have never seen the lighthouse. I have this uncanny ability to always go on the days it is closed: Tuesdays and Wednesdays. Of course, the drive, which feels like you're heading to the edge of the world, has never been a lost cause despite my initial destination being unavailable (you can park at the closed gate and hike to view the lighthouse, even when its interior and the visitors center are closed). Two trails are on either side of the gate: one heads north of the lighthouse and the other south. After watching a middle-aged couple take the southern trail, we decided on the northern one for privacy. This short and easy sandy trail led us out to a pinnacle on the cliff's edge. Sitting on a smooth boulder, having some lunch, and viewing miles of coastline with some of the most powerful waves I have ever seen, I honestly could not care less if I ever saw that lighthouse. *JD*

Kelley House Museum

45007 Albion St, Mendocino
937.5791
www.kelleyhousemuseum.org
Winter: Fri–Mon 11a–3p; Summer: Thurs–Tues 11am–3p

Named for one of Mendocino's founding fathers, William H. Kelley, the museum is a window into the lives of past residents. A comprehensive catalog of artifacts and an extensive archive of photos and documents provide countless resources for studying how the early residents and founders of Mendocino lived and reacted to the world around them. *DL*

Skunk Train

From Fort Bragg to Willits
800.866.1690
www.skunktrain.com
Schedules vary by season

All aboard the scenic Skunk steam railroad during the summer and have delicious barbecue and the steam-train ride together. The three hours through the costal mountains is never enough time for my 12-year-old inner child in a grownup body to be satiated. Unbelievably, a 90-minute trip is available for those who have time constraints or other adventures in this paradise. The train has different engines, depending on conditions, weather, and day of the week, but all are spectacular. From May to November, chugga-chugga, woo-woo! *IB*

Hughes Llama Ranch

Just north of the intersection of Highway 128 and Route 1 is the town of Albion. With its three major roads, Albion is a scenic small town. Drive slowly around curvy Route 1 so that you do not miss the Hughes Llama Ranch. Past the row of coastal cypress trees, nestled in the coastal headland flora, the road opens to a field dotted with many fuzzy, sweet, curious llamas. I stopped the car and scratched their silky foreheads. "Llamas will inherit the earth," postulated the ranch's owner, John Hughes. He seems to want to be asked about the historic Albion Crosses, which must have a special connection to his ranch and its contents. This is a great place to stop and stretch on the way across the Albion River, with the last wooden bridge still in use, and the Little Salmon Creek on to Navarro or Handley beaches. *IB*

Bodega School House

17110 Bodega Ln, Bodega Bay

876.3257

www.bodegaschool.com

Call ahead for tour times

Better known as the Potter School from the epic thriller *The Birds*, a visit to this white schoolhouse is a fun way to go down Northern California's film history hall of fame. Opt for a tour and get all the juicy details on the building and where each scene in the movie took place, or just bike by and grab a few postcards to prove you were there. *SB*

Will's Bait and Tackle Charters

1580 Eastshore Rd, Bodega Bay

875.2323

www.bodegabayfishing.com

Charters leave the dock at 9a, call ahead

Will's Bait and Tackle is your all-around Bodega Bay info shop and fishery resource. If you've come to town for a quick getaway and want to do some whale watching (when in season), or you want to learn how to fish, or you are more interested in just buying some local seafood that's been line caught that morning, you are in luck. I skip the big summer excursions, as I consider halibut not to be sustainable even when line caught in these waters, but in the winter the Humbolt squid fishing is a unique treat, plus you can rest assured there are plenty of squid to go around. On this excursion, you'll learn how to cut the squid correctly so you can have fried calamari rings without a black goopy mess. Ling cod is another sustainable treat to gather from these seas. During the winter and early spring months you can catch a ride on one of these boats to see the whales migrating. The helpful staff will fill you in on the details of what they've seen from year to year. Be sure to say hi to the baby whales when they go back north later in the spring! *SB*

Get Inspired

Museums, tours, and awe-inspiring exhibits—anything that aims to enthuse

(Ⓢ) Cuffy's Cemetery

Nathaniel Smith isn't the only one who was taken with Cuffy's Cove. The local churches, since America stretched over to the left coast, have been burying their loved ones overlooking this amazing viewpoint. I come here to escape the touristy atmosphere, to read a book while perched against an old gravestone, and to soak in the misty air without being bothered by all those pesky living people. There are pullouts near Cuffy's cemetery, or if you are on a bike it is even easier to take a break from Highway 1 and contemplate solace instead. *SB*

Torres Photography

43100 Iversen Rd, Gualala; 884.3380

Frame of Mind

39120 Ocean Dr, Gualala; 884.1949

Studio 391

39150 S Hwy 1, #2, Gualala; www.studio391.net

It's not easy to choose a favorite on the walls of these locally owned galleries. The photos change with the seasons, and you'll find classic images of coastal sunrises and sunsets, wildlife, and also creative art shots—a blur of colors.

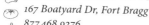 Navarro River Knits

 167 Boatyard Dr, Fort Bragg
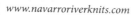 *877.468.9276*
www.navarroriverknits.com
Daily 9a–4:30p

Corn and bamboo fibers find their new place, not as sustainable flooring or biofuel, but on the checkered walls of Navarro River Knits in the old town hall of historic Fort Bragg. A rainbow of merino, wool, cotton, and these readily replaceable yarn materials get my creative juices bubbling up. I am always amazed at how many of these dramatic, brilliant colors I can actually see in the wild, from just outside this neighborhood shop. The hot green blend I've found is the same color as the fern buds growing at the perimeter of the hall. Choose a deep evergreen wool shade from a West Coast yarn producer or a hand-dyed alpaca from Sweden, New Zealand, or beyond. If you haven't already packed knitting needles or a crochet hook in your rucksack, you can find everything for your next handwork project here. *SB*

Mendocino Art Center

45200 Little Lake St, Mendocino
937.5818
www.mendocinoartcenter.org
Class schedules vary

The best place to be schooled in the arts on this slice of the Northern California coast is the Mendocino Arts Center. Pick up that pencil, paintbrush, or clay tool and get into it! Teachers are local artists, many of whom proudly display their latest creations in the cutesy galleries around town. I always like the feeling of learning a new pastel technique from someone and then looking at the bottom of a framed work the next day to see that person's signature. Learning the meaning of a watercolor wash in this community setting is a great way to look closer at your surroundings, slow down, and get into the subtleties of a truly beautiful place. You can even stay on-site if you've signed up for a class or workshop. *SB*

Mendocino Garden Shop

44720 Main St, Mendocino (just off Hwy 1, before the one stoplight in town)
937.3459
Mon–Fri 8a–5p, Sat–Sun 9a–4p

Looking for a last-minute housewarming gift? Want to make your car smell like lavender on your long drive? Need some eggs that come from the happiest hens on the planet? Head to the Mendocino Garden Center, a friendly gardening shop that sells eggs for $4 from a nearby farm (complete with a rooster, so the eggs are fertile and the farmers are early risers!). Head out to the side strip of vegetation and you'll see an array of potted herbs and perennials shelved on an old, rusted beater truck—my favorite public example of reuse in the town. Overlook the obvious hydroponic equipment and opt instead for potted lavender and seedlings of many varieties. Here you can also rent electric scooters, the best way to zip around town sans emissions (see page 188). *SB*

MacCallum House Inn & Restaurant Galleries

45020 Albion St, Mendocino
937.0289
www.maccallumhouse.com

If the nearby galleries are too kitschy for your liking, peruse this unlikely location showcasing some of the area's best photographers and painters. The historic homestead of the MacCallum family is curated by a wonderful photographer with an eye for the best creative takes on the Mendocino scenery. Poke your nose around the restaurant, along the halls, and in the bar area to see what is in store that month. *sb*

The Highlight Gallery

45052 Main St, Mendocino; 937.3132
www.thehighlightgallery.com
Tues–Sat 10a–4p, Sun 11a–3p

Voodoo Pink Gallery

10483 Lansing St, Mendocino; 937.2758
www.voodoopink.com
Daily 9a–6p

These are my two top picks for Mendocino art galleries. Neither is as cluttered or kitschy as others you'll find around town.

Voodoo Pink recently filled its front window space with a golden-tiled full-size cow statue, a modern take on mosaic art that makes me wish I had a huge high-ceilinged room to house it. The gallery's white walls are hung with select masks, portraits, landscapes, and the odd true-to-life statue like this glimmering moo-cow. The Highlight Gallery represents the best of the home arts, meaning useable artwork. Smooth carved wooden bowls and spoons, art glass that would be happy to house some dahlias from a Mendocino garden, and even handmade furniture are on display here. The artists behind these works are masters at what they do. *sb*

Mendocino Theater Company

45200 Little Lake St, Mendocino
937.4477
www.1mtc.org

It is an important event in town when a new show is staged at the Mendocino Theater Company. The innkeepers attend and tell their guests all about it, the local business owners are on- and offstage as part of the creative community spirit, and kids of all ages line up for the opening-night show. Check out what's on stage while you are up on the quiet coast and you'll get a slice of life in the town. *SB*

Gloriana Musical Theater

17800 N Hwy 1, Fort Bragg
964.7469
www.gloriana.org

Big-name musicals get face time with the Gloriana Musical Theater troupe, which exemplifies the true meaning of "amateur": someone who loves what they do. I'm not sure how that word got twisted to mean "nonprofessional"— my idea of the best profession is doing something I love—but whatever my issues with the concept, attending a show put on by Gloriana is a night out you won't soon forget. *SB*

Point Arena Tileworks

South end of Main St, Hwy 1, Point Arena
882.1931
http://pointarenatileworks.com

Just as you are leaving town, you'll see an array of colorful tiles pouring out of a garagelike building. Please heed the inner voice that says, "Stop here!" The clay possibilities seem endless, and any peek into the workshop will get you seriously considering redecorating your bathroom or kitchen with homemade tiles—no two are the same. *SB*

Get Active

Hikes, bikes, runs, and rapids—anything and everything to keep you moving

Ricochet Ridge Ranch

24201 N Hwy 1, Fort Bragg
964.7669
www.horse-vacation.com/DailyRides.php
Daily tours start at 10a; last tour is before sunset

Ricochet Ridge Ranch isn't just a fun-sounding alliteration. It is the best way to get out on the beach on horseback. The Ten Mile Beach Trail ride, which covers both the wave-fringed sands and the impressive redwoods, can be traversed in under two hours, so you have several chances each day to take this adventure. You can reserve a longer ride, or if you are totally horse crazy, an entire horseback vacation with the ranch's many options. *SB*

Doran Regional Park

201 Doran Beach Rd, Bodega Bay
875.3540

Just south of Bodega Bay, Doran Regional Park has the best beach for a sandy jog and a postjog picnic. The graceful grasses framing the beach temper the rough headlands like the shading in a watercolor painting between one color and another. This place is rarely crowded compared to some of the other coastal openings, plus it has a boat launch for ocean kayakers and camping, if you just can't imagine going back to a hotel after this elegant nature experience. *SB*

Anderson Valley Brewing Company

17700 Hwy 253, Boonville
895.2337
www.avbc.com/tour/discgolf.html

What do you do if you don't have enough people to play Ultimate Frisbee and you suck at golf? Combine the two and play disc golf at one of California's most fun places for the sport, Anderson Valley Brewing Company. If you rent the time and equipment for $10, you get a super discount on the beer tasting, or vice versa, so in the end you really get to play disc golf for free. There are some serious disc golfers around and some monkeys like me who laugh throughout the whole ordeal and try out backward spins and under-the-knee throws for extra style points. But if you do like to play it straight, there are plenty of people to join you. You can also find the game played at KOA Campground in Cloverdale and at Mendocino High School in Mendocino. *SB*

Bodega Bay Kayak
1580 E Shore Dr, Bodega Bay; 875.8899
www.bodegabaykayak.com

Liquid Fusion
32260 N Harbor Dr, Fort Bragg; 962.1623
www.liquidfusionkayak.com

Catch A Canoe
44900 Comptche Ukiah Rd, Mendocino; 937.0273
www.stanfordinn.com/innlight/canoe.html

Getting out on the water in a kayak is the best way to see the birds and sea lions of Mendocino. Bodega Bay Kayak gives lessons to people who've never set foot in a kayak or who don't think they have anything to learn. Liquid Fusion will show experienced paddlers the secret caves of the coast and also offers easy one-hour trips to the best birding spots. Catch A Canoe has the most beautiful traditional canoes, handmade from thin strips of wood.

Each of these spots is locally owned and strengthened by in-the-know paddlers and teachers. Rent a double kayak for a romantic trip on the water, or get on your gear and prepare yourself for a serious workout on the waves in a single kayak. *SB*

Veterans Memorial Park Tennis Courts
Laurel St between N Harrison and N Whipple sts, Fort Bragg
Bring your racket! These free public courts are ready for you to love—30 love, that is. Skip past the Vet Building and through the playground and you are sure to find a free court (I've never seen them full). *SB*

Bodega Bay Surf Shack

1400 Hwy 1, Bodega Bay

875.3944

www.bodegabaysurf.com

Apr–Aug

The most important thing I learned the first time I tried to surf was this: take a lesson! Thinking the smaller boards would be somehow easier, I had the toughest time managing my glide—that is, if I could get up on the board at all. The next time I took a lesson and used a long board, and boy was it a relief that I, too, could enjoy the ocean in an upright sort of way. Along the quiet coast are hidden surf spots aplenty and this great surf shack to take lessons if you aren't already in the know. For $100 you get a private lesson and 24 hours with an appropriately sized board and wetsuit (the board and wetsuit rental are a fraction of the cost without the lesson, but if you've never surfed before, you'll want some tutelage). When the tides are doing too much crisscrossing (rip currents can be dangerous with the uneven ocean bottom and shoreline variations), take a step on the wild side of the waves with the surfaholics at the Bodega Bay Surf Shack. If you want a slower adventure, rent a kayak or a bike—Bodega Bay is so beautiful it can be enjoyed at any pace. *SB*

& Bicycles, Too!
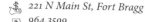

44900 Comptche Ukiah Rd, Mendocino

937.0273

www.stanfordinn.com/innlight/canoe_bike.html

Daily 9a–5:30p

This shop is right on the water and provides maps, electric bikes (that charge as you peddle), and lots of helpful tips. *DL*

Fort Bragg Cyclery

221 N Main St, Fort Bragg

964.3509

Tues–Sat 9:30a–5:30p

This cute, locally owned shop is staffed with gearheads and stocked with stuff to get you on the road for longer trips. Fort Bragg Cyclery also offers great, affordable tune-ups. *DL*

California Bicycle Tour Route

www.bitrot.de/bike_napa.html

Bike this route at your own risk! The web site details every step of the way for a good long loop, linked with campgrounds and pit stops, between the coast and Sonoma and Napa counties. It really is a great route, but you have to be prepared for it, and please, please dress like a dork and wear neon colors and reflective everything! DL

Farm to Table

Edible bounties direct to your tavola

Gualala Farmers Market

Gualala Community Center
46501 Gualala Rd, Gualala
884.3726
May–Nov, Sat 10a–12:30p

A seaside treasure at the south of Mendocino County is the Gualala Community Center's farm-fresh bounties. Come rain or shine for this indoor-outdoor market, which features nothing short of a cornucopia of the area's finest produce. I pick up local eggs and the area's famous chèvre with some just-picked herbs for a sunny weekend omelet after perusing the stands with the locals. The friendly smiles at the market make it that much easier to practice my Julia Child pan flips without getting grouchy after making a mess of the kitchen. SB

Oh! Tommy Boy's

5880 Carroll Rd, Petaluma
876.1818
Wed–Sun 9a–5p

Russian Banana, the superstar of fingerlings, the French Princess Laratte, and 20 other distinct varieties are available from October to March at the Coastal Fog Organic Farm and Oh! Tommy Boy's dry farm. I like the Black Beauty with sweet butter because of its color and texture. The farm has a limited production, so you have to get on the horn and place your order for a 30-pound box early in the season. I stop at the farm on my way to Bodega Bay to get a few varieties, which are so exotic that they make me an addict. It is amazing to imagine farming without irrigation, but that is what is going on here—it is called dry farming! *IB*

Cowgirl Creamery

80 Fourth St, Point Reyes Station
663.9335
www.cowgirlcreamery.com
Wed–Sun 10a–6p

Located in Tomales Bay Foods, a co-op of local produce and products, the Cowgirl Creamery dominates the building with its production center, visible through windows so customers can observe the cheese-making process. But if you can't watch, you can sample, which, in my opinion, is the better option of the two. While the Cowgirl Creamery Cantina has a small selection of sandwiches to go, as well as numerous huge bricks of international cheeses, Cowgirl's specialty is triple cream. The Mount Tam is award-winning, and Red Hawk is washed in beer from Marin. If you are there in springtime try the St. Pat's—it is the most divine, mellow soft cheese, wrapped in boiled nettle leaves for extra flavor and the green that inspires the name. *JD*

Other Mendocino Farmers Markets

For more information about these markets, visit www.mcfarm.org.

Boonville Farmers Market
Boonville Hotel
May–Oct, Sat 9:45a–12p

Fort Bragg Farmers Market
Spruce and N Main sts
May–Oct, Wed 3:30–6p

Laytonville Farmers Market
Good Food Store
June–Oct, Mon 3–6p

Mendocino Farmers Market
Howard and Main sts
May–Nov, Fri 12–2p

Redwood Valley Farmers Market
8920 East Rd, Lions Park
June–Oct, Sun 9:30a–1p

Ukiah Farmers Market
Alex Thomas Plaza, School and Clay sts
June–Nov, Tues 3–6p, Sat 8:30a–12p

Do Lunch
Outstanding midday eating of every sort

Laura's Bakery and Mexican Food
38411 Robinson Reef Dr, Gualala
884.3175
Mon–Sat 11a–4p

Organic burritos within earshot of sea lion howls and grunts? "Yupperdoodle," says I. Laura's Bakery and Mexican Food is the epicenter of yummy things in tiny Gualala. It's the perfect place to munch on an "ear" cookie while taking a break from the photography galleries. *SB*

Café LaLa
Cypress Village, Hwy 1, Gualala
884.1104
Daily 8a–4p

The atmosphere at Café LaLa is created by the Pacific Ocean and the Gualala River. It colors the sky and my-oh-my it colors the experience of delicious, reasonably priced food in a superfine alfresco setting. Azure light settles on my face and causes my taste buds to awaken. On cool days I choose to eat indoors by the fireplace, which is as wonderful as it sounds. My favorite menu item is Eggs Sinatra—"they do it my way" with soft-poached eggs and toast for $4.95. I also recommend the Red, White, and Bleu sandwich, a turkey-cranberry treat with a blue (cheese) surprise. *IB*

Mosswood Market

14111 Hwy 128, Boonville

895.3635

Mon–Thurs 9a–3p

The Mosswood Market is a good-looking place where you'll find a lavish spread of cookies and baked treats. You can try the food, too. The Moosewood Market features local, California-style cuisine, with pesto on the sandwiches and outside chairs to catch the rays. *IB*

Boonville Lodge

14161 Hwy 128, Boonville

895.3823

The Boonville Lodge is a choice place to stay, with beautifully appointed, spacious rooms and delicious meals in the restaurant. This is my favorite place to stay along Highway 128. The special rustic visual quality makes me feel as though I am hiding away from everything typical in my life, everything known and "normal." The superb, tasty treats at the restaurant make me want to stay here even longer. *IB*

Bruce Bread Bakery

17999 Haehl St, Boonville

895.2148

Hours vary

I do not speak "Boont" as many of the 1,400 residents of this idyllic valley do (rumor has it they invented the tongue to keep their stories from passersby and outsiders). No matter, as the Bruce Bread Bakery is ready to fill me up with more than just tales of days gone by. Terrific organic delectables are produced by Mary and her daughter Marissa, but this bakery's real attraction is its hot rolls—nothing tastes bad on them. *IB*

Cafe Beaujolais

961 Ukiah St, Mendocino

937.5614

www.cafebeaujolais.com

Daily 5:30–10p, Wed–Sun 11:30a–2:30p

Once upon a time I was a flower girl at a wedding in Mendocino, frolicking in my purple rose-covered dress and staying in a big white house with my mother. In the mornings we went down to the seaside to harvest kelp bulbs and filled the bathtub with them as props for bath time. When we got hungry, we walked to Cafe Beaujolais for fresh-squeezed orange juice and "morning food," a term the restaurant practically coined.

Now, on my return, Cafe Beaujolais is a lunch and dinner place, with only a *Morning Food* cookbook at the hostess stand as a reminder of the breakfasts of yore. These days you pop your head into the window at the Brickery across the garden for morning loaves of bread and crispy-crusted bagels. Inside the restaurant is food, real food, such as eggs Benedict with authentic Mornay sauce smothered over Red Seal Rye bread straight from the Brickery. The menu also features tasty vegan butternut squash risotto laced with locally foraged mushrooms and kale. Wine pairings from the Nelson Family and Esterlina vineyards were especially good, and I recommend you put your trust in chef-owner David LaMonica's hands with your vino choices. The annex, an elevated, glass-enclosed dining room, feels as though it were made for proposals or for giving a new shine to everyday romance. Fragrant climbing roses and veils of maroon maple and lacy juniper look as though they are about to envelope the room with junglelike lushness and sweet perfume. Cashew–poppy seed pie crusts and homemade ice cream seal the deal for dessert, giving David yet another opportunity to prove his prowess with pairing; the menu has many good dessert wines.

Follow the garden path to this special cafe—maybe not to gather kelp for your bath, but certainly to make your own memories. *SB*

 ## Station House Cafe

11180 State Rte 1, Point Reyes Station
415.663.1515
www.stationhousecafe.com
Fri–Mon 8a–3:30p and 5–9p (3:30–5p bar menu)

The little town of Point Reyes Station doesn't have too many places to grub, so thank goodness for the Station House Cafe. It's one of those nondescript cafes as far as atmosphere goes—neutral yellow and brick-red painted walls with wood panels and tables—but behind this simple modern decor is a wonderful array of classic cafe dishes, created from the wealth of local farmers. At this point in my trip, nothing sounded better than a burger, and boy was I pleased to get a Niman Ranch creation with Farmstead blue cheese and ripe Roma tomatoes, served with a homemade coleslaw, which may have been a little heavy on the walnuts and raisins but made a satisfying, ultrafilling lunch just the same. And if you're daring, try the Station House Cafe's homemade lemonade—this is not artificially sweetened lemon powder, my friend, but rather pucker-inducing, gland-salivating, jaw-twinging lemonade that only Mother Nature can provide. *JD*

 The Pine Cone Diner

60 Fourth St, Point Reyes Station

415.663.1536

www.thepineconediner.com

Daily 7a–3p

This is the kind of eating experience only a quirky small town can provide. A classic diner with sassy, tattooed waitresses, the Pine Cone Diner is a must-see. Located on the north end of town, the Pine Cone is best experienced sitting on a picnic bench out front, where you can watch people saunter in and out of the Citizen Newspaper and see cops strolling by on their lunch breaks, giving the impression that they weren't too busy, anyhow. Sipping my iced tea with the warm afternoon sun hitting my cheeks, which were elaborated by a huge grin on my face, it was one of those pivotal moments where I felt truly blessed to be a Californian. *JD*

Vines

Don't listen to anything but your own taste buds to discern your likes and dislikes when it comes to Wine Country's namesake

 Yorkville Cellars

25701 Hwy 128, Yorkville

894.9177

www.yorkvillecellars.com

Daily 11a–6p

Organic—yes, organic—vintners are right here along the winding, picture-perfect Highway 128, which looks more like a country road to my eye. Drive past fields dotted with sheep and solid sections of scented apple farms as you make your way toward the majestic redwoods and out to the Pacific Coast and the town of Mendocino. Here the Yorkville Cellars vineyards have been certified organic since 1986. I am sure that no pesticides or chemicals are being used on the land or the fruit. Stop at the tasting room, view the hundreds of awards, and then sip the wine and understand why it is so honored. I loved taking the tour of the property and the process—it made me feel a great respect for the wine made here. An overnight stay at the wonderfully accommodating rustic cottages in this scenic area completes the adventure. *IB*

Navarro Vineyards

5601 Hwy 128, Philo
895.3686
www.navarrowine.com
Daily 10a–5p

Navarro Vineyards used to be the only stop my family and I made on our way to the town of Mendocino, and it was the only real tasting room to speak of for some time. We went for the grape juices—there's a pinot noir and a luscious gewürztraminer—and for the rose-filled enclave picnic grounds, a last stop before the redwood forests closed in on us and beckoned for a quick hike and tree hug. These days the famous chardonnay and pinot noirs still shine on a visit to Navarro, but also hint that these guys have been in the game for a while. A polished tasting room also sells picnic fare and the pour staff are cuter than they are knowledgeable on wine. If you're lucky, you'll stop by when the winemakers are there themselves; they're fantastic and know just about everything there is to know about wine. Nonetheless, Navarro has been using sustainable practices since before it was cool to do so, and the wines are truly some of the best in a valley rife with competition. *SB*

Elke Vineyards

12351 Hwy 128, Boonville
225.7220
www.elkevineyards.com
Sat by appointment

Here's a real flip-flop: the Elkes of Elke Vineyards are the farmers, not the winemakers. Every Elke has dirt under his or her nails from growing organic grapes and apples, and guest winemakers come to do the showy part that most Napa and Sonoma families are gaga over. This is not to say the Elkes don't know a good wine! It's just that it is refreshing that at least one family is more into the grunt work than the glitz. I have to say I am with them there—nothing is better than watching something you've planted flourish and become fruitful. The Blue Diamond pinot noir is unstoppable! *SB*

Frey Vineyards

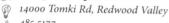

14000 Tomki Rd, Redwood Valley
485.5177
www.freywine.com
Daily 10a–5p

The wineries in Mendocino County are more tuned in to sustainability than elsewhere in the country, but Frey Vineyards was the very first to go organic, eliminating pesticides from its vines and sulfites from its vintages. When I grew up learning watercolor washes at a Waldorf school, I never dreamed I'd be drinking a bottle of wine with an anthroposophical painting on it. The certified biodynamic wines are all swathed in golden yellow pictures like the ones I grew up with. Sip the purplish syrah or the estate cabernet sauvignon with lingering cherry flavors and you'll want more of these special wines in your future. The composts and stews prepared for Frey's soil are enriched by diverse ecology and a carefully cared-for ecosystem at the winery. *SB*

Nelson Family Vineyards

550 Nelson Ranch Rd, Ukiah
462.3755
www.nelsonfamilyvineyards.com
Daily 10a–5p

I'll be honest, other than my adoration for dry rosé, dry gewürztraminer, and a select few extra-grassy sauvignon blancs, I am no white wine lover. But there have been more than a couple of instances on my Mendocino travels when my previous tastes have been challenged, and I have changed my mind. Nelson Family Vineyard's 2007 pinot grigio has got me doing flips for a varietal I was never gaga about—this crisp and lively white is the sexiest wine ever, and it is just $16 a bottle. I challenge you to find a better white for the price in this part of the country. Come in and meet the winemakers or the president, all Nelsons, and taste their complete range of small-production varieties. After all, wine tastes are different for each person, so as LeVar Burton says, "You don't have to take my word for it." *SB*

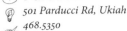 Parducci

501 Parducci Rd, Ukiah
468.5350
www.mendocinowinecompany.com/Parducci.html
Daily 10a–5p

The Mendocino Wine Company, the parent company of Parducci and its flirty chardonnays, is carbon neutral. Not only does the company use solar power and strict organic farming methods, but also its business structure maintains the local economy and takes care of employees in a way few other wineries do. All the grapes that go into Parducci bottles are from family-owned and -operated wineries, as the Wine Company owners are trying to reverse the statistics of shrinking family farms in the United States—at least within a 12-mile radius of the winery. You'll find Parducci wines at MacCallum House Inn & Restaurant, where I first enjoyed it, and at select restaurants, but a tasting here will get you started on the path to finding more sustainability in your wines and in your life. *SB*

Greenwood Ridge Vineyards

5501 Hwy 128, Philo
895.2002
http://greenwoodridge.com
Daily 10a–5p

What do baseball, sunshine, Frank Lloyd Wright, and great pinot noir have in common? You guessed it, Greenwood Ridge Vineyards! Just as the redwoods part and the rolling hills of Philo open up, you'll find the welcoming driveway of Greenwood Ridge, flanked by solar panels and corduroy vineyards. The octagonal tasting room is protected by the winery's mascot, a fire-breathing-dragon sculpture given to the Frank Lloyd Wright Foundation by the forefathers of Greenwood Ridge. The family has been a major part of local baseball legend, leading their division in the 50+ league—there's evidence in the hallway to the right of the tasting room, so get caught up in the story while you sip and swill. Full flight tastings include everything from an earthy pinot gris, to a crisp and sweet white Riesling, to the winery's famous pinot noir, winner of many accolades. The bottles are simply gorgeous, with their golden dragons wrapping the sides—a preview of the family-farmed flavors inside. *SB*

Handley Cellars

3151 Hwy 128, Philo
895.3876

www.handleycellars.com
Daily 10a–5p

The locals all stock Handley wines in their cellars, whether they have a treasure trove of hundreds of the sought-after bottles or just a few for when guests come through town. Handley Cellars practices sustainable farming, but more than that, the wines have an air of sophistication and elegance that sets them apart on the Highway 128 wine trail. Estate chardonnay and Anderson Valley sauvignon blanc are two whites that wow me, the cynical white wine drinker. This area of California is known for the subtle elegance of pinot noir, and Handley's is a fine example. There was even a bubbly rosé, something I'd love to see more of in this country, which quickly sold out, but I am sure tasters that give pressure to the family will eventually get them to re-create the magic of this pink and blissful celebratory drink. Cheers! *SB*

Pamper

Shelters from the hustle and bustle, simple enjoyments, and all things feel-good

Orr Hot Springs

13201 Orr Springs Rd, Ukiah

462.6277

If you've got time for a long, winding drive, be sure not to miss an appointment (everything must be scheduled ahead of time) at Orr Hot Springs. The series of natural hot baths here will make you feel as if all the area's original native peoples bestowed their healing powers on you, if you use your imagination and gaze up at the towering redwoods long enough. The first white settlers were astonished at the healing powers of these springs, and you will be, too, once you get there. I recommend staying at nearby Shambhala Ranch (see page 242) after a soak. *SB*

Roots Herbal Apothecary

250 Main St, Point Arena

882.2699

Mon–Sat 11a–4:30p

Looking for some ginger to chew on to prevent car sickness? Some valerian for a longer night's rest? All your natural health needs can be relieved at Roots Herbal Apothecary, which is located along Point Arena's short Main Street. Don't be afraid to ask questions—the staff will direct you to several solutions to aid with your traveling ailment. Everything here is either wild crafted or organic. *SB*

Bamboo Garden Spa

301 N Main St, Fort Bragg

962.0781

www.bamboogardenspa.com

For a relaxing couples massage, few spots top the skillful hands at Bamboo Garden Spa, a business owned by a couple who understand how dual pampering can benefit a relationship from the inside out. They've even started a school, Bamboo Garden School of Massage, that offers anatomy classes and various forms of massage. Their belief is that different massage styles complement each other, as opposed to the my-way-or-the-highway approach many masseuses employ once they have been trained in a certain technique. *SB*

The Inn at Schoolhouse Creek

7051 N Hwy 1, Little River

800.731.5525

www.schoolhousecreek.com

Story time! I love the writing of Pico Iyer. And I loved it even more when I heard about his idea to look at each individual when he's traveling as though he or she could be a prince or princess. As he explains, a princess of Thailand, who grew up in the palace with the whole nine yards, chose a different path than her predecessors and married a Danish gentleman. She is now roaming the streets of Los Angeles, keeping a low profile, and we could meet her and mistake her for less than a princess.

I forgot this concept today, after a morning of Highway 1 clamor. I had a lot to accomplish in this seemingly small place, which gets bigger and bigger for me when I look around each corner. I was on the move, and no delay could stop me on my mission to discover.

The Inn at Schoolhouse Creek was one of my appointments. I relaxed in the yurt massage room (complete with a composting toilet around the corner) with Gabi, who kneaded out my kinks from the previous day of winding driving. I left in a hurry, forgetting my swimsuit from my premassage dip in the ocean-view hot tub.

Later that evening, at a table laden with organic fruit kabobs and saffron risotto at the Brewery Gulch Inn (see page 245), in walks the woman whom I mistook for being "ordinary" in my rush for the door at Schoolhouse Creek, with my traveling swimsuit. I forgot, momentarily, Pico's sentiment about special people being everywhere. I wasn't even staying at the quaint blue cottages this kind woman oversees, and she went out of her way to get my swimsuit back to me.

Now I realize the real draw of Mendocino, besides the luscious organic wines, is more than the awe-inspiring views and the historic façades punctuated by weathered evergreens. It is the small-town mentality, the connected community that aims both to serve its visitors and to relate with each other on common ground, no opinions barred. Oh, and the massage wasn't bad either! *SB*

Sweetwater Spa and Inn

44840 Main St, Mendocino
800.300.4140
www.mendocinoinn.com
By appointment only

For a few bucks you can enter the baths of Sweetwater Spa and find yourself carried away to another place—a warm, cozy, wet place. Get steamed up any time of day for a reasonable price. Private wooden hot tubs with saunas are available for a few more bucks (they're free if you are getting a massage), or you can opt for the group tubs—there is no time limit on those, and you are bound to meet some interesting people. Sweetwater is my secret weapon for fully enjoying the coastal weather of this historic town: when the fog chills me, I hide away in these tubs and regain my love for the ocean air. *SB*

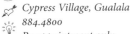

Healing Arts & Massage Center

Cypress Village, Gualala
884.4800
By appointment only

Not every massage is a good massage. But at Healing Arts & Massage Center in this blink-and-you've-missed-it town, the intensive training programs each of the therapists goes through ensure a quality healing experience every time. Whether you are looking for traditional deep-tissue massage or new-age somatic movement therapy, this nurturing spot is the kind of place where you can relax completely. Sit above Anchor Bay as your body undergoes a noticeable transformation. *SB*

Bookish
Reading retreats in every flavor

The Bookstore

223 E Redwood Ave, Fort Bragg
964.6559
Mon–Fri 10a–5p, Sat 10a–4p

You might speculate from the name that the proprietors of this business weren't really trying. And then you see the inside of the store, and the evidence that they were trying is literally stacked from floor to ceiling. The Bookstore is just that simple a concept: a store of books. This is my kind of no-nonsense store. The satisfaction is all in the search, and the most bookish of folk will surely share my love for the Bookstore. *DL*

Coast Community Branch Library

225 Main St, Point Arena
882.3114
www.co.mendocino.ca.us/library/coast.htm
Mon–Sat, hours vary

Don't overlook libraries, even in tiny coastal towns. In fact, this library outdoes itself on a regular basis with the traveling library branch, a big shiny bus full of books that makes the rounds up and down the coast. When Point Arena raised the funds to renovate the historic building, the ceremony included locals handing books in an assembly line across town and landing them on the new and improved shelves. Taking in the atmosphere of this cute town has to include a trip to the Coast Community Library—it is a community pillar to be sure. *SB*

Gallery Bookshop
Main and Kasten sts, Mendocino
937.2665
www.gallerybooks.com
Sun–Thurs 9:30a–6p, Fri–Sat 9:30a–9p

When did I first flip through the pages of a book from the Gallery Bookshop? OK, I admit, I was 3 years old. And I wasn't reading, I was listening. My uncle Chan, who was visiting us over on the other coast, gathered up a few gifts from my aunt, whose hubby opened the Gallery Bookshop after deciding that there was no other way to serve his penchant for all things literary. I was lucky to grow up in a family of bookish folk, but I also had my needs met in the area of flowery journals, amazing stickers, and picture books galore. Now as a Mendocino traveler, I am still awed by the collection here—from Thomas Friedman tomes to the latest from my Aunt Jolly's book club (most recently *Dewey: The Small-Town Library Cat Who Touched the World*). And the community ethic is contagious. On my most recent trip up north I overheard an author describing Vivaldi's celibate violinists, and the night after, a group of fourth graders were covering the store floor making foam swords, drinking fruity magic potion, and settling in for a midnight movie. I may be totally biased, but I bet you'll agree, this is one local bookshop you just can't pass over if you want an authentic look at Mendocino. *SB*

Imbibe
Where to sip and swill with a local feel

North Coast Brewing Company
455 N Main St, Fort Bragg
964.2739
www.northcoastbrewing.com
Free tours Wed–Sun 2–9:30p (Sat 12p)

North Coast Brewing Company, home of Red Seal Ale and the lighthearted Scrimshaw Pilsner, is the big small brewery in California. You can eat at one of two restaurants owned by the brewery or take home a six-pack for everyone to enjoy. I usually skip over the favorites listed and opt for the delicious California-style stout or the wheat beer called Blue Star. When I want just a tad of suds I mix Blue Star with Looza pear nectar, half and half, which is a take on my staple bar buy when I lived in Germany. *SB*

Patterson's Pub

 10485 Lansing St, Mendocino
937.4782
www.pattersonspub.com
Daily 5–11p

Boasting the best-stocked bar north of the Golden Gate, Patterson's Pub was conceived on a trip to Ireland and has since become a staple of the community. In fact, it has been said that without Patterson's, some Mendocino locals would die of food and drink deprivation. This is the perfect place to strike up a conversation or just sing a tune and be merry with your fellow man. *DL*

Anderson Valley Brewing Company

  17700 Hwy 253 (right off 128), Boonville
895.2337
www.avbc.com
Thurs–Mon tours 11:30a and 3p

Let's face it, there are lots of good beers in the world, and most serious suds enthusiasts reach for those not brewed on American soil. In my opinion, the beers from Anderson Valley Brewing Company can compete with the best of the world's beer, having tried suds in Belgium, Germany, France, England, and Japan (although I must say I'm not a fan of most lighter-style Japanese brews). I park, waltz around the brewery grounds waving hello to the horses and billy goats munching on grass, gaze up at the hops growing by the circular tubs of beer, and take a snapshot of the wall of kegs getting ready to be delivered across the country for all to enjoy. Inside the bartender explains disc golf rules before pouring me a tasting tray of 10 small servings of the brewery's best beers. I'm huge on the Barney Flats Oatmeal Stout and the famous Boont Amber Ale. This is a great place to meet friendly folks and talk beer, and then taste some that uproot jokes like "What do American beer and having sex in a canoe have in common?" "They're both f—ing close to water!" Not so here! *SB*

The Old Western Saloon

11201 Hwy 1, Point Reyes Station
415.663.1661
www.myspace.com/oldwesternsaloon
Mon–Sat 4p–close

It was still light outside when Angie and I peered into the darkness of the Old Western Saloon. The corner double-doors were wide open, but we could only vaguely make out figures sitting on barstools. Sounds of a tennis game blared on the bar TV. Angie motioned me to go in first. What a wimp.

Although no strangers to an after-dinner cocktail, nor to dive bars, we knew that upon entering this bar we'd be entering their world—the world of the locals. And sure enough, we were the only locals there. Of course, some tourist couples wandered in for one uncomfortable drink and split, but we really stayed, firmly planting ourselves on barstools, chatting with the regulars, and finding out who's going out with who, who drinks what, and most important for two young women, whom not to talk to.

This 1890s saloon is the only watering hole in Point Reyes Station, and if it weren't for the Budweiser racing flags or the Clash's "London Calling" on the jukebox, I would succumb to its ghost-town quality: an ornate wooden bar with a center mirror sporting roses and a pistol wrapped in a garter, the original cash register, a black turn-of-the-century stove, and figurines of cowboys and wagons lining the top of the bar, shrouded in cobwebs. Also above the bar, however, in pristine condition were large photographs taken a couple of years ago of Prince Charles and Camilla Parker Bowles sharing a pint with the bar's owner during their visit.

After my third generously poured vodka tonic, I had my chin in my hand as I watched a fly flit across the bar. A teacup Chihuahua ran up and took a sniff of my face before scampering back to his owner. An employee with frizzy, faded pink-and-green dyed hair was painting a pot plant in the cornstalk window mural. A sign on the bar said "Hangovers: Installed and Serviced." I should have seen it as a warning sign. *JD*

 Grey Whale Bar

45020 Albion St, Mendocino
937.0289
Daily 5p–close

Cocktails just don't receive the same attention as wines in these Northern California counties, except at the Grey Whale Bar, which was named for the whales that were found migrating the Mendo coast year after year. Follow along the path shadowed by the gray whale sculpture, and then take a seat in the glass-enclosed cafe or at the bar, both housed in the MacCallum House Inn & Restaurant. House-made bitters are a perfect celebratory toast mixed with local Roederer Estate Brut in the MacCallum signature cocktail. A Mata Hari, made with chai-infused vermouth and brandy, is a sultry combo with a late-night sweet treat; the dessert menu is served on request at the bar. Get exotic with an Absinthe Riddle with limoncello, possibly my favorite Italian import. The distinct flavors of the cocktails bring out the essence of each quality ingredient. *SB*

Stay In

The best take-out and take-home activities in town

 Piaci Pub & Pizzeria

120 W Redwood Rd, Fort Bragg
961.1133
www.piacipizza.com
Daily 2–10p

Fancy-pants pizza isn't isolated to the big cities of the golden state—you can find sautéed squid and fresh arugula leaves on a slice in Fort Bragg, too. Choose one of the many beers on tap and get serious about pizza here. When I am super-hungry I order focaccia slathered with Gorgonzola and pine nuts—yummy! *SB*

Upper Crust Pizza

39331 S Hwy 1, Gualala
884.1324
Daily 11a–close

Gualala's tiny pizza shop has always had significance to me, as it was the setting for a sort of last hurrah before parting with my cousins after a vacation at our grandparents' cabin in Anchor Bay. Although it has been over a decade since our last trip there all together, Upper Crust Pizza is still right across the street from the picturesque Pacific Coast and still serving up some delicious pizzas. *DL*

Tote Fete

10450 Lansing St, Mendocino
937.3383
Daily 10a–4p
$

Want a quick picnic? Grab salads and sandwiches, ready for you to take away, from Tote Fete. Everything is handmade in the tiny kitchen in back, and the chicken salad rivals my favorite big-city versions. Many ingredients come from the local farmers market, which takes place every Friday morning just steps away from this cute little sammie counter. *SB*

Pizzas & Cream

790 Port Rd, Point Arena
882.1900
http://pizzasandcream.com
Mon–Fri 4–9p, Sat–Sun 12–9p

The newcomer to the coastal pizza scene is making major headway with locals and travelers alike. Personally, I think it is because of Pizzas & Cream's Smoky Eggplant slices and handmade ice cream for dessert. If you aren't in a nightshade mood, opt for the Classic Cal with chèvre and sun-dried tomatoes, or the Goddess, which is covered with kalamata olives. *SB*

Casual Night Out

Dining and delighting in a relaxed atmosphere

Mendo Bistro

301 N Main St, Fort Bragg (upstairs inside the Company Store)
964.4974
http://mendobistro.com
Daily 5–9p

Owners Jaime and Nick are the ideal couple to meet on a trip to Mendocino's coast. Full of zing and familiarity, their food echoes their love of the place where they live and their desire to express their own jovial nature.

Homemade pappardelle, bucatini, and linguine are served in classically enticing sauces, all made from organic ingredients. Chickpea cake and catfish are two of the tastiest entrées and are also 100 percent sustainable. Heed the direction on the menu to save room for dessert—the chocolate and berry creations will make you wish you had two stomachs. *SB*

Coast Cinemas

167 S Franklin St, Fort Bragg
964.2019
www.thecoastcinemas.com

This is the movie theater—the *only* movie theater—in town. So if you aren't up for a video in your room or a DVD in your tent via solar-powered battery charger, head here with everyone else in Mendocino and Fort Bragg. If you've been in town more than a few days, you can count on seeing the lady behind the bakery counter, your server at Mendo Bistro (see page 231), or some other friendly face you've met once before. I chat with my aunt and uncle while we wait in the ticket line (get there early for popular flicks—as previously stated, this is *the* movie theater). *SB*

Rosie's Cowboy Cookhouse

11285 Hwy 1, Point Reyes Station
415.663.8868
Mon–Sat 10a–6p

When I heard the name Rosie's Cowboy Cookhouse, I was expecting to be greeted by a Black Angus–esque steakhouse and served baked beans in a bucket. To my great surprise, I found that Rosie's is a Mexican restaurant with burritos, enchiladas, and chiles rellenos on the menu. You can also get a cow burger with organic ice cream for dessert, if south of the border isn't your thing.

After we sat down, a colorful tostada salad decorated with sour cream and guacamole went by and landed at the table next to us. The lady who received it actually let out an audible "Woo!" in delight upon its arrival, so either she was really hungry or the food was that good. I confirmed it was the latter—total burrito bliss. But if you want tortilla chips and salsa, they're an extra $1.49. *JD*

Pangaea

39165 S Hwy 1, Gualala
884.9669

www.pangaeacafe.com

Tues–Sat 11a–4p and 6–9p

Everyone's favorite dinner out in the Gualala region is Pangaea. At least it is for everyone I've talked to, and I have a penchant for talking to strangers. Pangaea is a fresh spot for a cozy and possibly romantic dinner, if you want to spin it that way. Food comes from the owners' memories of their worldly travels, so the eclectic menu offers diners their own trip to foreign lands without leaving the smug coast of Cali. Take a date here and it'll have to go well. Take your parents and they'll be equally as impressed—it is the kind of place people will thank you for turning them on to. I order salmon, a rarity for me, but this stuff comes from Point Arena, so it's line caught a few miles away. Plus, this salmon is delicate and never overcooked, and it comes with fava beans and truffled golden beets in tow. For dessert I conquer the bittersweet chocolate cake and urge my honey to order a second dessert so we can share two different flavors. His strawberry tart is from heaven above. Everything at Pangaea is organic, most ingredients come from a few miles away, and if you still can't find a reason to order a meal here, tell yourself you want to discover the true meaning of the Yiddish word *zaftig*—that is, if your bubbula hasn't already taught you. *SB*

The Tides Wharf

800 Coast Hwy 1, Bodega Bay
875.2751
www.innatthetides.com/tides_wharf.asp
Mon–Fri 7:30a–9p, Sat–Sun 7a–9:30p

Casual grace with a view is what the Tides Wharf restaurant offers our group of mixed ages and lifestyles. Here is a place where we can all find something that we like in a setting that is both beautiful and historical. Every seat has a view of the Pacific. This is also the setting for the Hitchcock thriller *The Birds*. *IB*

Dress Up

Don your shiny shoes and head out to one of these fancy places

Terrapin Creek Restaurant

1580 Eastshore Rd, Bodega Bay

875.2700

www.terrapincreekcafe.com

$$ *Thurs–Sun 11a–2:30p, 4:30–9p*

Slow food can be fancy! The 30 miles around Bodega Bay are rich in yummy veggies and sustainable dairy, meat, and fish, so that is what makes it on the menu. Celery root flan, smoked trout rillette, local oysters, and burdock with sashimi are on the appetizer menu only for the lush fall season. Save room for an entrée of duck breast or organic chicken potpie, and then indulge in a showstopping finish of fig galette or chocolate tart. The restaurant focuses on regional foods, so it isn't extensive, but it's all done well. The kitchen's international influences find their way onto the seasonal menus regularly. This is my top choice for eating anywhere near Bodega. *SB*

MacCallum House Inn & Restaurant

45020 Albion St, Mendocino

937.0289

www.maccallumhouse.com

$$$ *Daily, hours vary*

Few things can prepare you for a meal like the one you'll have at the Mac-Callum House Inn & Restaurant. It is the most serious kitchen in the town of Mendocino, and in my opinion it rivals the fancy-schmancy dining in the other, more foodie-centric wine counties nearby. If you are going to opt for a tasting menu, this is the place to do it—that is, if you've reserved enough space in your stomach. Every day the menu changes based on what is freshest and tastiest in the mind of the chef, who has an obsession with duck (I recommend any way he prepares it). Pair little gem lettuce wraps with the seared fish of the day and toasted nuts with a Roederer Estate bubbly to toast by the firelight in the main dining room or by the window overlooking the MacCallum House gardens and croquet greens. Crab bisque is sinful, simply sinful, but it's the ideal way to indulge when you are elevated by the superior service and sultry atmosphere of this special-occasion restaurant. As I savored the duck breast seared in cider gastrique with endive and apple salad, I overheard the couple next to me toasting their 25th wedding anniversary, while on my other side a blonde woman extolled her own congratulations for having purchased a chunk of the Berlin Wall from Neiman Marcus.

The meat and fish preparations are supernal, although the sauces are well salted. If you love steak, don't miss the filet mignon here, which is dolloped with porcini butter and bourbon-glazed shallots. To end the meal on a fun-loving note, rather than a sophisticated tart, I recommend the ice cream from this kitchen—it is sensational, especially the rocky road rendition. If you aren't a local couple renewing your vows or celebrating a birthday, then I suggest getting a room here, which is equally as lavish and comfortable as the fine food, so you can saunter off to your room without a care in the world. *SB*

Mendocino Hotel Restaurant

45080 Main St, Mendocino
937.0511
www.mendocinohotel.com
$$$

Drew, the tattooed chef at the Mendocino Hotel restaurant, is extraordinary. When I entered the historic dining room the last thing I considered was that I would be served divine white gazpacho with grilled scallops and pesto-crusted salmon with truffle oil by someone with ornate tattooed sleeves and a penchant for body piercing. You'll have to set aside all your preconceived notions upon entering this romantic setting, known to some as the set of the Daryl Hannah B-movie *Shark Swarm*, and just get on the ride, so to speak.

Pastas are made fresh every day, and the soups made from scratch are outstanding, especially the house specialty, mushroom soup, and the aforementioned white gazpacho, which is buttery and cooling, made from deseeded cucumbers. Main courses are infused with the tenets of the slow food movement—the chef and hotel proprietor even check the boats they get their crab from to make sure none is harvested too small when still fertile, and only males are caught so that the local population can be maintained. Beef is raised humanely at nearby Star Ranch and is treated like royalty with herbed rissole potatoes plated with crisp filo pork belly and browned garlic escarole. Each wine course was another ovation in tastefulness, and biodynamic and organic wines are scattered across the rich vino menu.

Mendocino Hotel was one of the first places to chic-ify the olallieberry, a mystifying local berry that shines in a sweet pastry cobbler with house-made vanilla ice cream. And don't forget a glass of Mendocino port to further elongate the night—Meyers Family zinfandel port is a pleasant way to feel more a part of the time when this hotel was first up and running. Funny how a drink has a way of transcending centuries. *SB*

Stevenswood Spa Resort Restaurant

8211 N Hwy 1, Littleriver

800.421.2810

Daily 4:30p–close

$$$

Reviewed by many fine diners and reported as one classy place to dine, the restaurant of the fancy Stevenswood Spa Resort continues the resort's mantra of pleasure. Elegance is the bottom line, and each dainty plating of the chef's weekly tasting menus inside the redwood dining room reflects this ethic. Make sure to savor a local wine with your meal and plan to eat for a while—two hours is the average mealtime at this special-occasion restaurant. You may find, as I did, the cheese course was Ritz cracker–and–goat cheese ice cream. *SB*

Lodge

Great places to rest your noggin

Nick's Cove

23240 Hwy 1, Marshall

415.663.1033

www.nickscove.com

Staying at this cozy cove, just north of Point Reyes Station, is a slow way to vacation—slow in a good way. I like waking up early, before anyone else, and tiptoeing out on the lone dock to watch the birds flutter in the dawn light. Accommodations are comfortable, and most rooms have views of the water and plush white down comforters that are perfect to cuddle under. The fish restaurant sources most of its ingredients locally, though you'll want to avoid some pitfalls like big-fin fish and shrimp, which come from disappearing mangrove forests in Ecuador. Renting a waterfront or water-view cottage for an indoor paradise and then tromping over to the restaurant for barbecued local oysters is all I want from a stay in Marshall, and it is what I get at Nick's Cove. *SB*

Stevenswood Resort & Spa

8211 N Hwy 1, Littleriver
800.421.2810
www.stevenswood.com

This luxe lodge is like a piece of the big city in the middle of the redwoods. Service and style accommodate the pickiest of travelers, although I felt a little out of place even in my hand-me-down Versace blouse and Miss Maude shoes that I brought with me for the occasion. Things felt a little superficial, but I appreciated the attention to detail, the plethora of comfortable amenities, and the quiet of the retreatlike setting. *SB*

Stanford Inn by the Sea

44850 Comptche Ukiah Rd (at the corner of Hwy 1), Mendocino
937.5615
www.stanfordinn.com

The ridge of red rooms facing the sea is much more than meets the eye. This pioneering inn is a place where sustainability is a way of life. Whether you are chilling by the fire in the book-filled lobby, eating at Raven's Restaurant (see page 195), sleeping in, dipping in the pool, or perusing the grounds, each of these spaces has been touched by the gift of conscientiousness. There are flowers from the garden, forward-thinking books, and all-natural cleaning agents used in the lobby. The restaurant has the tastiest vegan and vegetarian dishes in town, most of which are made from ingredients grown on the property. The rooms are furnished with organic cotton towels and sheets, the pool is tucked away in a greenhouse that preserves heat and is treated with saline rather than the chemical alternatives, and the grounds are planted with either edible or native plants grown organically and sprouted from the inn's own nursery. All of this is hard to beat in a world where shiny and loud are often the best ways to get people's attention. The comfort of the inn and the relaxed atmosphere are genuinely Mendocino—a stay at Stanford Inn by the Sea is an authentic way to spend time in this coastal community. *SB*

Inn at the Tides

800 Hwy 1, Bodega Bay
800.541.7788
www.innatthetides.com

Providing easy comfort from a host of rooms with coastal views, Inn at the Tides is a casual place to overnight in Bodega Bay. It offers spacious accommodations that are upscale in a beachside setting with no extra charge for the fog horn! A complimentary breakfast at the Wharf is included. You can have something called the Tragger massage or a traditional acupressure, then it's off to the sauna and heated pool. What a great place for a wine-tasting trip. Find this treasure on the right side of the road after the 76 gas station. For family trips and surfing vacations with a touch of luxury, this inn does the trick. *SB*

Bodega Bay Inn

1588 Eastshore Rd, Bodega Bay
875.3388
www.bodegabayinn.com

Bodega Bay is more than a movie set—it has a small-town feel and folksy history just waiting to be soaked up by the onslaught of visitors that come here since Hitchcock made it famous. This inn has a quiet garden, and the small, local feel pervades. The large Dune Grass room is just over $200 a night during high season, but if you are willing to cross the hall to use the bathroom, you can stay in the Music room, complete with a piano, for just $69! This is probably the best deal in Bodega Bay. *SB*

Mar Vista Cottages at Anchor Bay

35101 S Hwy 1, Gualala
884.3522
www.marvistamendocino.com

My shoulders are starting to get sore from driving the twists and turns of Mendocino's coastal Highway 1. I've passed breathtaking views, salty beaches, stunning cliffs, tractors, windswept cypress trees, and today, a collection of paving trucks gurgling black asphalt for a new patch of smooth road. I've now wound my way down from Point Arena to an even smaller town: Gualala. At Mar Vista Cottages at Anchor Bay, with renovated Shaker-style cottages set back from the road, I feel a sense of relief. I have dirt under my nails, not from heavy garden work, but from picking the radishes and patty pan squash, arugula and wax beans, krim tomatoes and herbs, corn and purple peppers that will make up my dinner.

The cottage is private and comfortable, and of all the many spots at which I have laid my head along the coast, I have to say that this is my favorite. There is no infringement, no attitude, no clutter—just cozy, clean comfort. Then I find there is a soaking tub. As I soak, watching the white water crashing on Gualala's steep precipices to a soundtrack of barking sea lions, I flip the pages of my book until the sun sets behind the manzanita branches. Then I head to my cabin to make a feast of my harvests from Mar Vista's gracious u-pick garden. Sautéeing onion chives and the purple bell pepper with a little olive oil (since meeting Charles Crohare of the Olivina Ranch in Livermore, I never travel without it) releases the flavors and makes for a great soup base. I add corn and sauté for another few minutes. Broccolini and wax beans go in. Stir. Simmer. Baby kale and stemmed arugula in. Wilt. I feel more alive already, with the help of the peaceful tub and the garden beds at my beck and call.

My Mendocino travels have been vastly different from those in the other Wine Country counties. I'm fed mostly vegetables, and I'm talked to with more integrity and intelligence. I am more than a journalist—I am a person, too, and everyone here wants to appeal to my human sensibilities.

Supper tonight was one of my favorite types of travel souvenirs: the nonmaterial kind, the ideological kind. *SB*

The Weller House Inn

524 Stewart St, Fort Bragg
964.4415
www.wellerhouse.com

Reliving the logging days of yore is easy from this quiet street on coastal Fort Bragg. The beautiful Weller home is a great vantage point from which to see the shades of history of the surrounding area, from the original Western settlers, to the midcentury logging boom, to the hokey community that now flourishes. Walk to breakfast places, bars, and bookstores—Fort Bragg is just steps away and has much less of a hoity-toity atmosphere than the town of Mendocino, which is always cluttered with tourists of the well-dressed, shopping-bag-in-hand type. I love the romance of this working town, the friendly neighbors who know each other's names, and the restaurants and pubs. Headlands Coffeehouse (see page 199) is just steps away and has live music every single day of the year. The rooms at the Weller House Inn alone are worth a trip, not to mention the Sunday brunch, which requires a post-dining nap in my opinion! *SB*

Manchester Beach KOA

44300 Kinney Ln, Manchester
882.2375
www.manchesterbeachkoa.com
Besides being one of the most highly rated camping resorts in the KOA system, Manchester Beach is a prime location to spot the seasonal migration of gray whales. It also happens to be the home of a famous driftwood beach, and I feel compelled to visit the campground just to find some interesting specimens. *DL*

Coast Guard House Historic Inn

695 Arena Cove, Point Arena
882.2442
www.coastguardhouse.com
Want to make believe? Then stay at the Coast Guard House Historic Inn and pretend you are a sea rescuer of old, who listened for the call to duty for ships in need of help. There's no such call to action here any longer, just private cottages right on the bluffs or whirlpools overlooking the azure sea. History buffs will delight in the rich stories to come from this old Cape Cod–style house, and vacation bums like me who want to turn off their brains for at least a night will enjoy the plush bedding and mesmerizing views. *SB*

Bodega Bay Lodge & Spa

103 Coast Hwy 1, Bodega Bay
875.3525
www.bodegabaylodge.com
Nestled on a hillside just a stone's throw away from the undulating currents of the Pacific Coast, Bodega Bay Lodge & Spa can accommodate just about any kind of retreat, whether it be family, business, or romantic. Panoramic ocean views abound, from the private balconies to the multiple conference facilities. The on-site Duck Club Restaurant offers award-winning seasonal menus highlighting fresh local seafood and ingredients. *DL*

Blanchard House

8141 Coast Highway 1, Little River
937.1627
www.blanchardhouse.com

With a single guestroom, Blanchard House caters to the experience of a romantic and peaceful home away from home. The private entrance and balcony give it an extra air of seclusion, and a homemade breakfast made from ingredients found at the Mendocino Farmers Market is brought right to your door. Transformed from a wild landscape, the garden at the Blanchard House has taken a number of shapes over the years, and the many native varieties of rhododendron and flowering perennials make it worth seeing more than once as the palette of colors changes. All the more reason to return to this romantic getaway. DL

Lighthouse Inn at Point Cabrillo

45300 Lighthouse Rd, Mendocino
937.6124
www.mendocinolighthouse.pointcabrillo.org

Painted in turquoise, lima bean, and antique white, the official colors of Coast Guard housing, according to the educational plaques around the group of historic buildings, this is one special place to stay. Sit in the sunroom overlooking the lighthouse and cliffs beyond and listen to the ocean crashing in. If you are a guest you can drive the single-lane road out to the lighthouse, which day visitors must walk, and you can stay in the high style of decades gone by with a friendly staff and loads of rocking chairs ready for a quiet sit or a bookish adventure in the most picturesque bed-and-breakfast in Mendocino. SB

Mendocino Hotel & Garden Suites

45080 Main St, Mendocino
937.0513

A place as old as this should have gone through many incarnations (and behind the scenes, it has), but the look and feel of the late-1800s inn and saloon is as intact as an old Western film. I stepped under the yellow clapboard façade and entered like I myself was a logger of old, searching in the dim lights and musty aroma for a bottle of whiskey. Instead, I found cheery Deena behind the beveled-glass reception desk and a blush-colored canopy bed in my room facing the ocean. The wallpaper, light fixtures, bathtub, and armoire all echo days gone by, the very days that have gone by in this seaside village. But that is a good thing when it comes to sustainability—the furnishings are lovingly maintained so that their antique beauty lives on, and the wallpaper is hand-screened, not made with corrosive vinyl.

It is lovely to experience not only a far-off place, but also times gone by. Walking to shops and restaurants is a breeze since "the hotel," as it is called around town, is the central landmark. And it is where locals come to grub, too (see page 235). When I searched for Internet access in the woodsy-colored lobby I chanced upon several bubbly Mendo residents taking their supper in the window-side wingback chairs. Calling down to the desk for help with bathtub plugging and directions might require a few tries, but service is friendly. The proprietor has been doing green management, including switching out toilets in the early 1990s for low-flow ones, decreasing overall water use at the hotel by 80 percent. I recommend room 24, which is not a suite but is equipped with the best view I've yet seen in this town as well as a private footed bathtub. *SB*

Shambhala Ranch

21200 Orr Springs Rd, Ukiah
937.3341
www.shambhalaranch.com

As the saying goes, "It's not the destination but the journey that matters"; so too with Shambhala Ranch, named for the owners' dual vision of heaven on earth. Getting to this remote spot is a prerequisite for the abundance of peaceful, serene beauty that could only be had at such a distance from civilization. I rounded the bald, golden mounds of soil and sandstone, and the fringes of evergreens, passing Orr Hot Springs and several fluttering quail to find the carved wooden sign and the welcoming oak tree at Shambhala's entrance. Tara was in her garden as I pulled up, and before I could get my bearings I was eating tomatoes from her carefully pruned plants. Inside, an eclectic collection of masks from around the world and Tibetan thangkas hung from the redwood structure, made from wood felled on the land. We walked to the private beach and waterfall at Big River, ate apples and figs from her orchard, and found Jupiter and Cassiopeia even in the night light of the full moon.

Seventeen years ago Tara told her friends about her dream to open a retreat center, and they gave her the digits of a friend from whom they'd heard the same vision. A year and a half later Tara and Stuart were married and looking for land, and when they found this place they knew it was their Shambhala. Later, when they contracted an archaeological inspection, they found areas where native American rituals had taken place for 2,000 years. Apparently, they weren't the only ones who felt this place had a certain spiritual *je ne sais quoi*.

Here I dine with the person who cooked my food and the gardener who grew it. I gaze over a pond, hoping to see the otters play. It is a grand place for a total retreat, where 40 acres of preserved redwoods shelter the stumps from trees floated downstream for timber 100 years ago. And sleeping in a bed in a place with no electric current provides a deeper, gentler night's rest. The place is a living home, with ample space for many kinds of gatherings, from shrinelike outdoor sleeping quarters, to an indoor dance studio, to a sur-round-sound porch. There aren't many frills, and interaction with others stay-ing there is unavoidable, unless you are the only guest, which could be the case on a mid-week off-season night. Stay for at least three days, hike the property, bathe in the river, and get back in touch with nature and yourself. *SB*

The Old Schoolhouse Compound

Point Reyes Station
415.663.1166
www.oldpointreyesschoolhouse.com

My eyes hadn't even opened yet, but I knew it was morning by the sound of the silky rooster crowing. The window shades of the Barn Loft were illumi-nated with what was already powerful sunlight for 7am, and as I drew up each one I was happily struck by the warmth and delighted by the view of the sun slowly rising above the grassy hills in the east.

As my companion remained asleep in the loft bed—a small, single space with a sleeping bag and lantern that she quickly darted up the ladder to like a kid at camp calling the top bunk—I sat at the cozy bay window, sipping complimentary coffee, gazing upon the awakening countryside, and writing notes for this very review.

The Old Schoolhouse Compound has this amazing ability to create the outdoors, indoors: wreaths made of twigs, fresh farmers market wildflowers in every room, photographs and paintings (some done by the inn's owner, Karen Gray) adorning the neutral-colored walls, and VHS videos and exten-sive libraries to educate guests on everything wilderness, from bird-watching guides to videos on the mysterious creatures on the ocean floor.

Home of the town's old schoolhouse from 1879 (which is now the Grays' vacation home, also available for guests), the compound offers Jasmine's Cot-tage, a secluded getaway with a colorful garden and country charm; the Barn Loft, which is ideal for a romantic weekend for two; and Gray's Retreat, which can sleep six plus a baby (there's room for a crib) and has a great western patio for sipping wine at sunset. And if you rent Gray's Retreat, you can add the Sheep Wagon to your package. Parked next door, this authentic wagon (it sleeps three) has original 150-year-old running gear, a traditional shepherd's dining table, and, you guessed it, books on shepherding. *JD*

Brewery Gulch Inn

9401 N Hwy 1, Mendocino
937.4752
www.brewerygulchinn.com

Mendocino's Brewery Gulch Inn is the redwood oasis you dream of when you think of the California coast. The luxe accommodations are built of redwoods, but not the freshly chopped kind. These logs were the largest ones, some with 15-foot trunks, which had sunk when they were originally felled in the late 1800s. When these trunks were discovered at the Big River bottom, they were hauled to the surface once more, and instead of being shipped down to San Francisco to become a new pink lady, they stayed here to become one of the most sought-after hotels in the area.

Brewery Gulch has more tricks up its sleeve: recycled corkboard under the carpets help to dampen acoustics, organic cotton towels and bedding make the rooms pesticide-free, and chemical-free cleaning products and local produce in the kitchen are a few other measures the hotel has taken to tune in with the surrounding environment.

Between the epic gulch view from the cozy back porch and the wild turkey–dotted lawn out front, the place is lush with life. Brewery Gulch is best suited for couples or writers needing a respite from the busy world. Daily wine hours include a buffet of local seafood, fresh vegetables, and organic fruit, plus the winemakers themselves show up on summer Fridays to chat with visitors. Breakfast is just as luxurious: homemade hollandaise bennies and rich mango lassies share the menu with healthy fruit and granola and smoked salmon scrambles.

Use the place as a jumping-off point for winery excursions south on 128 or to explore the town of Mendocino, or just stay in, warm your toes by the fire, catch up on all those books you've been meaning to read, and take a plunge into the best video collection I've yet found at an American hotel. *SB*

Jenner Inn and Cottages

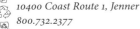

10400 Coast Route 1, Jenner
800.732.2377
www.jennerinn.com

Story time! Driving just miles north of the busy Bay is my new response to stress. Forget the worries, the urban wilderness, the traffic jams, and the rivers of people, and trade those memories for the Russian River and the quiet volcanic cliffs that look as though the Pacific Cookie Monster took a bite out of the land and left a few crumbs for the waves to wash over.

I've driven along the gentle, winding roads, just off Highway 101, by calm cows and glimmering sunlight trapped under the rolling ocean-chilled fog that dapples everything it touches. Once I got to the end of Valley Ford Road, I passed quickly through Bodega Bay, stopping only to feed a seagull the crusts of my sandwiches and watch the fishermen haul in their crab cages. I stopped above Arched Rock Beach to put my bare feet in the ice plants and snap a shot or two.

I found respite at Jenner Inn and Cottages—out of the way in the best possible sense. I was relieved of the city's hold on me, ready to tackle anything. It was a clear night and the stars were fully visible; below the deck some tiny chirps from nesting coots could be overheard.

The next day I followed the narrow band of land to Bodega Head, where I chanced upon two stags, munching away with their doe brides following close behind. The surf at the head was rough and powerful, but it didn't deter the multitude of birds and mammals that call this special place home. I tip-toed toward the edge of the sandy rocks to see the waves flushing through tide pools, waving a tangle of kelp to and fro as it drained back into the next wave.

Once back in Sonoma Beach State Park, I retraced my tracks along the row of beaches and coves—Schoolhouse Beach, Miwok Beach, Salmon Creek Beach, Portuguese Beach, the list continues . . . Shell Beach was brimming with vehicles, and I wanted to know what the buzz was, why this lot was full. Some trail signs denoted the break in the Kortum Trail, or Sonoma Coast Trail, which leads along the coastal bluffs from Wright's Beach up to Goat Rock, passing through Shell Beach at about the two-thirds point of its 13-mile stretch. I carefully descended the wooden-planked stairwell, passing boulders of greenish serpentine and clumps of sea grass on the way. At the black sand beach, I walked away from the crowds, in search of shells. After filling my pockets I took my turn tossing a starfish back into the ocean from its dry perch on a worn stone.

Back in my room I was happy to be greeted by a large Jacuzzi-style bathtub, and I watched the sunset from this warm and bubbly vantage point over the streaming Russian River. A playful seal popped its head up as if to say goodnight, and my coastal journey came to an end for the day. *SB*

MacCallum House Inn & Restaurant

45020 Albion St, Mendocino
937.0289
www.maccallumhouse.com

Next time my honey bear invites me to dinner and a movie over a long weekend I'm jetting up to Mendocino to show him my idea of a good time. I'm determined to take him to MacCallum House and its wine-savvy restaurant, which finally does justice to the many world-class wines produced in their home county. I've long been working on a hypothesis that the reason it has taken so long for California's viticultural greatness to be known all over the globe is because the all-too-often watered-down taste buds of chefs and eaters alike have underestimated the wines. Food hasn't been good enough to stand up to the wines, especially in rural areas, Mendocino included. But a slice of city elegance, foodie snootiness (if you'll allow me), and local charm is encapsulated in a MacCallum experience. (All the restaurant needs to do is donate its unforgivably thick wine glasses to a worthy cause.)

Staying and dining in unison is a must. The rooms—the Barn lodging's my favorite—include stone fireplaces with ready-made fires built with kindling and newspaper plus a few logs so all you have to do is light a match (even if your hubby is an Eagle Scout like mine). Plush beds and pumps of lemon-verbena paraben-free soaps and lotions are easy on the environment, and all of the cleaning products are tested thoroughly for eco-friendliness before being put into use. Jetted tubs make the garden-enclosed hot tub unnecessary.

In the restaurant, housed in the original MacCallum home, built circa 1886, the wine-tasting menu is a must. Executive chef Alan Kantor, himself a New York–trained culinary guru, likes local Liberty Farms duck more than anything and glazes and braises it to perfection. I can, and will, commit to a complete breakdown of his prowess, which fully lives up to the wines he pairs, like fine Titus zinfandel, among California's top incarnations of this easy-to-spoil American grape, or sultry chardonnay from the Santa Lucia highlands.

Whether you blindfold your honey and steal away to MacCallum, or you're here for just a typical vacation, there's no way a spot like this can come and go in your life story without a few punctuation marks—my guess is that they'll be exclamation points. *SB*

Camping the Coast

Sonoma Coast Camping

Call 565.2267 to reserve a spot at one of the following locations. None allows RVs.

Doran Park

201 Doran Beach Rd, Bodega Bay

This is Sonoma County's largest campsite, with 112 reservable spots and lots of showers and toilets.

Gualala Point

42401 Coast Hwy 1, 1 mile south of Gualala

This campground has 20 campsites and showers and toilets on-site.

Stillwater Cove

22455 Hwy 1, 15 miles north of Jenner

This campground has 17 campsites and showers and toilets on-site.

Westside Park

2400 Westshore Rd, Bodega Bay

This campground has 39 campsites (7 are open to people with no reservation) and showers and toilets on-site.

Mendocino Camping

Call 937.5804 to reserve a spot at one of the following locations:

Hendy Woods Campgrounds

Hwy 128, 8 miles northwest of Boonville, in Philo

This is my favorite inland campsite. It includes 100 acres of redwoods, and has cabins and tent sites.

MacKerricher Park Campground

Hwy 1, 3 miles north of Fort Bragg in Cleone

You'll find the best birding beach here and horseback riding, too. The campground includes two lakes and over 100 campsites.

Manchester State Park Campground

Hwy 1, north of Mendocino, just north of Russian Gulch

This campground has 750 acres of beach and dunes with two creeks.

Pomo RV and Campground

17999 Tregoning Ln, Fort Bragg
964.3373

This RV campground has all the necessary hookups and covers 17 acres.

Russian Gulch Campground

Hwy 1, look for state park signs just north of Mendocino

This is my favorite place to camp on the coast. It has creek-side tent sites and a group campsite for larger parties.

Union Landing State Beach

Hwy 1, Westport, follow signs to state beach

This campground has 46 campsites on 3 miles of coastline.

Van Damme Campground

Hwy 1, look for state park signs at the bend just south of Mendocino

Van Damme covers 1,800 acres, with more campsites than other Mendocino area campgrounds.

The Quiet Coast Calendar

January

Crab and Wine Days

Mid-January through first week in February
Mendocino Clinic, 822 Stewart Street, Fort Bragg, and other locations

February

Mendocino Film Festival Oscar Night

Third week in February, evening of the Academy Awards
St. Anthony's Hall, Mendocino

March

Mendocino and Fort Bragg Whale Festivals

First and third weekends in March
Various locations, Fort Bragg and Mendocino
www.mendowhale.com

April

Redwood Coast Whale and Jazz Festival

First two weeks in April
Point Arena Lighthouse and Gualala

May

Boonville Beer Festival

Second Saturday in May
Anderson Valley Brewing Company, Boonville
www.avbc.com/news/boonbeerfest.html

Mendocino Heritage Days

Second week in May
Various locations

Anderson Valley Pinot Noir Festival

Third weekend in May
Various locations

Mendocino Film Festival

Last weekend in May
Crown Hall, Mendocino
www.mendocinofilmfestival.com

Kate Wolf Music Festival

Three days in late May
www.katewolf.com/festival
Black Oak Ranch, Laytonville

June

A Taste of Redwood Valley

Father's Day weekend
Various locations
www.atasteofredwoodvalley.com

July

Willits Frontier Days
Fourth of July and closest weekend
Various locations
www.willitsfrontierdays.com

Woolgrower's Barbecue and Sheep Dog Trials
Third weekend in July
Mendocino Fairgrounds

Mendocino Music Festival
Throughout July
Various locations
www.mendocinomusic.com

August

SolFest
Second weekend in August
Solar Living Institute, Ukiah
www.solarliving.org

Yorkville Highlands Wine Festival
Mid-August
Various locations in the Yorkville appellation
www.yorkvillehighlands.org/festival

Point Arena Harbor and Seafood Festival
End of August
Point Arena main drag

Vibrant Living Expo
Third weekend in August
Living Light Center, Fort Bragg
www.rawfoodchef.com

September

Pure Mendocino
Labor Day weekend
Various locations
http://puremendocino.org

Studio Discovery Tour
First and second weekends in September
Various locations
http://studio-tours.com

Winesong!
Third weekend in September
Mendocino Botanical Garden, Fort Bragg
www.winesong.org

Mendocino County Fair
Mid-September
Mendocino County Fairgrounds
www.mendocountyfair.com

Earthdance
Mid-September
www.earthdance.org/laytonville

October

Ukiah Pumpkin Fest
Second Saturday in October
463.6712

Hopland Passport

Mid-October
Downtown Hopland
www.hoplandpassport.com

Day of the Dead Festival

Last day of October
Little River Inn, Mendocino Coast
707.962.2210

November

Mushroom Festival

Second full week of November
Mendocino Botanical Garden, Fort Bragg

Festival of Trees

End of November, throughout December
Mendocino Botanical Garden, Fort Bragg

December

Candlelight Inn Tour

Third week in December, Thurs–Sat
Various locations
www.mendocinoinntour.com

Index

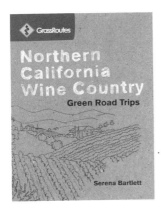

GrassRoutes Travel offers a new kind of guidebook in which green travel, sustainable living, youth culture, and authenticity take center stage. These energetic guides tap local scenes at their best: from indie shops to late-night eating spots, from getting around sans car to getting creatively inspired, from the hottest music venues to the quietest places to open a book and read.

"Like toting along a local eco-minded friend on your travels."
—*The Virtuous Traveler*

"Forging a new standard."
—*Oakland Tribune*

"Deftly compiled and highly recommended."
—*Midwest Book Review*

Online at grassroutestravel.com

Wherever books are sold

SASQUATCH BOOKS
www.sasquatchbooks.com